THE ENGLISH CLIMATE

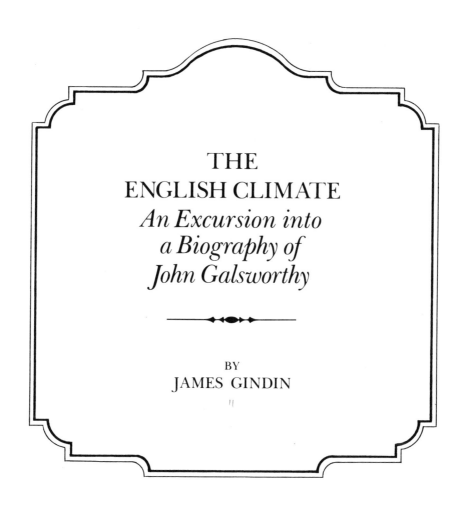

THE
ENGLISH CLIMATE
*An Excursion into
a Biography of
John Galsworthy*

BY
JAMES GINDIN

Ann Arbor
The University of Michigan Press

Library of Congress Cataloging in Publication Data

Gindin, James Jack, 1926-
  The English climate.

  Includes index.
  1. Galsworthy, John, 1867-1933. 2. Authors,
English—20th century—Biography. 3. England—
Description and travel—1971-   I. Title.
PR6013.A5Z5673   823'.9'12 [B]   79-9860
ISBN 0-472-08349-X

For my father, Jac Gindin, 1901-78

Acknowledgments

More than most, this book is dependent on the generosity of others, on their willingness to devote their time and their memories of Galsworthy to my interests and questions. I am particularly grateful to members of the Galsworthy family, who, on numerous occasions, were as helpful and as hospitable as they possibly could be. No literary executor could have been any more warmly accommodating than the late Mr. Rudolf Sauter. No relatives could have taken more trouble in welcoming me, in responding to what I asked, and in sharing their recollections, both verbal and written, than did Dorothy and Ralph Ivens. I am no less appreciative of the generous welcome and responsiveness given by other relatives, particularly by Miss Muriel Galsworthy and by Mr. and Mrs. Hubert Galsworthy.

Those outside the family were also unfailingly helpful in sharing with me their memories and their insights into Galsworthy. I should like to record my gratitude to Joan and Jack Dean (as well as to Mrs. Dean's sisters, and to her brother-in-law, Henley), to Dwye Evans, to Mr. and Mrs. Edward Grinstead, to Miss Rosamond Lehmann, to Charles Pick (the managing director of Heinemann's), to Mrs. Pat Scrivens (now, since Rudolf Sauter's death, Galsworthy's literary executor), to the late Dame Sybil Thorndike, to Mrs. Marjorie Watts, to Dame Rebecca West, and to Donald Wilson. They all provided whatever information they could, as well as an interest and personal kindness that went far beyond expected boundaries.

I have also had considerable aid from public collections and institutions. The Galsworthy Collection, established and donated viii

in 1962 by Mr. Sauter at the University of Birmingham Library, is conveniently organized and well maintained. I am grateful for many favors to B. S. Benedikz, the Head of Special Collections at the University of Birmingham Library, and to Miss Christine Penney, his assistant. I have also been helped by material readily available in the Scribner Archives, donated by Charles Scribner's Sons to the Princeton University Library, and wish to thank both Scribner's and the Manuscript Division of the Princeton University Library. Time for this study and the opportunity to conduct interviews was generously supported. I am grateful to the National Endowment for the Humanities for a senior fellowship in 1973-74, and to the Horace H. Rackham School of Graduate Studies at the University of Michigan for a summer fellowship and travel grant in 1975. I should also like to thank Miss Stacey Olster for skillful, rapid, and intelligent typing.

More strictly personal gratitude is also a pleasure to acknowledge. Robert Super's careful and sensitive reading saved me from a number of factual mistakes and instances of tonal clumsiness. Donald Hall, who read the manuscript twice, combined enthusiasm with sharp and direct criticism. His knowledge and acuity, both of and about England and prose style, helped me make extensive revisions, and I may well regret that I did not, in every instance, follow his sympathetic and tough-minded advice. My most pervasive and deepest gratitude is to my wife, Joan Gindin. She suggested this kind of book in the first place, then carefully read and worked over each of the various drafts. No one could have better combined both involvement and distance, been both a character central to the concept of the book itself and a reader able to see, from the outside, directions and implications that I could not. She is, intimately, part of both the subject and the authorship.

Ann Arbor, Michigan
14 July 1978

Contents

Painting of John Galsworthy by Rudolf Sauter, 1923

PART I
February–June
1974

THE SOFT AIR that gently sweeps across southern England from the Atlantic seems to act as a moderate preservative, like the way in which Mediterranean sun and sand have preserved many of the relics of antiquity. England's westerlies are in constant movement, sometimes stormy, sometimes with the quick brush of clarity, sometimes vague and wistful, accommodating themselves to the changing landscape just like the village buildings, often clustered in valleys, that seem to have grown naturally or always to have been there. English villages are seldom assertions or challenges; rather, they are accommodations to space, disclosing a detailed variety, a block of Georgian symmetry, the swelling angle of a half-timbered house, a minute example of Victorian proliferation. And the westerly weather demonstrates the same variety, the same movement, within a confined space. Driving into Salisbury from the East, near dusk one rainy January day, I saw the cathedral spire, drenched in sun, seeming to throw a rainbow across the darkness toward our car. It looked as if arranged by a supernatural lighting director, but such rapid shifts of light are, in fact, frequent. Sometimes, lumbering in from the Continent, the weather becomes static for days—what the television weatherforecasters dryly call "anticyclonic." The weather from the Continent, or the East, is more searing, more transfixed, certainly more capable of producing extremes of heat or cold, holding the landscape in the kind of suspense that suggests intensity or destruction, injecting the aura of possible cataclysm into the English atmosphere. Often, in Victorian novels, the East wind portended acute misery or death or the contagions of continental dogma. Yet, invariably, in both fact and fiction, the prevailing westerlies have reestablished themselves. They seem to preserve the green and gentle contours of the

land, the varieties of weather and movement, the villages content in their carefully apportioned space, and, as I became increasingly aware during the 1973-74 year when I lived there,
the lives of the people.

My work for the year, doing research for a critical biography of John Galsworthy, made me more sensitive to weather
and climate than I had ever been previously. My initial interest
in Galsworthy began with his fiction and drama, as an attempt
to understand and illuminate it thoroughly. Galsworthy's work
has received scant critical treatment in recent years, has been
consigned to its dates or its presumed audience, or blandly ignored, or summarily relegated to the category of high-level soap
opera on television. Yet, I was also interested in Galsworthy
himself, in the perspective and the vision of the man who created the fiction and the drama. I did not want to restrict myself to the convenient abstraction of literary analysis, valuably
sound as that discipline often is; nor did I want to confine my
biographical treatment to what could be entirely verified
by documents, to the biography of the laundry list. Rather, I
wanted to get some sense of Galsworthy as a writer, of the
fusion of the accidental man, his times, and his conscious art-
istry, of all the elements that created the work. In order to do
this, I wanted to talk with as many survivors, friends, and relatives who knew him as I could find, and I knew that, obviously,
they would all be considerably older than I, all have lived
through many years of the English climate, been weathered and
made sensitive in ways that I had not been. In talking with
them, I would want to absorb as much as I could, to learn their
versions of Galsworthy, knowing that I would be able to reflect
and react later, and hoping that the eventual selections that
would shape my own conception of Galsworthy would be based
on as much insight as possible. Yet I also knew, even before I
started, that the process of first listening and then reacting supposed too easily that I could turn various portions of my mind
on and off like water faucets. How I came to know or understand something would be part of what I knew, and I would
therefore find it wiser to acknowledge and speculate about my
own subjectivity, at almost every point, than to assume the ob-

jectivity of myself and others. The eventual aim was to understand John Galsworthy, the writer's perspective, visible through others, through documents, and through the fiction and the drama itself, that created a considerable amount of literary work. The method, involving reading whatever I could and talking with anyone who knew him, was necessarily more subjective and self-involved. The necessary subjectivity added a further complication: I would try to understand what I suspected I could never fully verify or document, attitudes and shapes that I could only see partially (and with significant amounts of distortion) through myself. The process of discovering what I could of John Galsworthy would be, in part, a process of self-discovery, but, I thought, I had better begin by imposing myself as little as I consciously could.

I also knew that, in living in England for the year, I would have to go back to an England older than any I had encountered at any length before. I had lived in England for three widely separated years and numerous summers, had had at those times other and more contemporary forms of absorption and points of focus. A student year settled on appreciating warm beer, plays, and cricket, and on developing a permanent veneration for all the attempts and achievements of the first socialist government after the Second World War, what J. B. Priestley had described as a "new" England moving haphazardly, often drably, but peacefully, toward a new concept of social justice. A year working as a civilian for the Education Branch of the U.S. Air Force in England, the first year of my marriage, had a double and somewhat contradictory focus. At work, my wife and I devised and taught courses that might allow airmen who had had little education or learned little from it to qualify for better jobs or for reenlistment. We saw, with some amusement, that large institutions like the military could support diversity and projects that we thought worthy which were not strictly germane to the institution's purpose, a perception that violated some of our earlier preconceptions about an Eisenhower government. We speculated that large governments might ultimately be healthy in abrogating provincialism and forwarding a kind of charitable internationalism. In contrast, we also developed a more private sense, formulated in pubs, university common rooms, and café expresso bars, nourished by the plays we saw and the novels we read, that the individual had to exist cautiously within the framework of a larger world he could never fully understand or control. A later year, in the mid-sixties, during which my first child was born, was spent teaching in a northern university, at Sheffield, learning more about the National Health Service, all its complications, its nobilities and inequities. I also watched buildings and education escalate, wondering, somewhat ambivalently, if I might not be part of a profession and a generation perhaps more sensible than some others. In all of these years, I was basically comfortable with my contemporaneity, and felt, even more strongly when I was in England than when in America, that I shared with others of my generation a perspective that was uniquely post-Second World War. In none of these years did I much notice the weather—in fact, I always took the Englishman's opening gambit of "Don't you find our weather miserable?" as mere defensive politeness and ignored the issue as quickly as I gracefully could.

In 1973-74, I spent most of the first six months or so confined to libraries, for I wanted to read all the books, manuscripts, letters, and documents I could, just as a matter of doing my homework, before visiting those who had known Galsworthy. Even at that, age and older customs kept impinging on my consciousness, beginning with the bent but sprightly gentleman who scrambled nimbly about the catwalks introducing me to the London Library's archaic and unique cataloguing system. Early in the year, quite to my surprise, I decided to take my children to see the Changing of the Guard at Buckingham Palace, an event I had stigmatized as "touristy" and never seen before. A group of older women who came down from Sheffield annually to see the event helped hoist my children onto the stone lions rampant on the Victoria Monument so that they could see the parade more easily. An aging man in a polished version of the clothes of a country gentleman, a thin line of campaign ribbons on his chest, explained the various colors to us and, as we left, handed us his card with his name followed by a regiment and a string of initials. My family and I lived for the year in Chelsea, only about four blocks from the chromium boutiques and strobe lights of the Kings Road, yet I kept noticing the weather in all its variety and older people in their astonishing vitality. The newsagent's shop at our corner, its floor lined with clean sides from cardboard cartons every morning, its crowded shelves piled with stationery, pens, paper napkins, wrapping paper, twine, tobacco, and such, was owned and kept by Miss Watson, a tiny woman of eighty-seven. She never blamed the new computer system for newspaper distribution that sometimes mixed up her orders so that she would be short of one paper and inundated with another—she'd merely say "We must give it time to get used to things." Wrapped in a cardigan several sizes too large for her, and wearing, during the winter, a woolen hat pulled down over her ears and mittens with the finger-ends cut out so that she could give change rapidly, she often commented on the headlines of the newspapers she sold. Perilous warnings about the "energy crisis" (English newspapers never quite reached the skepticism of American newspapers in always referring to the "so-called energy crisis") or the implications for industry of the three-day week, always brought out something like, "Oh, we may be going through a bit of a bad time now, a bit of silliness. But it'll be all right. We'll be all right. You're comfortable, aren't you? . . . Oh, I'm so very glad to hear it." When I tried to peg her assurances to a party or political program, she was invariably evasive, for it was always England that would be all right, the weather that would turn, people that would be kind. She kept her money on the counter, a large board with deep circular grooves for the coins of various denominations, pound notes slid underneath. My next-door neighbor, a handsome architect, modish in denim suits, said how foolish she was, "what a relic," and marvelled that she hadn't been robbed and mugged. She told long stories about her family, her sister who "could have been a concert pianist," her mother who had grown up in the country. Her abiding interest was genealogy. Once she lowered her voice and told me confidentially that "my mother's name is one of the five or six oldest in the country. My name, now, Watson, my father's of course, is solid, Scottish, nothing distinguished, but my mother's is one of our oldest." When I asked what it was, she smiled coyly and forty years seemed to vanish, as she said, "Now I would have to know you a great deal better, for years and years, to tell you that."

If Miss Watson's shop was invariably neat, structured to withstand all winds, Mr. Holland's ironmongery across the road reflected all the chaos of changing times. Drainboards and piles of sponges leaned against trays of light bulbs or forgotten cans of paint, all tumbling on huge bags of cat litter or puce, hard plastic garbage cans. The various wares usually spilled out into the street and it was difficult to pick one's way into the center of the shop without tripping over a paraffin heater or a large, old spool of copper wire. Yet Mr. Holland, daily lamenting the growth of the chain stores, could find anything in the shop his father had established in 1898. His conversation was a dramatic litany of all the impositions a demanding world faced him with: "Now, Mr. Holland, she says, I'll have that bathtub fixture and please come round at ten on Saturday night to show my husband how to fit it properly"; "Well, he phones for two gross of cat litter to be delivered by hand and I've never seen him before in my life"; "Well, he says, the chains don't carry that Mr. Holland, and so I'll have to get it for him because you know there's only two of us independents left between the river and the Fulham Road." Yet, as several neighbours told me, Mr. Holland did all these things, installed the fixtures, got whatever the customers wanted, without ever making an extra charge. When television reporters announced during the three-day week that toilet paper might be in short supply (a fear events never justified), it suddenly disappeared from Mr. Holland's rickety shelves. He explained, "I've a bit, a few rolls, but I'm saving them for the old people, the shut-ins. I'll start with the same people I helped out during the war. Still a number of them about." Mr. Holland never expressed the wish that 1942 would return, was never explicitly nostalgic; rather he just saw his shop and his own grumbling ("of course, I grumble, I've always grumbled," he would say, eyes smiling, corners of his long white mustache rising) as the kind of local center he had been brought up to think a shop should be.

When I felt secure enough to emerge from the libraries, the first person I contacted was Rudolf Sauter, a nephew of Galsworthy, his principal literary executor, and a man who was always close to his uncle, living in the same house for Galsworthy's last seven years. Mr. Sauter has written a short and sensitive book on the uncle he knew. Several phone conversations had prepared me for his elaborate politeness, his concern for my convenience, his insistence that, since I would be passing near his house in Gloucestershire, just outside Stroud, on a short holiday with my family, I should bring my wife and children along for tea. I also knew that he was a painter, almost seventy-nine years old, and I suspected, because he had not referred to her, that his wife (who had been more than ten years older than he) was now dead. What surprised me, however, after finally finding the right road out of Stroud, passing the tiny village common and making the three-hundred-degree turn after the third telephone pole onto the partly paved track, was the spring and energy in the walk of the slight man with full white hair and heavy white sideburns who came rapidly out of his gate to welcome us. I was also impressed by the view, the house horizontally stretched and perched on the side of the hill, overlooking a long, deep, green valley that included Stroud and its few factories, several small villages in which buildings seemed huddled together for comfort and protection, and jigsaw fields in variously modulated shades of green. The day was bright and warm, a soft and gentle westerly although the calendar (often irrelevant in England) showed the end of February, so that my children, who had prepared for silence in possible bad weather with coloring books and several volumes of Enid Blyton, could explore the hills and fields behind the house while we went inside to talk.

We were soon joined by Mrs. Scrivens, an attractive, blond, and warmly expressive woman of fifty or so who has been close to both Mr. Sauter and his late wife for years and who later provided us with their usual tea of cakes and several kinds of honey sandwiches. As we talked, Mr. Sauter was in constant motion, alternately leaning back as he reflected and remembered, perched forward right elbow on armchair, right hand supporting his head, peering at me as he listened, jumping up to punctuate the conversation by showing me one of his paintings stacked in various corners around the room or the sheet music of the songs that Galsworthy and his wife had written (he the lyrics, she the music) and published or the tape recorder on which he, Mr. Sauter, was currently writing a play. A good deal of our conversation went back beyond the range of either memory, back to what might have made Galsworthy, coming from a background of upper-middle-class prosperity and complacence—a Forsyte background—become a writer and begin to question the axioms on which he'd been brought up. The standard middle-class movement from commercial success to art in two or three generations seemed too general an explanation, and nothing in his career at Harrow (where he was head prefect, and the kind of boy who is captain of the football team without being the best athlete) or in his rather indolent and dandified years at Oxford, wearing lavender gloves and studying racing handicaps, seemed to provide much of a clue. (I later learned at Oxford that, although Galsworthy was at New College at the same time Ernest Dowson and Lionel Johnson were, he refused an invitation to join their Essay Club.) Mr. Sauter's replies at that first interview concentrated on his own father, a very talented Bavarian painter named Géorg Sauter who had come to England in the 1880s to copy the Old Masters in the National Gallery and to paint portraits, and who had met Lilian, Galsworthy's older sister, while he was copying Titian's *Bacchus and Ariadne*. Géorg Sauter had infused the whole Galsworthy family, some expressing greater receptivity than others, with a sense of Art, of the Continent, of a wider and more intense scheme of perception and values (a theme central to *The Island Pharisees*, one of Galsworthy's earliest novels).

As the son developed the story of his father's influence, I began to notice the piercing intensity of his blue eyes (eyes that another relative later described as different from the characteristic Galsworthy soft, absorbent grey) and the deep lines holding his firm chin downwards (lines that Mrs. Scrivens laughingly remarked repeated those visible in the pictures of his father's fierce and uncompromising face). Mr. Sauter also talked of the First World War, when his father, who had never bothered to become a British subject although he lived in England for thirty years, was interned in a camp for enemy aliens for almost three years. None of Galsworthy's connections or friendships with the political establishment helped, and, despite Galsworthy's dinners with Churchill, C. F. G. Masterman, even Asquith himself, Géorg Sauter was not released until the war was over. And, then, as jingoism became more frightening and intense in the late stages of the war, even Rudolf himself was interned for nearly a year. Born in 1895 when his parents were on an extended honeymoon viewing Géorg Sauter's origins in the German Alps, his 1918 imprisonment seemed the long-delayed end in a chain of events beginning with the doubtless sensible disinclination of Victorian women to travel while pregnant. Mr. Sauter speculated on how these events had affected Galsworthy, had shifted his social and political concerns. Before the First World War, Galsworthy had represented a kind of benign and ameliorative Edwardian Liberalism manifested in his leadership of the campaign against the Lord Chamberlain's censorship of the drama, in his advocating more humane methods for slaughtering animals, in easing solitary confinement for prisoners (Galsworthy had helped write the reform bill, introduced by Winston Churchill, then the Liberal Home Secretary, after Churchill had been impressed by a production of Galsworthy's *Justice*), and in organizing among writers a 1911 protest against the use of airplanes in time of war (a protest G. B. Shaw regarded as "pious piffle"). After the war, however, his only causes were international—a strong advocacy of the League of Nations (even to the extent of writing a long letter to the senior Henry Cabot Lodge, passionately pleading for America's joining the League) and a great deal of work for the international Poets, Essayists, Novelists (and Dramatists), or P.E.N. Club as president for almost twelve years. This internationalism made him seem increasingly remote to some of those most interested in social and political issues in England during the 1920s.

After tea, Mr. Sauter took us downstairs, where the wide windows revealed an even fuller view of the valley around and below, as if we were momentarily suspended within it, to show us many of his father's paintings. These ranged from colorful, impressionistic portraits against full and rich Vuillard-like backgrounds to stark studies of mountains and searing light. He also showed us a good deal of his own work: drawings of English houses and scenes, drawings dependent on the rectilinear curves that seem to signal Art Deco and that still characterized much of his lettering, dramatic depictions of the Grand Canyon, abstractions painted in the sixties of sun and mountain and ice. As we looked and talked, gazed back and forth between the window views of the gentle English valley and canvases of the Grand Canyon or Alpine summit, we more and more began to connect the sense of landscape with a sense of life. When first I praised the view from the window and Mr. Sauter replied, "Not much, nothing in comparison to your Grand Canyon," and I countered that "really, I prefer this," I thought that I was simply responding politely to an exaggerated form of hospitality. But I soon realized that somewhat self-consciously, half-humorously, I was adopting Galsworthy's role in a good-natured dialogue that had been part of a frequent interchange between uncle and nephew. I assumed the role that, of course, the Grand Canyon must be seen and appreciated, but that it could not really be believed; it was something essentially inhuman and a great deal less rich, comfortable, and interesting than the varieties of soft English panorama. The other role maintained that, although the English landscape had its quiet charm, it was a comfortable evasion (within which one could well live eighty or more years) from the more soul-like intensities of canyon, peak, sun, and ice. We were, in miniature, recreating a past I had come to learn about, and I was also learning that the past is not entirely isolated within a moment on an historical continuum.

As the sun vanished behind the valley, we talked more of novels and voices and the distances of art, Mr. Sauter giving me his sense of when Galsworthy's art was relatively close to life and when it was not. He thought old Jolyon as Galsworthy's father the closest approximation of fiction to biography. He recognized that his view might be distorted because of his own fondness for his grandfather. The old Victorian patriarch had

separated from his wife for his last two years, had lived with first
one daughter, then the other (Mr. Sauter's mother), and died
when Mr. Sauter was only nine and a half. As we tried to define
this relationship between life and fiction, we knew how provi-
sionally we were staking out the distance from Galsworthy to
his nephew and, with a much greater leap, to me. Long after the
February darkness had come and our children had returned happily from an upper field announcing they had found some sheep,
we collected ourselves to go. My daughter said it was her half-
birthday and Mr. Sauter insisted on going back into his kitchen
to find a gift for her. He walked out with us past his gate. In the
darkness, I could not start our rented car and felt a keen twinge
at my own well-known mechanical ineptitude, an apparent resemblance to Galsworthy that was totally unfeigned. Mr. Sauter
ran back to get a flashlight just as, quite accidentally, I managed
to start the car. As we drove away in the confusion of repeated
laughter, embarrassment, thanks, and farewells, I thought how
I from America and the time of abstraction had praised the
English scene and its concretion, how I (thinking I might be acting out of consideration to someone of another generation) had
rejected the idea of using a tape recorder only to find one in
operation there and my host far more familiar with its intrica-
cies and problems than I, and how I, in contrast to all his quickness and efficiency, couldn't punctuate the day appropriately
by starting the bloody car when I should have done.

Landscape was less useful in recreating the past two days
later when, down in Devon, we drove out to see Manaton, the
village of twelve or fourteen widely separated houses, and
Wingstone, the farmhouse in Manaton where the Galsworthys
lived about half the year, permanently renting five rooms and
the wide veranda from the farmer who shared the house and
worked the farm, from the time of their marriage until 1923.
The farmer's wife who had come from Yorkshire originally and
who spoke Spanish as well as English and read a great many
books, cooked and cared for them. The soft, warm weather
held. Even with a fairly detailed road map, Manaton took some
time to find. As we drove through the narrow lanes, almost covered by high hedgerows, backing up or being backed up for

whenever a car came in the opposite direction, we would come to occassional T-junctions at which a white sign on a wooden post might or might not point toward Manaton. Every so often, the hedgerows receded as we climbed along the edge of Dartmoor, covered with a low brownish furze that seemed endless; then, the road would dip again, as the hedgerows climbed to border small fields and pastures. We finally reached Manaton, its houses widely spread apart on a plateau protected from the moor by a dense, green wood. We asked a woman walking along the road for Wingstone, and she looked after us quizzically as, following her directions, we made another right-angle turn. I drove confidently down the track between rows of beeches I had read about and ended in a muddy pen, sheep dogs yapping against the sides of the car, thirty or forty sheep somnolent and unconcerned. A young man who'd been shoveling compost a few feet away, the current farmer's helper, had no idea why I had come and told me that the farmer, who I later discovered leased and worked the land for a corporation, was in Bovey Tracy for the day. The yard was so thick with mud and compost heaps and so enclosed by half tumbled-down wooden fences, the dogs so clamorously insistent that we were aliens, that I decided not even to walk around to the veranda on the other side of the farmhouse to see the memorial plaque or the view that friends as various as Hardy, Conrad, and Shaw had been so impressed by more than fifty years ago. Instead, I turned the car around, tires churning in the mud, and drove my family, justly satirical about my form of nostalgia that would erase half a century, to another nearby village, one of clustered old houses and shops rising to an old, squat, half-timbered market cross that now housed both a room for town meetings and the public lavatories. My family knew that one could buy china figurines of animal families, made individually on a local farm, at very reasonable prices at a shop in the village. Sometimes, tourism is a sane and necessary retreat.

We wanted to see more of Devon on our own. Since a general election was to be held later that week, we rather gravitated toward North Devon, the constituency of Jeremy Thorpe, then the media-genic leader of the Liberal party. Throughout the preceding weeks, we had watched campaign speeches on television, equally unimpressed by the ponderous simplicities in which both Edward Heath and Harold Wilson, then the party leaders, asked for the electorate's trust in the "current crisis." Fuel-saving and the three-day week, as we had seen these measures in London, had not seemed to affect life at all. Houses, hospitals, and schools were never without heat, and the winter was generally a mild succession of gentle westerlies. Like many others we spoke to, we could never decide whether the mandatory absence of Christmas lights was a boon or a deprivation. Back in the early and middle fifties, we had praised the relative austerity of English Christmas decorations, more as our own reaction against what we saw as excessive American trumpery and commercialism than as any kind of aesthetic feeling. Yet, in 1964, coming down from the north to a Christmas in London, we had welcomed the lights and the spidery illuminated reindeer of what seemed then a more affluent and tasteful civic gesture. In 1973, however, the lack of lights served more as a talking point, an introduction to possible debate, than as any means for the expression of feeling one way or another. Other measures for saving energy were more visible. Shops not dealing in food could only use electric power half the day, the half varying in a complicated weekly regional rotation that almost no one mastered. My daughter's shoes needed new soles, and I went twice to a nearby shoe repair shop on the half of a day during which the machine could not be used. When I returned a third time with my daughter, wrong again, she, unworried at seven about being thought an "ugly American," turned her large hazel eyes at the repairman and said, "But I need my shoes." He laughed and said, "Oh, to hell with it. I can't keep the times straight either," and turned on his machine. In addition, shops illuminated by candlelight in the early winter dusk seemed attractive, more conducive to careful and enjoyable selection of clothes or books than is the harsh fluorescence of the more usual lighting. We were like tourists, enjoying the complexities and difficulties in shops, the interchange generated in buying even the most mundane necessities—but then so were many of the English we knew.

We had to warn ourselves, consciously, not to be complacent. We were aware, from newspaper and periodical accounts, that possible implications of the coal miners' strike and the energy shortage might eventually be disastrous, depending on the amount stockpiled, which neither political party ever reported knowledgeably and honestly. Yet, industrialists and businessmen, sometimes in public, more frequently in private conversation, acknowledged that most factories produced just as much in three days as they had in five. Food, we heard, might soon be short—according to the American newspapers we saw, some of which have taken a patronizing tone toward the "suffering" or "benighted" British ever since the Second World War prevented them from hating the imperialists, food already was short—but shelves in all the London shops were full. And American newspapers were not the only alarmists: the wife of our architect friend next door had originally come from Holland and her family sent them a Christmas food parcel that even included several loaves of bread. The political debates, the cries and counter-cries of crisis and impending disaster, seemed remote to us and to almost everyone we talked to. One bright January morning, I met a novelist friend in the reading room of the London Library. He tapped the copy of the *New Statesman* he had been reading and asked if we had experienced any of the dire inconveniences the leading article discussed in such shrill terms. When I said that we hadn't, he replied that he hadn't either, "but I just wanted to check with someone not English to make sure I'm not becoming too insular and 'all's well with England.'" As election discussion continued on television and in the newspapers we realized that, on the specific issue of the miners' strike, Labour had the better argument. Miner's pay was shockingly low in relation to other wages and prices (and, as it later turned out, the Tories recognized this and professed they had based their "firm stand" on a mistaken statistical calculation). But, beyond this, both major parties' dramatizations of the reasons for a "clear choice" in their favor invoked abstractions of an imminent apocalyptic future that we found it difficult to see in the landscape about us.

On that late February holiday, we drove around Exmoor, visiting villages and the local churches distinguished by square towers, wood-beamed high-arched ceilings, and heavy, richly textured stone. We also saw Tintagel, the Arthurian series of rocky thrusts from the north Cornish coast, a bleak network of shelters and trails, on a cold, grey, windy day. The rapid shifts of light, the momentary fierceness or relaxation of the westerlies on this rocky coast, seemed so easily able to blaze into an "Excalibur" which would vanish a moment later that the coast convinced me that it was an appropriate origin for the fashioning of myth and legend as a bastion against the sea. I recalled something of the same feeling during a week spent in Aberdeen more than twenty years earlier, long before the discovery of oil fields beneath the North Sea. Aberdeen had fascinated me then, a grim, grey, dour city maintaining its granite as a bastion, a tenacious structure solidly posing itself against the unknown. Britain, I thought, might need its carapaces at the extremities, its rock edges, to protect the green and vulnerable rolling land within. Back in the softer realms of Devon, we spoke to people in shops, hotels, and pubs, who were invariably pleased to hear what we liked about Devon, its quiet, its color, its landscape, its pace, but were worried that it would soon change. One older woman who ran a shop told us, "When the new motorway is finished next year, it won't be the same. Birmingham to Exeter in three hours or less. We'll be over-run with tourists, and it's bound to change things. Some say it's good for business. And you can't blame people for wanting to come down here. For myself, I'd rather not have the money and keep Devon the same. But, then, it isn't up to us, is it?"

On the day before the election, we were caught in the traffic surrounding Thorpe's final luncheon rally in Barnstaple. Enthusiastic crowds welcomed him, and the series of tiny reception rooms and lounges in the local hotel were jammed with television cables, camera equipment, and crews sent from London. We stayed, however, about six or eight miles out in the isolated north Devon countryside at a hotel. The owners, hiring friends and neighbors to help as needed, converted their large Victorian house of odd corners and angles into a hotel as the only way to retain it. Large bay windows in the bedrooms revealed a view of patchwork fields and fences, all in different shades of brown, yellow, and green, that led up to the rich darkness of Exmoor beyond. The owners served delicious French meals and kept a blazing log fire in the large, central hall. We watched the election returns grouped around the television set in a small, cold anteroom. My eight-year-old son sat on the floor, coloring each constituency on his large map a bright Tory blue or Labour red or Liberal yellow or Scots or Welsh nationalist green as the result was announced. A handsome, quiet, and articulate old couple from Hampshire visibly beamed when the news came through that Jeremy Thorpe had retained his seat. But more typical, perhaps, was the view of a young schoolteacher from Yorkshire, with an upright look and a silent, admiring wife: "I don't think Thorpe can be a very responsible politician. Isn't he friendly with actors and such people?"—although my wife and I did not get the point at the time, a tight-lipped and probable reference to the homosexual scandal that, revealed more than two years later, finished Thorpe's career as party leader. Some time later, when almost everyone had gone to bed, the owners and another couple, who had been out celebrating a birthday, came in to look at the returns. They were in a jovial mood, and the owner finally confided to us: "I'm really very pleased Thorpe's back in. But I can't say so publicly, not around here. Most of the farmers are staunch Tories." The woman of the other couple chimed in: "Oh, yes. Don't tell anyone around here, but we put lots of Thorpe posters, you know the ones on posts and telegraph poles, back up when the farmer next door to us had torn them down." She laughed, and told us, "We're really renegades out here. So's Jeremy." The owner added, "You know he said he'd come out here to lunch on Sunday if he won." None of them really believed he would, and he didn't.

At about noon the day after the election, we went into our favorite pub in the nearby town of South Molton to watch the final returns of the indecisive election. The waitress, who was about sixty, brought sandwiches for our children into a small room away from the bar. A day or two earlier, when we had first stopped there and the pub was less crowded, we had talked to her for quite a while: "I'd really be worried living in London now with that IRA and their bombs. I lived in London all through the Blitz, through the whole war. Worked as a waitress in the Houses of Parliament. But it was different then. We were all together and you knew who your enemy was. The war was the best time . . . I've lived down here a long while. My daughter grew up here and had a horse. Couldn't have had one in London. Now she has one where she lives in Pennsylvania." We moved into the bar, and the gregarious pub-keeper cleared a space so we could watch the television set and bought us a drink: "All you romantics are attracted to Thorpe. Mind you, I'm glad he kept his seat and there should be someone like him in Parliament just to keep the place alive. But, nationally, if he ever had any power, he'd be just like the rest. This Liberal revival is a pipe dream." Later, with almost all returns in, television coverage finished and the pub was soon almost empty. The pub-keeper came out from behind the bar and joined us for a last drink, sitting on one of the wide, deep chintz-covered armchairs next to the fire. "Oh, I like it down here. My own boss. Open or close the bar when I like. Know everyone in town. Nothing much changes, and most people in Devon like it that way. But it's a tiny corner, it's not the world. And the world will catch up with it one of these days. That's why something like the Liberal party is silly, though Thorpe's a nice enough man personally—who hasn't his skeletons? But the world is changing, and Liberal dreams and the dreams of most people in Devon aren't up to it. I wish this election *had* been decisive. One of them soon will have to be or we'll all go under." He looked at his watch. "My God, it's already three-quarters of an hour past closing time. The police will run me in," he laughed, as he rose to close for the afternoon.

A few days later, on my wife's birthday, we were having a farewell post-closing-time drink with the pub-keeper, still discussing the election, when the dish-washer rushed in hastily to tell the pub-keeper that Tiny and his boys had arrived from Cornwall. The pub-keeper's normally rosy face blanched and his lips tightened. Tiny, who stood about six feet five and weighed well over two hundred fifty, with the flattened face of an ex-prize fighter, came in exuding the false joviality that barely covers menace. The pub-keeper signalled us to leave, and we quickly flashed a silent thanks and goodbye, wondering to ourselves if the rest of the world hadn't already caught up with Devon. The next day, as we drove back to London, I kept thinking of Devon, and the pub-keeper, and his assertion that some election soon had better be decisive. I wasn't so sure. I had, I decided, been mildly pleased about the slim Labour majority, more as a puncture to Tory pretense than as any hope for wiser or more beneficent government, and the close result seemed to parallel the closeness of my own sense of the party divisions. Impossible-to-elect third parties absorbed most of my sympathy. Certainly, my vicarious Labour support carried none of the enthusiasm, none of the sense of victory or defeat, that I had felt when coloring in election maps during earlier stays in Britain. I recalled the 1951 election that narrowly turned out the Attlee government. At the time, I was a graduate student on a year's grant at the University of Glasgow. During the campaign, I had gone down to Glasgow's Central Railroad Station to see Winston Churchill, a dim figure then, the large head scowling and shrunken into his overcoat, arrive to give a speech. Boos and hoots, as well as an occasional harmless tomato, greeted him from the crowd of noisy workers, remembering not the war leader but the earlier cavalier attitude toward unemployment and the dole. The workers had been jobless for most of the decade before the Second World War. I did not stay to listen to more than three minutes of his grumbling and irrelevant orotundities. Later, I heard the election returns on the radio in a student dormitory through a long night, as only one seat changed, always to the Tories, every two hours or so. I watched the gradually growing smiles on the faces of the Tory students, the engineers, and those who could quote from memory the times of any trains listed in Bradshaw's Railway Guide (in just the tone of latching on to certainty that some American students use to quote baseball averages), and the periodic explosions of disgust or resignation on the faces of the Labour students, the sons of Scottish dockers or crofters and most of those who came from England. I kept waiting for a rush of news or emotion to reverse the result, but that never happened. I recalled, too, the 1964 election, the campaign in which Sir Alec Douglas Home, the Tory Prime Minister, asserted that he could plan the economy as well with a box of matches as Harold Wilson and the Labourites could with all their charts and statistics. Sir Alec seemed anachronistic, the parody of an older Britain, harmlessly eccentric, but incompetent as the head of a complicated contemporary government. Clearly, by 1974, confidence in Labour's economic management had come, in turn, to seem naive, yet that confidence was, even in retrospect, no worse than the attitude that had seemed to radiate from the U.S. Embassy at the time, an attitude which saw the English election as a struggle between the stable Tory forces of tradition, order, and sensible accommodation and the subterranean Labour forces of upheaval and potentially dangerous Leftist connection. As a Fulbright lecturer that year, I was, with my wife, in London attending Fulbright orientation sessions during the early days of that political campaign. After one such session at the U.S. Embassy, we went to dinner at an English friend's. My wife, asked to describe a Fulbright political "briefing," replied with a metaphor that, although accurately representing the tone of a speech we had heard, was literally false: "The State Department would be much more comfortable with Sir Alec. Wilson, as an Oxford don, like Harvard professors, might be out of it at an LBJ barbecue, whereas Sir Alec, as an aristocrat, would know how to fit in anywhere." Her audience smiled, and the conversation passed to other official lunacies. Three days later, when I arrived at Sheffield, I found multiple messages, at our hotel, at the university, at a professor's house, to phone a London number. It was the *Sunday Times* correspondent, Atticus, who began by asking me, "Is it true that the American ambassador said that LBJ would be more comfortable with Sir Alec elected because of how he'd behave at a barbecue?" When I explained the metaphor and the falsehood, he said, "Oh, that's all right. Think nothing of it. My wife always lies at dinner parties, too." Later in the year, brought together by mutual friends, we traded stories about the poses and follies of politics and government at another dinner party, one at which all the women had been given Victorian wedding dresses to wear for the evening by the hostess who had found them in a sale of used film properties in an antique shop in Greenwich. That, too, I thought in retrospect, was part of 1964, a kind of sprightly irreverence with an underlying confidence that people and their governments generally wobbled through things for the better. And now I knew that *that* Atticus, Nicholas Tomalin, was dead, the only foreign newsman killed in the 1973 Arab-Israeli war.

Back in London in the early spring of 1974, in the weeks that followed the first visit to Galsworthy's nephew and the trip to Devon, I spoke with publishers and editors who provided me with necessary and helpful information, although none of them had known Galsworthy. My subject seemed to be receding again, settling back into historical generalizations, buried beneath lost records of publishers' accounts, or hidden within Devon farms or changes in government. Through friends of friends, and then a phone conversation with her daughter, I did, however, establish contact with Mrs. Marjorie Watts, herself the daughter of Mrs. C. A. Dawson Scott who conceived the idea of the international P.E.N. Club in 1921, founded it, and persuaded Galsworthy to become its first president. I knew that Mrs. Watts had written a brief history of the international P.E.N. published for its fiftieth anniversary and was now beginning work on a more ambitious biography of her mother, who had achieved some distinction as a novelist, essayist, and reviewer before the First World War turned her energies toward organizing groups and places where writers could meet. Several telephone conversations led to my arrival in Hampstead on a cool, grey May afternoon. I walked up Heath Street, past the new white concrete slabs that, facing in different directions, house some of the newer shops; I continued up the hill, around the old church and into Hampstead Square, then dipped down into the well of Cannon Place. I deduced the missing number I wanted from those on either side of it. I thought, as I rang the bell, how very different this crowded, submerged part of Hampstead looks from the large Georgian cottage spaciously astride the heath only six or eight streets away, which was Galsworthy's London home from 1918 until his death. But Hampstead is deceptive. Mrs. Watts, a short, brisk, energetic woman in her late seventies, answered the door and quickly led me up a flight of steps, out of the well, into a large, comfortable room with a huge bay window revealing a spacious garden full of tulips and large clumps of wisteria, with the rhododendron, in massive buds, just about to bloom. After a few brief comments on the weather, the grey clouds that had altered her morning's plan that we sit in the garden, she told me about her recent holiday in Cornwall where she had had to rush her twelve-year-old grandson to the hospital in the middle of the night for an emergency appendectomy. She made many favorable observations on the skill, comfort, and consideration the National Health Service provides, then ushered me to a comfortable sofa and perched herself on a chair opposite, smoothing down her skirt, and saying, "Well, what about Galsworthy shall we talk about?"

She began talking about her mother and Galsworthy working together, arranging dinners, collecting members, striving to overcome national boundaries, during the initial days of the P.E.N. She thought their characters complementary, her mother's impulsive, enthusiastic, bursting with new ideas every moment, Galsworthy's calm, judicious, tactful, although they shared the same aim. Here, Mrs. Watts jumped up to get a copy of her book in order to read the words that best described what they shared: "a deep belief in internationalism, a dislike of grandeur and show, snobbishness or racial prejudice—and they both loved the underdog." She smiled broadly as she clapped the book shut. Mrs. Watts had herself worked as the full-time secretary for P.E.N. for over five years until the impending arrival of her first child, and she had many anecdotes to illustrate Galsworthy's wisdom and generosity, his ability to keep an organization of temperamental and often difficult writers working smoothly toward the same purpose. She saw him frequently, corresponded with him almost daily when he was in England (for Galsworthy was far from simply a name on the organization's masthead), and could recall many of his words and gestures on particular occasions, most often those involving smoothing the ruffled ego of an Eastern European or calming an excitable delegate from France.

Mrs. Watts's Galsworthy was invariably "noble," and, as we talked, he seemed to become more distant, more an abstraction

of temperate virtue. Mrs. Watts began to discuss Galsworthy's
wife, Ada, whom she was most anxious to defend, quite justifiably I think, against rather crude charges of hypochondria that
have reached print in the last dozen years or so. Basil Dean, who
played the lead in the Manchester production of Galsworthy's
first play, *The Silver Box*, and who later became a producer who
staged about a third of Galsworthy's twenty-five plays, regarded
Ada as a hypochondriac who drained most of Galsworthy's energies, caused him to refuse invitations to meet theatrical connections, and impeded his career. Then in his eighties (I was unable
to meet him before his death, just short of the age of ninety, in
early 1978), Basil Dean published his autobiography in 1970,
adding to a feisty account of his own career a number of references to the fact that, whenever Dean wanted to see a good deal
of Galsworthy about some production, Ada "dragged him away
to the Continent to exercise his nursing skill upon her current
indisposition." An earlier book, published in 1963 by Dudley
Barker, adopts the same point of view and depicts Ada as a selfish hypochondriac. Barker is also irreverent and iconoclastic
about another aspect of Ada: her role as victim in a loveless and
possibly brutal first marriage to Galsworthy's cousin, Arthur
Galsworthy, the story that became the crucial event impelling
so much of *The Forsyte Saga*. Barker concentrates on Ada's
selfishness and villainy by recording interviews with Arthur
Galsworthy's second wife that show him a gentle and harmless
soul, interested only in the Essex Yeomanry and a few hours of
quiet bridge in the evenings, a man who never suspected that his
wife was having an affair with his cousin for ten years, during
three of which he was off in South Africa defending his country.
Mr. Sauter and the other relatives are quick to defend against
the Dean/Barker point of view. They point out that Ada's illnesses were real and that Arthur Galsworthy long knew of his
wife's affair, or at least passively acquiesced to his wife's complete independence, for she established herself in her own flat,
close to the houses of her two good friends, John Galsworthy's
sisters, as early as 1898. Arthur did not seek a divorce because,
in their view, he did not seek anything but peace and quiet. Mr.
Sauter was, in fact, so annoyed at the appearance of the Barker

book that it became the subject, he later told me, for the only letter he wrote to the *Times* in his more than eighty years.

Mrs. Watts, having heard the Dean/Barker point of view expressed publicly at a meeting celebrating the Galsworthy Centenary in 1967, a meeting that apparently engendered more hostility than illumination, was eager to convince me to credit none of it. Yet her own memories of Ada seemed rather shadowy, portraying her as "elegant," a kind of symbol, "why, for me, she *was* Irene." Then, in a sudden moment, Mrs. Watts realized how remote and distant her version of the Galsworthys was, and her face broke into a slower, warmer smile than any I had seen all afternoon. "Yes, I suppose I really didn't know them very well, in spite of all the meetings and P.E.N. dinners and dinners at their house. Oh, of course, I worshipped him, and her, too, but it wasn't a worship that anything could ever have come of. I wouldn't even have imagined it. I had my own life to lead. I was young and in love—with lots of young men in the first few years, very much so with my husband in the last two years I worked. I guess I never did really give any emotional energy to Galsworthy, nor he to me. I was just too young, and in love, and quite pretty." The last point I can verify by a picture of herself she'd published in her book. The long skirts and drab contours of the 1916 uniform of the Women's Volunteer Service and the grim determination to master the semaphore flags she's holding at outstretched arm's length do not in the slightest obscure the high cheekbones and regular features of a very pretty young lady.

Mrs. Watts, striding quickly and surely, carried the tea from the kitchen on a heavy, antique, silver tea service and set out the sandwiches and cakes on a three-tiered Edwardian dark wood stand, "just the very few pieces my mother left me." Once I was served, she seemed to relax, leaning back in her chair as we talked of children's education. She wanted to know how my children found school in London, comparing it to the experience of both her English grandchildren and that of her American grandchildren in Vermont. We talked, too, of the social services, the Welfare state, the curious revival among British Tories of the thirties' fear that Communists were about to take or had already taken control of the industrial unions. She also told me a good deal about herself. Her husband, an artist for *Punch*, had died in a civil air crash in 1935, leaving her with three young children and little money. Most of the next thirty years had been spent in raising the family, educating the children, keeping things together. She had never written or been much interested in writing. And now, economically secure, she said, for the first time in her life, she had suddenly realized a few years ago that she must write her mother's biography: "All the information I have, all the letters, the stories, the people I remember. No one else has it. When I die, it will all be gone, permanently lost, if I don't get it written down. Maybe no one else cares—and I didn't for a very long time, I had other things to think about—but I feel I ought to get it down." As she walked me back down the well to her front door, her efficient briskness returned and she looked as if she had another ten or twenty years in which to set the record straight.

A day or two after I saw Mrs. Watts, she wrote me a letter, modifying slightly one of the anecdotes about Galsworthy and J. B. Priestley she had told me; she wanted to be sure that the information I had was accurate. And she telephoned a number of times in subsequent weeks, extending generous invitations and wanting to make certain I didn't miss the rhododendrons in Queen Mary's Garden in Regents Park, particularly fine that year, or neglect the gardens at Kenwood House. We also talked a good deal about her mother and biography, enough for me to sense that her interest in writing her mother's life was less an act of homage to the past than an act of self-definition, a process of setting straight her own record in terms she had not considered before.

May flourished in its brightest effulgence, chestnut blossoms everywhere along the route, on the day I went to Stroud to visit Mr. Sauter again. This time, by myself, I took the train, and a chipper, smiling Mr. Sauter was standing in the sunshine on the station platform when I arrived. He guided me to his car, opened my door, whippped round to the driver's seat, then pushed open the sliding roof as he quickly negotiated Stroud's narrow, precipitous streets on the way out to his cottage. He told me that his wife had always liked the roof open, especially in weather like this. We drove up the hill and, as the breeze filled the car, he took off his hat and tossed it into the back seat. When we reached his closed gate, he stopped and jumped out to open it, explaining that, at this time of year, the village cattle grazed the open common by right and an open gate was an invitation to return and find a stray cow among one's paintings and papers. Once inside, we talked of Galsworthy's relations with his sisters, Lilian and Mabel, and with his brother, Hubert. He described a generation breaking out from conventional upper-middle-class Forsytism. Lilian, the eldest, was the most "philosophical," and he showed me parts of his mother's early diary which mixes notes taken on Kant and Schopenhauer, analyses of family relationships (often directed against the interest in clothes, tidy housekeeping, and "exteriority" shown by her mother), and speculations about ethics, "truth," and the nature of art. After her marriage, Lilian's home became a kind of salon with visitors like Mark Twain, the young Ezra Pound, and Richard Aldington, not all of whom, by any means, praised the early literary efforts of young John Galsworthy. Then, Mr. Sauter smiled warmly: "But I think I missed most of the best evenings. All those people talking about art and music and literature, while I was off by myself being miserable at school." Mabel, the youngest, was interested in music. She later, having married a prosperous businessman, befriended and supported musicians such as Myra Hess, who, for a number of years, played the piano at her house almost daily. Only Hubert, in Mr. Sauter's terms, was "rather the odd man out." Quick, mechanical, owning the first motor car in Torquay, and very much an English patriot, Hubert had little interest in the artistic and the intellectual. "But," Mr. Sauter added, "you'll get a much better idea about Hubert from his children, my cousins Muriel and Hubert. I'm sure they'd be delighted to talk with you."

Over gin and tonic, our conversation drifted a generation back to Galsworthy's parents, Mr. Sauter's grandparents. Galsworthy had always written fondly of his father, both in fiction and in biographical essays, suggesting a strength and generosity not easy for a young man to measure himself against or to supplant. Mr. Sauter expanded on his memories of the old Victorian patriarch with a long white beard in his last years, a highly successful solicitor, "with a good brain and an open mind," fairly wide interests, and a demonstrative fondness for and curiosity about children. "But no interest in literature or art, almost none at all. The annual performance of Handel's *Messiah* at the Albert Hall was his limit." Mr. Sauter remembered the old man's last years well, when they lived in the same house, and retained, as his uncle did, his devotion for the kind man who could value activities and commitments he would never have engaged in himself. Old Jolyon was a widower even at the beginning of *The Forsyte Saga*, whereas Galsworthy's mother outlived her husband by more than ten years (she was twenty years younger than he). But Galsworthy seldom referred to her, and the fictional portraits that can, somewhat more hesitantly, be attached to her and the one short biographical essay are considerably less affectionate than those of the father. Mr. Sauter uttered a few phrases about her tightness, her conventionality, her less open mind, but then added, "again, you'd better talk to my cousins about her. You'll get an entirely different picture, especially from Muriel. They were very close." And I felt myself, momentarily, retreating slightly, as if, as a guest, I needed to be careful to avoid taking sides in a family alignment of forces that had been going on for three generations. There was no animosity now, no bitterness, but each Galsworthy still had a role on one side or the other.

We drove through Stroud and the valley and up the steep hill on the other side, into a cul-de-sac surrounded by chestnut blossoms, to Mrs. Scrivens' for lunch. She welcomed us heartily and took us up the stairs of her modern development house to show us the new shower she was having installed. She had made a moussaka for us, experimenting with the recipe she had found in a newspaper for what she guessed was an "old Swiss dish." As we ate the thick, tasty food, and drank the white wine, we talked about Bury House, the large home in a small Sussex village where Galsworthy had lived with his wife and Mr. and Mrs. Sauter for his last seven years. Galsworthy died in early 1933, was cremated and, two months later, as he had requested in a poem called "Scatter My Ashes," his wife and Mr. Sauter hired an airplane to scatter his ashes on the South Downs, where he often rode his horse above the village of Bury; the process was repeated for Mrs. Galsworthy in 1956, and again for Mrs. Sauter in 1969. Mr. Sauter has, in recent years, written his own poetic version of "Scatter My Ashes." Mrs. Scrivens thought I would like to see the Downs and Bury, many of the former servants still living there, and she particularly hoped I could see the studio near the house that Mr. Sauter had largely built for himself. At this point, her son, a young man who ran a local car-hire firm, came in to join us briefly for lunch. He wanted to know if I knew anything about Miami Beach. As I tried to rummage among recollections almost thirty years old, for I have not been to Miami Beach since I was stationed near there with the Air Force toward the end of the Second World War, Mrs. Scrivens interrupted, laughing, to say, "Oh, he's only interested in the girls who'd be lying *on* the beach," and poked her elbow fondly into her son's side. Over coffee in the lounge, a long room with low, square sofas in vivid red, purple, and beige, a room that seemed thick and warm, the three of us returned to the subject of Bury and decided that we might all, joined by my wife if possible, go down there for a few days to see the house and speak with the servants and other villagers. We began to make tentative arrangements, who would drive, pick up whom where. Mrs. Scrivens had recently been ill, and was still not sure how well she might take such a trip. Throughout the discussion, Mr. Sauter was the liveliest of the three of us, the one most full of possible suggestions, most considerate in thinking of everyone else's comfort and convenience, almost like the careful organizer of an expedition in a novel by Jane Austen.

Back at Mr. Sauter's, we found that the sun was high and hot, and we decided to sit outside, placing chairs on a shaded concrete ledge at the end of his garden, looking out over the valley. I quoted a 1910 diary entry in which Galsworthy mentioned a long political "argument" with his brother Hubert. Mr. Sauter replied: "1910? That might well still have been over the Boer

War. They disagreed about that fiercely. Hubert believed in it, was chauvinistic, he might even have been something or other in some Yeomanry. JG thought it was tragic, stupid, a Kiplingesque farce." This led us to a discussion of Galsworthy's politics, his interest in Edwardian causes, like easing solitary confinement for prisoners. Mr. Sauter himself, also strongly influenced by the First World War's disillusions and internments, was primarily interested in the postwar internationalism, and asserted that his uncle lost interest in domestic causes: "Except, of course, for Foggartism—you know, the emigration scheme he develops in *A Modern Comedy*. But he was only half-serious about that, knew it wasn't practicable." He had always been a Liberal, but, increasingly, as the Liberal party broke apart in the 1920s, he found no political locus in England and viewed English party squabbles as insular and provincial. I brought up the point that some other, younger writers (such as J. B. Priestley from whom I had recently had a letter politely saying that he had no wish to see me because he had nothing to add to his published opinions that Galsworthy's later novels were far inferior to his earlier ones and that although "a man with a tender conscience and genuine humane feelings, . . . he had not the natural fellow-feeling that men like Wells and Bennett had") might have resented that change in Galsworthy, might have viewed that early reformer as becoming indifferent, self-elevated, or the captive of a kind of complacent establishment. Mr. Sauter found that partly true, but added that the views of others might have been based on the sense that Galsworthy hadn't changed, hadn't any important and new emotional experience after the drama of his affair with Ada, the drama central to *The Forsyte Saga*. Later, around 1911 and 1912, Galsworthy had a flirtation with Margaret Morris, a young dancer and actress who organized and trained a troop of young girls who performed classical dances. In 1967, Miss Morris, then nearly eighty, had written a book, telling of her love for Galsworthy and Galsworthy's attraction to her. The only tangible result was a long, passionate kiss in the back seat of a taxi, although Miss Morris had been quite willing to go much further and claimed that only Galsworthy's consideration for his wife prevented an affair. Miss Morris had wanted the three

of them to live together as a "deeply passionate and happy tri-
umvirate." "Yes," Mr. Sauter said, "that may be a silly book in
some ways, but Margaret Morris mattered to him. I'm sure she
did though he never talked of it. He could put that behind him,
control it because he wanted to control it. He just wouldn't let
it shape his life, damage what he had with Ada."

We returned to talking of politics and control, of what
Galsworthy thought man could control and what he could not,
of his view of the impact of an individual's work and concern
on the general state of things. After a while, Mr. Sauter leaned
back in his chair and closed his eyes. "No," he said, "I'm not
tired. I'm thinking." He sat up and leaned forward into the sunlight, the lines on the side of his mouth deepening downward.
"What do you think JG would feel about things today? The
Bomb? The young? Vietnam? The way the world has gone in
the last forty years?" I replied in terms of the balance and control we had just been talking about, said I thought he would
have understood issues broadly, would have been one of the survivors. "No," said Mr. Sauter, shaking his head sadly. "I don't
think so. You're probably right that he'd have listened to non-
violent student radicals carefully. And he'd certainly have hated
Vietnam, like the Boer War. But you've missed the other side of
him. The sensitivity to suffering, the capacity to feel deeply
what others were feeling. He couldn't have stood the war, the
late thirties and after. The Nazis, the concentration camps, the
Bomb. They would have shattered him. Shattered. I often think
of him in that way, that he couldn't have stood it, was too sensitive for all that happened then. Sometimes, too, I think he saw
it coming in the early thirties. He was gloomy his last two years.
Not the slump, maybe not even his illness we all didn't really
recognize, but the world, Europe, Fascism. Maybe that even
hastened the end." Galsworthy died the morning after the
Reichstag fire he never knew about.

As the shade lengthened against the whole garden, we put
away the chairs and went inside for tea. I had already missed
the train I'd planned to take, and Mr. Sauter went to his bright
red telephone to find out the last train that would bring me
to London that night. As we drank tea, he talked of Ada

Galsworthy, the closeness of the marriage in which she, the only secretary he ever had, was always an intimate part of his work, and read and talked with him about everything he read. She was an accomplished pianist, "could have had a career of her own." She was often ill with asthma and bronchitis, genuinely ill Mr. Sauter knew, and Galsworthy rather enjoyed taking care of her, making her drinks and hot milk at night, insisting that they go to warmer climates each winter for her health. They had both, somehow, never expected that he, the physically invulnerable one, the calm one, would die first, and she was distraught when he did. She seemed to Mr. Sauter suddenly changed, for a time, strangely intense, "almost unbalanced." She wanted to destroy Galsworthy's favorite horse, and only his nephew Hubert's buying it prevented that; she destroyed all his letters to her and, apparently, a number of years of his diaries. After a short time, she and the Sauters decided to leave Bury, and she moved into the London house, sorting out and annotating Galsworthy's papers, while the Sauters went off on their own. During the Second World War, she was persuaded to move to Torquay to get away from the bombing. Although no bomb came near the Hampstead house, one exploded frighteningly close to the house in Torquay. Her eyesight had begun to falter even before Galsworthy died, and no longer able to play the piano (she permanently injured a finger separating two dogs who were fighting), she lived with a companion who sold a number of her valuable portraits of the family and Galsworthy's books for very little. Surviving the companion, living on in Torquay until she was nearly ninety, Ada Galsworthy, according to her nephew, seldom talked of the more recent past, of Galsworthy and their marriage, but, almost to his surprise, she would often recall the quiet cruelty and insensitivity of the first husband she still could not forgive.

The scent of chestnuts lingered in the soft, darkening light as Mr. Sauter drove me to the railroad station. We passed a cricket match just ending on the village common. Having read in his diary that Galsworthy had taken his nephew to the annual Eton-Harrow match at Lord's every year before the First War and recorded his annual disappointment at Harrow's nth successive loss, I asked Mr. Sauter if he had, in those days, shared his uncle's interest and loyalty. He laughed, "Lord, *no*. I was just polite and usually pretty bored. And, if my uncle had been about, you'd better have said the Harrow-Eton match instead of the Eton-Harrow. But he once came out with a funny theory. I haven't thought of this in years. After Harrow had been badly beaten again, he asked me how the food at school was. Like any schoolboy, I said it was terrible. 'That's it,' he replied. 'Terrible in my day, too. That's why we never win at cricket. I must write the headmaster about it.'" While we waited for the train on the station platform, Mr. Sauter briskly wrote out a number of addresses and phone numbers for me. As the train pulled out of the station into the night, I could still see him upright and smiling, waving good-bye.

On my next train journey south and west, a week or so later, I watched thick, dark clouds in swirling shapes, alternating with bands of intense blue, a sky like the background of a series of Gainsborough paintings, through the windows of the train. It never did rain that day, the background just providing a panorama of all the weather's possibilities, while my attention was concentrated on Miss Muriel Galsworthy. Miss Galsworthy had arranged to meet me in Westbury, a town in Wiltshire still on the main line after the reorganization that has closed many English railway stations, although she lived in the larger town of Warminster, a few miles away. She had phoned the evening before to confirm arrangements and to describe herself as rather small and grey-haired, but, when the almost empty train pulled into Westbury station, she was the only person waiting on the long platform. She walked up to me quickly and decisively as I left the train, a small and energetic woman with large, soft grey eyes and a rather wide mouth and full lips that added both warmth and humor to her face. She later asked me not to mention her age: "If you're going to write about me, you can say what you like but not that. I think it's a little bit rude and certainly lazy for a writer to rely on someone's age. He ought to be able to describe better than that." As we walked rapidly to her car, she asked me to have faith in her driving, "I may go fast, but it's safe. Very quick reactions. Like all the family, except Uncle Jack. He never drove you know." We glided smoothly through several small Wiltshire villages, clusters of hump-backed, thatched-roof cottages, surrounded by thick grey cloud. And the conversation turned to sport, as we compared our reactions to watching the recent football Association Cup Final on television and talked about the changes signified by the introduction of one day cricket matches. She told me that her father, Hubert Galsworthy, would never have approved of one day county matches, would have thought them un-English. She described him, in old age, during his last summer, the summer of the end of the Second World War, on the houseboat moored on the Dart River in Devon where he had lived alone for over thirty years, blind, twisting the dials of his wireless to get the latest county cricket scores of a hastily and only partially resurrected season.

We drove into Warminster, parking on a road perpendicular to the High Street in front of a row of Georgian cottages separated from the curb by only a few feet of sidewalk. But space expanded the moment Miss Galsworthy opened the front door, revealing a large hall with a step halfway up into a bay furnished with two comfortable armchairs in front of a large Palladian window that looked out into the garden. The hall, the bay, and the angled staircase that rose from one side of the bay all gleamed with highly polished wood, small colorful rugs, and carefully arranged pictures and pieces of china, a composite in miniature of all the surfaces appropriate to an English country house. Miss Galsworthy led me into the drawing room, painted a pale green with white trim to preserve its Georgian lines, although containing a large, comfortable sofa covered with a floral pattern and several antique cabinets. She asked me to help myself from any of the bottles arranged, almost like a Dutch still life, on a silver tray standing on the large, polished wood secretary. We sat down, I on the sofa, she on an upright armchair almost backing on the fireplace that looked as if it could have been designed by Robert Adam, and Miss Galsworthy began to talk about her grandmother. She described a tiny, tidy woman, always perfectly and elegantly dressed, fastidious and conventional, who never lost her dignity and was called, with respect, the "little Marquise" by the other residents of one of the hotels on the South coast where she lived during her last years. Miss Galsworthy moved briskly to the mantelpiece to fetch and hand me a miniature in a circular silver frame with elaborate scroll work, a drawing that she, as a teenager, had done of her grandmother's face. The fine drawing looked French in its simple lines and pastel elegance and revealed, in the delicately sharp features, a sense of severe compression and unvarying presence in facing the world. But her grandmother was also, Miss Galsworthy pointed out, invariably kind and considerate. Miss Galsworthy explained that her own mother, a Spanish girl who was "warm-hearted, lively, responsive to life though sometimes mystified by it," had been very close to her Galsworthy grandmother. Hubert and his Spanish wife had not, after the first few years, got on very well and had amiably resolved to go their separate ways, Hubert soon settling in his houseboat on the Dart. And her mother, Miss Galsworthy continued, had felt a bit frightened with two children to bring up in an alien land, one with all sorts of class divisions and difficult rules, and had relied more and more on the elder Mrs. Galsworthy. "In a way, my grandmother took over. She felt someone had to, and my mother was grateful. I remember, when I was five, my grandmother took me to an hotel for the holidays, the Imperial Hotel at Exmouth. I had to repeat every word I mispronounced. Strict, but it gave me an ear. She spoke so beautifully, every word sounded perfectly without anything stagey. And another time I'll always remember, when I was three, my grandmother visited, and was shocked to hear me talk. 'You must do something with that child,' she told my mother, 'she's speaking Cockney.' It was the nurse, and, of course, my mother, whose English was never very sensitive, simply didn't know. My mother argued that the nurse was such a kind woman and so good with my baby brother. But grandmother wouldn't budge, wouldn't change her standards. The nurse had to go—with a generous salary bonus—but no reprieve." We discussed the possible influence of such a woman on her own children, and we agreed that we could easily see how her children might revolt, especially daughters, and particularly the older daughter, Lilian, who, Miss Galsworthy said, "had Uncle Jack's brain with an added quickness Jack didn't have." But, she went on, the influence on sons must have been more complex. Her father had maintained an almost fanatical sense of order and precision on his houseboat. And, in her uncle, she thought the influence of his mother visible in his language, his own sense of dignity and balance, his sense (as he once, in print, rather off-handedly acknowledged) of both literary and behavioral form.

This conversation led to my speculation about another question. In 1894, Galsworthy began to see a great deal of his cousin's wife, Ada, whom he had met briefly at a family dinner celebrating her wedding more than two years earlier. For his family, young Galsworthy carried the aura of a world traveler, having, in the intervening two years, been around the world, sent by his father ostensibly to learn maritime law. Yet, for Galsworthy, the greatest value of the tour was the long all-night talks with Joseph Conrad, first mate on the *Torrens*, the ship on which Galsworthy returned from Australia to England. After his return, encouraged by both his sisters, who thought that the brilliant and musically talented Ada was wasted on a dull Army officer like Arthur (other cousins referred to him as "a cold fish"), John and Ada saw more and more of each other. They became lovers on September 3, 1895, an anniversary that, in his later diaries, calling it "de facto," Galsworthy noted more often than he noted the anniversary "de jure." The ten-year affair was well known to his sisters and to literary friends like Conrad, Ford Madox Ford, and Edward Garnett. Both John and Ada presumably hated concealment and subterfuge, but they would not go through the public process of her divorce and remarriage because of the anger and the pain the scandal might cause old John Galsworthy. They apparently agreed entirely on the motive for silence. When Ada revealed the affair publicly through the medium of H. V. Marrot's official biography of Galsworthy, published soon after Galsworthy's death and written with Ada's careful and apparently unceasing collaboration, she intended to suggest that the agreement between the two that his father could not be hurt was total. Marrot wrote that "one of them," although he doesn't say which, wrote a letter saying that "neither of them could grieve the declining years of his father"—a statement that preserves an unnecessary obscurity around who wrote what letter to whom. But the attribution of motive certainly seems unquestionable. In fact, the time between old John Galsworthy's death in December, 1904, at the age of eighty-seven, and the marriage between John and Ada Galsworthy on September 23, 1905, is, given the requirements of proof of adultery, a court hearing, and a lapse of time, within days the minimum then allowable by law. Yet, in all this consideration for the father, I could not find a word about the mother still alive, about what she might have thought or felt. I asked Miss Galsworthy about this. "Yes," she said. "My grandmother didn't talk about it, of course. But she accepted it. They didn't live near her, and she was always at Torquay, or at Menton, in France, in the winter. You see, she was more religious than the others. Church of England. The only religious one in the family, none of her children were. Maybe that helped her to accept it, even to welcome Ada. Yes, curious. One thinks he was the more large-minded, but, maybe, after all, it was she."

In the dining room, up two more polished steps from the bay, with a wide window showing large bushes of blooming forsythia and spirea in the garden, we ate cold salmon, boiled new potatoes, and salad, while occasional sudden shafts of sunlight made the dark wood table glisten. Miss Galsworthy talked about her father. The most direct, least complex of the Galsworthys, the family thought of him as a "clean potato," she laughed, urging me to help myself to seconds. She thought that a 1910 argument on politics between the brothers might just have been the usual party difference over any issue. John Galsworthy had always been a Liberal, Hubert a Conservative so staunch that his children both recall that, at one point, they were not allowed to go to the village tailor or bootmaker because these tradesmen supported the Liberals. Even during the Second World War, Winston Churchill's heroism and long Tory service were not enough for the older Hubert to excuse earlier Liberal heresies. And, in addition, Churchill "was less a gentleman" than Chamberlain. Miss Galsworthy described her father as thinner, slighter than his brother, with a "weaker mouth," though the same soft, grey eyes—each had one weak eye, John's the left, Hubert's the right—although, unlike his brother, Hubert never sported a monocle. Hubert was much the better athlete, a good shot, good golfer, yachtsman, highly proficient at billiards, football, cricket. Yet he was lazy, never went to University and had never intended to. He read a good deal of fiction and empathized strongly with a few characters: Thackeray's Colonel Newcome, his brother's Soames Forsyte. Although Hubert was impatient with ideas and thought his brother "heavy," too inclined to suffer over tragedies he could do nothing about or too pained by things like treatment of animals in slaughter houses, he was, thought Miss Galsworthy, always rather in awe of him. She repeated her father's favorite story, an account of the time in Vancouver, where both had been sent to conclude some business for their father's firm. They had been out on a lake in a canoe and waves from a larger boat had swamped them; John Galsworthy had been thrown in the water, and Hubert had pushed down his paddle, then reached in to pull his brother up by his hair. John emerged, face still expressionless, dignity unruffled. "It was the calm," Hubert would say, "not a muscle of his face had moved, not a hair out of place." Miss Galsworthy told another story of a later time when Hubert invited John and Ada to lunch on his houseboat. Anxious to repay their hospitality, which had always been aided by cooks and servants, he spent days preparing the meal and went miles to find the appropriate wines. But they, temporarily on a diet they had heard about, wouldn't drink, and they spent a good share of the lunch, wrapped in their own world, carefully modulating the pronunciation of "charabanc" back and forth to get the French shading exactly right. Hubert's fury, according to his daughter, lasted for years.

When, after serving me two portions of a subtly flavored delicious trifle and a dish of fruit prepared in case I, as an American, could not abide trifle, Miss Galsworthy asked if I liked my coffee weak or strong. I said strong. "Good," she replied, "Uncle Jack always took his strong. I think men should, though I prefer it weak." She then went on to describe coffee and evenings at Wingstone, a very different Wingstone from the one I had seen a few months earlier. The farmhouse had neither gas nor electricity; a large and intricate wrought-iron stand in the center of the drawing room held forty or fifty candles which Mrs. Galsworthy would light ceremoniously every evening, casting a glow on the paintings by deSmet, a Belgian refugee in the First War whom Galsworthy befriended. The farmhouse also had no bathroom, although the farmer's wife was always willing to carry a tin bath full of hot water up the stairs. Galsworthy himself was always the kindest host, carefully picking books to put on the bed table of each visitor, making sure that Miss Galsworthy and her mother knew the times of masses at the nearest Roman Catholic church and that the car was ready to convey them. "Uncle Jack was really *noble*. He was *never* petty or small-minded, and he got bigger as he got older." Miss Galsworthy told a number of anecdotes to illustrate his generosity, his aid to neighbouring villagers, his insistence on the best and most expensive care when her brother was ill, and his care for all the family in handling the money that he, the older son, had inherited in trust for the others from his father. On her twenty-first birthday, she told me, her uncle confided to her that her investments had not done as well as had some of the others, and he volunteered to make up the difference annually so that she would always have a sufficient income. As he became older, she thought, he was also less and less interested in politics, "although maybe I just didn't listen when politics were talked about. Oh, but he did like the Prince of Wales. The one who became Edward VIII. I think they shared a sense of suffering, a sympathy for all those people whose lives were so very different from theirs. He was so pleased that his O.M. was conferred by the Prince of Wales."

By this time, I had run out of cigarets. Miss Galsworthy apologized for not smoking and not having any fresh ones on hand, as if any possible form of comfort or guest's idiosyncrasy ought to have been anticipated. She did have some old cigarets, but told me that when her brother, Hubert, had last visited several months earlier and had run out of cigarets, he had tried a few and pronounced them unsmokably stale. I decided to walk into the High Street to try to find some while she prepared our tea. By this time, the grey clouds had thickened and a cold wind blew through the High Street. Not a shop was open—early closing—not a person about in this sudden moment of winter on the 22nd of May. I was glad to return to "the Chesnuts," as a small polished bronze plaque on Miss Galsworthy's door announced, to be greeted by the warmth of polished wood and the whistling kettle. As I carried the tray into the drawing room, carefully watching the steps, Miss Galsworthy said, "I'm glad to see you're cautious. That's the only thing that worries me about this house. I or someone else may slip on that polished wood I love so much. Broken hips can get serious." She quickly darted past me to open the door and clear a space for the tray on the table in front of the sofa. When we had settled again into talk, she spoke of Ada. She, too, had resented the assertions that Ada was hypochondriacal, thought she was often really ill and tried to ignore it as much as possible, never complaining. She also shared Galsworthy's generosity, and once, when Miss Galsworthy was at school in a convent and wrote requesting some old and unneeded things for a convent bazaar, Ada had gone to Harrods and ordered huge baskets of sweets, fruits, and delicacies to be sent to the convent. She had similar baskets delivered to Sherborne where Galsworthy had sent the younger Hubert to school. Yet she also protected her husband, answered a lot of the silly letters, like one from a woman who sent her picture and wanted Galsworthy to exchange it for one of his. "We all roared at breakfast when Aunt Ada said, 'Let me deal with that one.'" Sometimes, Galsworthy was defensive about his generosities, as if his wife might not permit them. Miss Galsworthy recalled one day at Bury when he came in to tea with a beautiful Windsor chair saying that one of the villagers had given it to him. It took Ada, laughing all the while, about twenty minutes to drag out the fact that he had bought the villager's cottage, under foreclosure, allowing the family to continue living there, and been given the chair as a token of gratitude. "Some people might have found her hard to get to know. Although she was always kind and could do very generous things, they never knew if they were coming or going with her. Not always. I remember one American woman, very hard, very brittle, my mother and I met somewhere and took there to tea. She was one of the few who liked Ada better than she liked Uncle Jack, thought she seemed to know more about life, less easily fooled. But it was the other way around with most people. Like my father who preferred my mother's warmth, her 'giving out,' which Ada never had. She just wasn't my father's 'cup of tea.' He once said, 'her eyes never meet yours.' And I suppose that was true. Her eyes were dark, off somewhere. She didn't seem quite real. She *floated*, yes, floated. She seemed, sometimes, to be talking to the walls, but what she said was very apt, sharp, to the point . . . No, she never talked to me about Arthur Galsworthy. Maybe she thought she could change him and found she couldn't. Was he some sort of roué? You probably know more about that than I do . . . But she and Uncle Jack did have a *real* marriage. They were together, and I've seldom seen one quite like it. They did all sorts of things for each other, without speaking about it, and she was part of his work, not just a scribe. I remember once, near the end, I was staying with them in London, and Aunt Ada asked me to invite some of my girl friends to dinner. It was quiet, rather formal, then, after dinner, while Aunt Ada was playing, Uncle Jack said 'play something common for these young girls.' She played 'I'll Be Loving You, Always.' After a time—it always took him a while—he warmed and got up and started to dance with one of the girls. And he laughed—he was slow, but when he laughed, finally, it went all the way through. And she did, too. They could always catch each other's mood perfectly." They never, however, according to Miss Galsworthy, talked of children. He seemed shy around children, although teenagers venerated him because he would talk to them as if they were grown up. When Miss Galsworthy once had a troop of Cub Scouts under her care, her uncle politely refused to talk to the group, saying he wouldn't have the slightest idea of what to say.

The late May twilight was still the same dense, cold grey as we moved back to the kitchen and Miss Galsworthy talked of her own life, her interest in religion, her work as a driver for the blind, taking them to jobs or to doctors' appointments, her interest in her house and her garden. She was still close to her brother and sister-in-law (several of her sister-in-law's paintings hang in the house), her niece and nephew, and her cousin Rudolf. She wanted to know if I had seen Rudolf's house and his garden. When I said I had, she replied, "A shame you hadn't seen it earlier. It was lovely when his wife was alive. The house was beautiful, and she did the gardening all herself. Now, he has paintings stacked all over the place. And then he had some hippie gardener who just let the place go to seed. A forty-year-old hippie, long auburn hair, beard that made him look Christ-like. Rudolf taught the gardener to paint, and the gardener talked to him about Zen and things. Very intelligent, really very nice—but, then, nobody paid any attention to the garden. For a while, the gardener, Ken I think his name was, tried a commune, but it didn't work so he came back to Rudolf's. Now, I think he's gone again. He married, one of those hippie flower ceremonies that Rudolf said he enjoyed. And he and his wife and her teenaged daughter went bicycling off to India. The daughter went as far as central France and came back. I don't know what's happened to Ken and his wife. Rudolf's garden still, I suspect, hasn't recovered."

Miss Galsworthy gathered her keys and carefully turned on lights because, intending to visit a friend after taking me to the station, she wouldn't be back until after dark. We talked of the recent television production of Galsworthy's play *The Skin Game*, one we both had liked, although she had some reservations about casting. When we reached the station, she insisted, like her cousin, on coming to the platform with me and waiting until the train pulled away. As we waited, she said, "I just remembered one more story I hadn't thought of in a long time. It's really more about my mother . . . when my mother was first married, she once came up to London to shop. Uncle Jack met her at the station with a dozen roses. He wasn't married then, and she knew nothing about Ada. He said he wanted to take her to meet a friend of his for tea. When they reached the house, my mother said some instinct made her leave the roses downstairs. They went up, into a large room, almost bare except for a big grand piano. Ada was very gracious and formal, served them tea, her two little dogs squeaking a kind of grace before tea. Then she played for a while. When my mother and Uncle Jack left, my mother picked up the roses and said, 'You see, I left these so the lady wouldn't see them.' Uncle Jack smiled, but he never said a word. And my mother was convinced that she would never understand England."

Arrangements to see Miss Galsworthy's brother, Hubert John, had to be more tentative, for, in the spring and summer, depending on the weather, he lives either on the farm near Winchester that his uncle bought for him more than fifty years ago or on the boat, moored at Maidenhead on the Thames, that he has since bought for himself. The last week in May was warm and beautiful, soft hazy blue weather, and Hubert phoned inviting me to spend a day with him and his wife on the boat. A quick train from Paddington brought me to Taplow, the nearest railroad station to the boat, and I phoned the boat yard. When I had waited outside the tiny station, scanning the advertisements for one-day excursions to Brighton and Southend, for about the expected ten minutes, a car drove up and a heavy, jowly, tired-looking man, who seemed in his late sixties, laboriously extricated himself from behind the wheel, managed a smile, and came toward me. I was relieved to find out that this was not Mr. Galsworthy, that this man had come to meet someone else. And, a moment later, I saw a thin, wiry, grey-haired man, dressed in a double-breasted blue blazer, almost running across the overpass from the other side of the tracks, and recognized immediately both the Galsworthy face and the characteristic energy. Within two minutes from the narrow station road, surrounded by overhanging trees, we were on a broad six-lane motorway; within two more, we were on the narrow, rutted strip of river bank so that we could park as close to the boat as possible. As we pulled up near the boat, Mr. Galsworthy asked if I remembered the scene in *A Modern Comedy* in which Soames, just shortly before he dies, goes to Devon to trace his ancestors and the chauffeur lands the car in a ditch. "Well," he continued, "the very same thing happened to my uncle. In 1922. He went down to Wembury to trace the Galsworthys and, almost sideswiped in the rain, the chauffeur landed in a ditch. No one hurt. The vicar took care of him, brought him all the parish records. Exactly like the novel." As I got out of the car, I saw a line of boats moored alongside the Thames, all in the shadow of Maidenhead Bridge, a chunky stone structure the foundations of which date from the thirteenth century, although the bridge and roadbed are only two hundred years old. It was being repaired, supported with a structure of iron pipes, so that the increasing volume of traffic wouldn't undermine the foundations. Away from the bridge, the Thames curves gracefully, a line of boats stretched along one side, heavy elms and willows interspersed along the opposite bank, the few buildings subordinated to the trees which are constantly in gentle movement, and the water far cleaner and less polluted than it was only a few years ago. The gentle curves, and the thickness of color and texture, made me think that this might be a day closer to Constable than to Gainsborough.

The boat itself was trim and comfortable, wood and fabrics in muted colors. The Galsworthys planned to spend most of that summer moored at Maidenhead, for Mrs. Yvette Galsworthy, many of whose other paintings are of flowers or still life, was then working on views of the Thames and found numerous possible views she wanted to paint without moving from the top deck of the boat. She was a rather large woman with a square face, high cheekbones, large, brownish-hazel eyes that scrutinized one intensely as she talked. Looking at the two Galsworthys, I thought of John Galsworthy's classification of English faces into two types: the long, thin face, angular and composed, often reflective; the heavier, square face, showing solidity and determination. I did not, however, want to dwell on John Galsworthy's taxonomies of physiognomy too fondly, particularly since these included the pair of calipers that, at one period in the twenties, he kept on hand to measure the head of every visitor in order to gauge his or her cranial capacity. As soon as Hubert Galsworthy brought drinks out from one of the wooden cabinets and mixed them, he began to talk of current politics, saying that he was distressed by the Watergate revelations because he regarded Nixon as the best president the United States has had since Woodrow Wilson. When I asked him why, he talked of foreign affairs, détente, trips to Russia and China, along with the posture of "law and order," the insistence on discipline. He went on to say that, perhaps, it was really Henry Kissinger he valued most, for he could think of no public figure currently more valuable and effective. Mrs. Galsworthy joined the conversation: "Yes, it's really Kissinger. All the intelligence and the drive. That's because he's Jewish. No other race can combine intelligence and drive so well. He just never stops, never gives in, until he's made people see reason. He's tireless."

Varieties of conservatism led us back into the Galsworthy past, and Mr. Galsworthy confirmed his sister's view of their grandmother, underlined not only her sense of presence but her broad-mindedness, and repeated that standard accounts of the family background had not done her justice. Mrs. Galsworthy added that her own grandmother, long before her family had any connection with the Galsworthys, had once described the author's mother, whom she had met in the south of France, as "more regal than the Princess Marie Louise." Mr. Galsworthy wanted to stress the other side of his grandmother, saying that although it must have been a "shock" to her when her eldest son, who could have been so successful at the bar, became a writer, she did appreciate his work. Her pride, unlike that of the Galsworthy clan, was not simply connected with his financial success. We then shifted to the two Galsworthy brothers, as always, to the son and nephew, "mentally poles apart, although genuinely fond of each other." Mr. Galsworthy continued: "It wasn't just politics. Conservative and Liberal. They just approached everything in an entirely different way. My father rushed to join a League for Air Defense that started in '20 or '21, when Uncle Jack wanted to obliterate flying altogether. And I remember once, with my father, taking Uncle Jack on a boat trip up the Dart River to Totnes. My father tried to show him how to handle the boat and pointed out the scenery on the way. But Uncle Jack didn't care much for the scenery, still less for the boat. He only wanted to see what he'd heard was the thickest yew in all of England and measure its trunk. When we got there, he kept walking around the yew, measuring it with outstretched arms, and my father just couldn't see the point. But the real irony concerned money. My father thought Jack 'a fool with money, no idea of it at all, never talks about it,' yet it was my father who lost his patrimony. He had an income of £350 a year when he married, not bad at all for those days, but he invested it badly. Uncle Jack had to bail him out, later gave him an annuity, and he constantly helped my mother after my parents separated, sent both my sister and me to school. Uncle

Jack gave lots of money away. Didn't seem to think of it. The chauffeur at Grove Lodge once told me that tramps had a sign on the wall saying 'You'll be given something here.' But his investments, his patrimony, always seemed to accumulate."

Over a lunch of cold salmon, potatoes, strawberries, and lots of beer, Mr. Galsworthy continued expressing his reverence for his uncle. "No man's ever touched him." "A terrific influence on my life." "Really taught me to think things through for myself." He thought that Galsworthy's greatest distinction as a man was his capacity to listen, to absorb experience. Galsworthy had spoken very softly, judiciously, had always been able to understand how or why others felt as they did. "I remember Hugh Walpole—do you know his novels?—at lunch one day. He held the stage, talked all afternoon. My uncle just listened tolerantly, never said a word even though I'm sure he knew that most of what Walpole said was nonsense. That's why my uncle was a better novelist. I've always tried to listen, to learn things. Just the other day a chap in the pub over here told me that the Russians were short of rubber during the Second World War. So they planted acres and acres of dandelions to get rubber from the roots. I didn't know that. Did you? . . . Uncle Jack could always understand what he didn't approve of. He'd long since given up shooting, out of conviction, but when I went down to Bury he bought me a gun in case I might want to shoot. I did. He bought me the place at Winchester, set me up in farming, but he never made me feel that I owed it to him to take his advice . . . Yes, the farm still runs," Mr. Galsworthy laughed, "not an investment he'd have lost on." In later years, Mr. Galsworthy had also become a professional photographer. I remarked that, with the exception of a few photographs taken by E. O. Hoppé about 1912 or 1913, all the photographs I'd seen of Galsworthy had him facing the camera, ramrod straight, as if he wasn't going to flinch before the firing squad. "Yes," replied Mr. Galsworthy, "that's a shame. I only took up photography after he died. I think, had he lived longer, I could have persuaded him to relax more in front of the camera. I am sorry for that. It might have been the one thing I could have done for him."

Every time we passed away from reverence or opened the tab of another can of beer, we returned to the theme that Galsworthy had been slow-moving and unmechanical. He was always "awkward, he thought of how he would do something and then did it the wrong way, soft-handed." Galsworthy had really hated airplanes, would never fly, was ill at ease on boats, and would have been horrified at the idea of tape recorders. "It was always safe to get him a watch for Christmas because the last one was sure to have broken down. Even his pens always scratched." A few moments later, as I was struggling to flush the boat's toilet properly, trying to follow the directions I'd been so carefully given for synchronizing the pulling of two levers, watching the water gurgle but simple refuse to replace itself, I felt my own identity with Galsworthy grow to its strongest pitch.

Like his sister, Mr. Galsworthy watches any dramatization of a Galsworthy play he can and reads everything written about his uncle. He was particularly disturbed by a C. P. Snow broadcast about Galsworthy's work, "making it sound so wooden, missing everything humanitarian about the books." He wanted to know what I thought of Lord Snow's own fiction and was pleased that we could relegate it into a category. We talked of government officials and Parliament, and the way they saw things in a different perspective, as if everything could be controlled. He had known and corresponded with Sir Gerald Nabarro, the outspoken and eccentric Tory M.P., a dedicated individualist, who had recently died. "We corresponded because he loved Uncle Jack's work. Read it all over and over. But, still, he couldn't have understood it all that well. He wasn't nearly as wide. He wanted to abolish smoking. Uncle Jack could never stand people abolishing things for others." He shook his head and lit another of his cigaret-sized cigars, while his wife and I smoked cigarets. Mr. Galsworthy told me that he had once thought he might go into politics, had ideas about the country. But his uncle had convinced him that politics, especially party politics, was "a very dirty game." He twirled his little cigar in his fingers, stopped and thought. "Maybe, the really talented never do go in for politics. Like my uncle who gave up trying to do things through

politics pretty early in his career. Or my cousin Rudolf, whom
you know. Rudolf was an amazing boy, a painter, could write,
top boy at math at Harrow as well. He could have done anything.
You should have seen the dining room at Bury. Rudolf painted
various types of Africans and people in each panel of the dining
room wall. Marvelous. But they're all gone now. Don't know
what happened to them. I'm sure Rudolf doesn't himself. He
had too many talents and no direction, doesn't care what happens to his work. Strange chap. Maybe what my uncle had that
no one else in the family did was judgment. Yes, judgment."

Mr. Galsworthy and I went out on the narrow back deck to
catch more of the fading breeze, while his wife prepared tea. He
talked of some of the other boats moored along the Thames,
and waved to the owners, sunning themselves or working on
their decks. He talked of his days as "number one" on a minesweeper during the Second World War, his interest in the ship
as a disciplined community, his willingness to argue with the
Admiralty for conditions he thought his men deserved. When his
wife brought out tea and joined us, we began to talk about Ada
Galsworthy. They were not as upset about the book charging
her with "hypochondria" as the others I'd talked to had been.
"Hypochondria would be going too far," Mr. Galsworthy said,
"but she was spoiled. And she loved the attention she could
get when she was ill, and going abroad every winter. But she
was a marvelous hostess, often more at ease with new people,
especially men, than Uncle Jack was. She wasn't domestic, always had a housekeeper, and Vi Sauter took care of everything
at Bury. She was an intellectual—understood everything quickly,
read and thought a lot, intelligent and practical too, always
saw what people were up to. I was really very fond of her."
Mrs. Galsworthy was clearly somewhat less fond of her husband's aunt. "Of course," she added, "I only met her once, but I
thought her selfish, stone-cold, probably to everyone other than
JG. But even then, quite some time after his death, you could
tell they were attuned emotionally and intellectually, really one
being. They were attuned astrologically as well, a Leo and the
cusp between Scorpio and Sagittarius. Only a Leo could have
lived with that combination, and she realized it." We talked
about astrology for a time, Mrs. Galsworthy asking me my sign

and those of the rest of my family, sympathizing with my wife for a concatenation of planetary influences undoubtedly hard on her. Mr. Galsworthy brought in the fact that Ada had become very much interested in astrology in her later years. "Not only astrology," he went on. "When she didn't go to Mt. Dore, the mountain in south central France supposed to be good for bronchitis, one winter, in 1935 or maybe '36, I introduced her to a quack I knew in London . . . maybe you take the word 'quack' to mean something more dishonest than I do. I mean a 'quack' as using homeopathy or herbalism or ESP—things like that—they weren't allowed to practice after the National Health Service came in in '48. At any rate, Ada got on very well with this chap. He cured her, or at least helped her, and she never went abroad for the winter again. You see, not really hypochondria, because she really was ill. But who knows the sources of illness? And she kept up with this chap, this homeopath. He still often went down to see her in Torquay. She helped him write his book, which became quite well known, something about man's unknown journey—he had all these theories but he couldn't write very well." I asked if Galsworthy had had any interest in astrology or homeopathy. "No, not really," said his nephew, "but he was very interested in cures. You know, I'm sure, about his work as a masseur in France during the First War. Even before that, my sister was once ill, had a hole in her stomach for six months. He had specialists for her. And then he got on the phone to Germany, to have the first mercury vapor or ultraviolet ray lamp seen in England sent over. It worked. The doctor later bought the lamp from my uncle, made a fortune with it in Eastbourne, and retired by the time he was forty-five."

The sun, now lower in the west, came out from behind a large willow and hit us squarely in the face, so we went back into the cool shade of the cabin and Mr. Galsworthy drew the curtains over the portholes. "I was very fond of Ada," he repeated, "but I felt I never quite got through to her. She wasn't warm, didn't show any *continuity* of feeling. The time I remember most was a visit I made right before the war. Probably 1938, but before Munich. We were talking about the Germans. I said I thought their viciousness was exaggerated, that they weren't as bad as people said. Aunt Ada was furious. She said, 'You just *don't* know what you're talking about. They're dreadful. To Jews. To anybody.' We had a real falling out, and her anger at me lasted a long time. But of course she was right. She had traveled, had first-hand information, friends, people she helped. She did know what she was talking about, and I didn't. I didn't see her again until after the war." We talked, then, of the Nazis, the current tendency to romanticize them or to repeat, slavishly, the slogans about efficiency or discipline that lulled so many into insensitivity in the thirties. "Yes," Mr. Galsworthy said, "we sometimes do that, we English. We want discipline so much that we sometimes don't see what it can mean. Uncle Jack saw it all, though. He was very worried about the future, felt war was coming in '31 and '32. I think it killed him. He made me read a book called *Wars and Weapons* which argued that we were unprepared, and he said 'the British make up their minds but always just too late.' He worried more than people knew or understood. Hypersensitive and sound judgment, too."

The breeze began to pick up slightly as I crossed the plank from the boat to the riverbank. Mrs. Galsworthy leaned out to say good-bye and said that I must bring my wife when I came to visit them again, next summer if we couldn't manage it later this year. "Yes," Mr. Galsworthy echoed, as he drove me back to the station, "next time, when you and your wife come down, we must cruise down the river. We'll move a bit, not just talk about my uncle, though of course I'm always delighted to answer any questions about him. Once a fellow in a pub, a good friend, said hadn't it been hard on me growing up in the shadow of such a famous uncle. 'Not a bit,' I said, 'not at all. He couldn't have been kinder or more understanding. I feel lucky to have had such an uncle. Learned a lot I wouldn't have otherwise.'" On the train back to London, I thought that the day had not been quite as straightforward a route into part of the past as I had perhaps anticipated. I could not always distinguish, as easily as rational models for research suggested, gentle eccentricity from insight, and I realized that both were combined in the imagination of the England I was trying to understand.

❧

Back in London, letters and telephone calls further defined the planned trip to Bury. Unfortunately, Mr. Sauter and I should have to go alone. Mrs. Scrivens was still not feeling well enough to join us, and my wife could think of no one easily available with whom she would feel comfortable leaving the children for two days. My wife and I agreed to let baby-sitting decide it, which would leave Mr. Sauter and me more room for the play of identities. Until a few weeks earlier, a loquacious, elderly Scottish nurse who lived in the neighborhood, had stayed with the children when we left overnight and fed the cat while we were away. But she had recently been forced to move from her Chelsea flat to a distant section of London by a property developer eager to evict and remodel so that he could quadruple rents. Eviction took the form of refusing to make repairs, boarding up other flats in the building as they became vacant, and employing noisy demolition crews, gradually making it intolerable to live in a deteriorating shell. Miss Beattie had left, with her cats and her vast collection of postcards of Edinburgh and Fort William, still hoping that the Labour government she enthusiastically supported would set things right. Mr. Sauter and I made arrangements to visit Bury alone. Having decided to travel to London by rail, he looked up with meticulous consideration all the times of possible trains and carefully explained the alternatives. The projected journey back more than forty years began to dominate my imagination.

Close as the village was to London, the trip to Bury also represented a point of focus on an England that I had known little about in previous years. As June began and I realized how little time I had left on this visit, scenes and images of southern England absorbed my attention. I recalled my images from past years, beginning with the year in Scotland and its sense of the dour and granite fortress built against the sea. I thought, too, of the year spent working for the U.S. Air Force, my wife and I living mostly in Cambridge, shuttling between weekends spent punting to old pubs along the Cam and weekdays bringing some of our Cambridge friends out to the base to join in teaching the classes on history (by reading newspapers) and math (my wife shooting craps with her students) for the educationally deprived airmen, relishing each jolt that close observation of one group gave to the stereotyped judgments of the other. I pictured the year in Sheffield in architectural images: the sturdy, heavy, Victorian brownstone houses in brewer's baronial style that stretch toward Derbyshire in one direction and the cramped, huddled terraces that cluster alongside the licensed betting offices and steel mills along the muddy river toward Rotherham in the other. In the midst of these images, I recalled another, a dark, gloomy summer's day in 1960 when, driving across the Yorkshire moors and then down through some of the West Riding mill towns, a poet friend and I passed through Hebden Bridge, noticing men wandering the streets in front of closed mills who resembled, with their cloth caps and threadbare jackets, the pictures of the unemployed in the thirties, as we heard, on the car radio, the news that Aneurin Bevan had died. I realized that my past images all carried political implications, found sympathy for and value in various British qualities that could be opposed to some vague sense of a central or "establishment" Englishness. It was as if I, as an alien, had been more comfortable with mild rebellions from the left, had given a peripheral and political cast to my Anglophilia, avoiding too self-consciously, perhaps, the possibility that I might be mistaken for one of those ascotted young American academics who tries to pass as Oxbridge.

During this year just past, I had recognized that the images peripheral to a central Englishness and to southern England would not do as an attempt to understand Galsworthy. I was old enough not to be afraid of poses. In the effort to get closer to what Galsworthy was and what he represented, I had needed to get closer to a sense of southern England. Accordingly, this had been a year of thatch, of rolling green hills, soft landscapes, and low stone walls. My wife and I had visited Devon and Wiltshire a number of times during the year. We had shown the children the cathedrals at Salisbury, Winchester, Gloucester, Wells, and Exeter, letting them roam to outline with fingers in the air the traceries of stone or the space of vaultings, to watch the changing colors and reflections as sun moved against stained glass. They became so interested in stained glass and churches that we frequently stopped at smaller ones, like the church of St. Mary the Virgin in Fairford, a small Gloucestershire town, where the exceptionally rich stained glass tells the long, sequential Biblical stories of Genesis and Exodus. As sun and cloud alternated late on that cold early March afternoon, after having spent an hour watching all the variations in the stained glass, the children were fascinated as a sexton in the empty church showed them how to do brass rubbings until the cold cramped everyone's fingers. We also planned, before we left England, to take a week in Kent, a slow week of abandoned castles, churches, country houses, and cricket matches. Strongly as I sympathized with Miss Beattie, my attention, as I worked out what journeys time would permit, was drawn toward the southern counties, particularly toward Bury and the Sussex Downs where Galsworthy rode and wrote on almost every day he could during his last seven years.

Just two days before we went to Bury, I went down to Ham, on the southwestern edge of London, to see Mr. Dwye Evans, who had recently retired from Heinemann's, and whose father, C. S. Evans, an editor and essayist, directed the firm and was close to Galsworthy both personally and professionally. I took the London Underground to the end of the line at Richmond, reading Michael Foot's biography of Bevan on the way, then a taxi from the suburban town center, crowded and bustling on the clear summer morning, out to Ham. As we neared Ham Common, we passed rows of detached, red brick Georgian houses, each set carefully behind clumps of landscaped bushes and trees, often topped by an individual white-framed circular window or set off by painted sashes for windows and doors. As metaphors for Dutch painting began to form in my mind, the taxi driver interrupted, "Is there an American colony around here? You're the third American I've brought out from Richmond station in the past two days." We quickly found the white Georgian house at the end of the Common, although, until I had walked through the tree-shrouded entrance under the glass-covered portico, and made a right-angle turn, I could not really see the spacious and symmetrical proportions of the house built in 1770. Once inside, I was shown down two steps into the drawing room with a large bay overlooking the back garden, just as Mr. Evans, a tall, balding man in his early seventies, bounded down a short flight of steps from another direction at the back of the house. After he greeted me, he opened the photograph album he had been carrying to show me a series of informal snapshots taken at Manaton in the summer of 1919 or 1920. Most of the snapshots centered on a makeshift cricket pitch, showing a burly and enthusiastic C. S. Evans, bowling or throwing out his arms, an elegant Ada Galsworthy, smiling but never getting too close to the wicket, and a composed Galsworthy, bat in hand, facing the bowling, but, as always, ramrod straight, as if the photograph were a prelude to losing his wicket with dignity. Mr. Evans told me how Galsworthy had loved to organize games, which everyone enjoyed, and I began to see how the photographs faithfully depicted one who would always assume the role of straight man in any form of amusement, but who needed the game as he needed the shape of a novel or play. Mr. Evans then described how, as a young man, one of his jobs was to organize a cricket side from among Heinemann's employees and transport them down to Bury for an annual match against the villagers led by Galsworthy himself. The matches were events measured by elaborate lunches, teas, and suppers supplied by the Galsworthys, long tables set out on the lawn overlooking the smooth local cricket pitch, and ending ceremoniously with a silver cup passed to the winning side. Mr. Evans couldn't remember what had happened to the cup, but he was sure that Heinemann's had won the last match in the summer before Galsworthy died.

Mr. Evans began to talk of his father who, as a young editor and writer working for another firm, had known Galsworthy well. When, in 1915, C. S. Evans, rejected for military service as physically unfit, had a number of offers from various publishers, Galsworthy urged him to accept the one from his own publisher, Heinemann's, because he thought the firm the best publishers of current fiction. The two remained very close from that point on, together editing *Reveille*, a periodical dedicated to rehabilitating men coming out of the services that the Ministry of Pensions supported at the end of the First World War. The journal published poems and stories as well as articles concerning pensions and new forms of treatment available for wounded ex-servicemen. As Mr. Evans expanded on the relationship between the two, he resolved what had been, for me, a minor biographical puzzle. Other sources had, I understood, publicly and privately credited C. S. Evans with the idea for expanding *The Man of Property* (published in 1906) into *The Forsyte Saga*, carrying the same characters through further novels and further years, yet Galsworthy had committed himself to such an extension in his diary in the summer of 1918 without mentioning the advice or opinions of anyone else. "Oh, the *idea* was entirely Galsworthy's own," Mr. Evans said authoritatively. "My father's contribution was simply the publishing venture, putting the first three novels into one, suggesting Galsworthy might provide linking narratives, like, you know, 'The Indian Summer of a Forsyte,' and calling it all *The Forsyte Saga*. He suggested this in 1921. At first, Galsworthy objected, thought the large volume might hurt the sales for individual volumes, but my father convinced him and published *The Forsyte Saga* in one volume in May, 1922. It was the first of the omnibus volumes, and omnibus volumes in general did well, almost came to dominate the publishing scene between the two wars. But the idea, the continuation of the characters, was all Galsworthy's. No one could or would have dictated to him, or even suggested, about something like that."

As we sipped black coffee, Mr. Evans, who himself joined Heinemann's in 1927, talked of Galsworthy personally, of his kindness, his representation of the word "liberal" in every sense, his refusal to be snobbish, his quiet friendliness with and concern for packers, shippers, secretaries in the office. Mr. Evans thought that Galsworthy's visits to Heinemann's office provided the attitudes visible in his characterization of Bicket, the young packer in *The White Monkey*, the first volume of *A Modern Comedy*. Unable to support his ill wife, Victorine, on his salary, Bicket steals books to sell on his own, while Victorine poses in the nude for a painter, a violation of her husband's code of morality, as the only way she can help to support herself. We both thought the depictions of Bicket and Victorine sentimentalized, an example of Galsworthy's sympathy for a class he did not understand very well, a sort of benevolent liberalism from a distance.

When Mr. Evans went back to his kitchen to get us another pot of the thick, black French coffee, I thought of how I had also, to myself and to others in stories I told, sentimentalized and made a class representative of a woman who also posed in the nude for painters. I could understand how I had done so, how vaguely and vicariously I had appreciated a world so clearly not my own. During my year in Scotland in the early fifties, I had, whenever I visited London, stayed in the small house of the mother of an actor friend, one of the only houses on a rubble-bordered street, just off the Brixton Road not far from the Kennington Oval, that had not been bombed out during the Second World War. She was poor, and the job posing for students at a London Art College that she had found through some other friends of her son was her only source of income at the time. She felt herself too heavy and weary to char any longer as she had before and during the Second War. Still, she would refuse to let me pay more than one pound ten a week for bed and breakfast on my frequent visits. And, on the table in her old green, wood-panelled kitchen, she invariably left a single boiled egg she had hoarded from her ration, and a steaming pot of tea, late at night, so that I would not go to bed "peckish." On nights when I was not too late, I had developed the habit of stopping at the off-license on the corner on my way back to buy a small bottle of gin. We would drink it neat, as I ate my egg, and she would tell long and elaborate stories, accompanied by many gestures and exaggerated changes in facial expression, stories about her childhood in the country, about her days as a young barmaid in London around 1919 or 1920 and all the attempted assaults on her virtue that she put down sharply though with understanding, about her later years as a widow bringing up the two older children she had been left as well as her illegitimate son, my friend, by working as a char in clubs and a barmaid at the refreshment tents at race meetings, stories of her fear during the Blitz when she would gather all her favorite possessions under the narrow staircase, mimicking the official phrases like "London can take it" and "stiff upper lip," stories of later adventures like hop-picking in Kent. I had loved her stories, repeating them often to others. I realized that I had little way of knowing what in them was a record of her own experience and what had been derived from the radio plays she listened to almost every day, repeating the dialogue almost word for word days or weeks later. Her dramatizations would rush from Thomas Hardy to J. B. Priestley to Noel Coward, all mixed with her own experiences. The stories of her past were never sufficiently consecutive to allow one to trace any kind of biography through her comedy and drama, even to tell to which of her several principal men she had married and which she had not. Whenever I would try to string stories together or would ask her questions directly, she would frown with mock severity, hold out an index finger, and say, "No, no, ducks. Let's not get into all that. Let the past stay buried and tell me again that story you told about those thieving watch merchants in Italy." I, like the art students, simply called her "Miss Quartz," an entirely fictional name she enjoyed; more formally, she used the last name of her actor son, the child she was proudest of, although it had never been hers. Eight years later, I went to visit her when she was working in the bookkeeping department at Simpsons, Piccadilly. Changing times and the need for an income larger and more stable than one earned by posing for art students had led her to a job as a cashier in a Lyons Corner House; an unsuspected talent for computing accurately and a sharp eye for possible financial cons had led to better jobs. At Simpsons, in 1960, her hair that had been almost white now glistening with a bluish rinse, she took me to the staff lounge for tea and told me that she had recently gone as a spectator to Epsom on Derby Day, where she had tended bar several times more than thirty years earlier: "Yes, ducks, I saved all winter. I went like a Lady. Bought myself a grey dress and a grey hat, a return ticket on the train, all fixed up. I even had a few pounds left over to bet, which I lost, like a Lady. But don't you ever tell my son. He'd never approve." As I thought of her, I realized that I had, for years, in my stories, made her my representative of the healthy earthiness of the London poor, their sense of vitality, of sexuality, and their talent for survival. Fond as I was of her and genuinely as I enjoyed her stories, I had, in my own mind, made her into a sociological generalization about a time and place that was not my own. I had not sentimentalized her personally, but I had sentimentalized the class representation. In my literary imagination, I had sometimes combined her with Joyce Cary's Sara Monday, although I hoped my attitude had never been as condescending as Cary's. My distortion was, on its very different level in terms of art, really politically closer to Galsworthy's. Both Galsworthy and I appreciated and respected the individual woman who had had a rough time in a rough world. But we each made too much of that social world that was not our own, Galsworthy in those impossibly noble and symbolic private conversations between Bicket and Victorine, I in focusing on symbols of a class. The inevitable distortions of fiction can be evasion or projection as well as heightened and selected truth.

When Mr. Evans returned briskly with a fresh pot of coffee, he shifted the conversation to the practical aspects of dealing with Galsworthy. Apparently, Galsworthy was a publisher's ideal of a writer, never haggling about money, always (unlike some of his contemporary authors) loyal to the firm that published all his work except at the very beginning. "But that doesn't mean he and my father always agreed," Mr. Evans continued. "Galsworthy had strong views about prices his books should sell for, about appearance, other things. He was ambitious for a bigger readership, for popularity in the best sense, not for money, which he didn't need." Mr. Evans had liked and respected Ada, but had not known her very well while Galsworthy was alive. Afterwards, however, he had worked with her often, in connection with both Galsworthy's books and the two short books, one about their dogs and one about their travels, that Ada had later written, and he had found her extremely efficient and intelligent. "She was never just tough. Very gracious and elegant, yet practical, always coming back to the practical point." Mr. Evans rose, walked briskly to a cabinet to find a few letters to his father, some from Galsworthy, one from Joseph Conrad about an article he'd written about Galsworthy, which were carefully kept in an album beneath plastic covers. After I had read the letters, he closed the album and tapped it with his fist. "Letters don't really show much about Galsworthy. Always more formal and polite than he really was. Women who knew him could tell you that—he was always very attractive to women. That austerity everyone talked about was a front, you know. He was quite shy, really, and women always liked him. In some very quiet way, he responded. But it was sex. That's in his writing. It's really all about sex, though in the most thoughtful and dignified way possible. Sex held together by form. Not at all like some of the dreadful stuff on today's market which combines sex and commerce, sex to make money. One of those writers couldn't understand why we rejected her first novel. And it sold fantastically. Then, when apparently things didn't go well with her English publisher after the first, she sent us her second novel along with sales reports on the first. When we said no again, she was dumbfounded, just couldn't understand at all, thought we were crazy. Galsworthy of course wasn't like that. He cared very much about literary value, about art, about how it was done. But underneath, the subject matter of the novel, it was really all sex. And he knew it." As both Mr. Evans and I realized, focus on sex, intelligent, sympathetic focus, was a statement that could universalize experience, that might help to counteract divisions of class and background.

We sat down again, and Mr. Evans leaned back in his chair talking of popularity and sales, as well as of the problems of publishing. He pointed out that Heinemann's had helped persuade the BBC to film the twenty-six part, immensely successful version of *The Forsyte Saga*, adding that he himself had argued for the black and white version because at that time, in 1966 or 1967, the Public Broadcasting System in America would not have taken it had it been in color. He thought that Heinemann's really owed Galsworthy a good deal. During the slump, he recalled, he had, several times, ordered another ten thousand copies of *The Forsyte Saga* just to keep the presses going and the printers working, and the firm had always managed to sell a considerable number of them. Our conversation then drifted toward his cottage in the south of France, just a few miles from the Mediterranean, where he and his wife would soon go for three or four months. He talked, too, of his children, one in Dublin whom his wife was currently visiting, another married to a professor in Lawrence, Kansas. "We like that now. Like to travel, live in different places. One of the advantages of the modern world—its internationalism. But now our new government announces it will tax not only money aliens earn here, fair enough, but also heavily tax money they bring into the country to live on. Terrible. Stupid. Young couple next door, Americans. I've only met them a few times. Pleasant enough. But they're leaving, I hear, and I gather it's because of this new taxation. Firm he works for can't hold out against it, so they'll just up and leave. Terrible. It'll leave us all just stuck in our own provincial holes." He shook his head sadly, quickly, as if trying to shake off the return of an old xenophobic disease visible again just when the society had seemed safely immune.

Before he drove me back to the Richmond Underground station, Mr. Evans carefully put back, each in its appropriate cabinet, the albums, the books, and the framed poem in manuscript that Galsworthy had once sent him. "I wasn't always so careful about these things," he explained. "In his will, Galsworthy left me a manuscript of one of his *Five Tales*, one of my favorites. It was bound in leather, beautiful job. Later, in the slump, when I was really hard up, I sold it. £200 or 250, I don't remember. Now, of course, I wish I hadn't. None of our authors left me anything like that until John Masefield died. He left me the pick of his library." As we settled into his bright, new, sporty Peugeot, I thought that my original connection of the houses on Ham Common with Dutch painting suggested nothing more than an exterior physical fact. Thoughts of Mr. Evans's car and the south of France, and a last look at the brilliantly colored azaleas in his garden, brought Matisse to mind, but I decided that was incomplete and uncharacteristic as well. I realized I had better abandon my painting metaphors. Soon, we were talking of my plans and back in the center of Richmond. Mr. Evans smiled cheerfully and shook my hand.

Two days later, on a bright, very warm morning with a hazy, blue sky, the westerlies seemed momentarily suspended as I drove through Hyde Park to Paddington to meet Mr. Sauter. I was in good time to watch his train pull in, see him jump down from the carriage, suitcase in hand, and stride rapidly down the platform, wearing a neat and restrained brown plaid suit, camera

and light meter draped over his shoulder, a large maroon handkerchief in his breast pocket. Both of us were eager to get going,
and, discussing the best possible ways to avoid the traffic jams
that encircle London, we started off. "I couldn't possibly drive
in London now," Mr. Sauter smiled broadly. "Every road I remember is one way, always in the wrong direction." As we were
stuck in a long, narrow file trying to escape from the choked
center of Hammersmith, behind huge brewery lorries and furniture vans taking right turns, I began to talk of my other interviews since I had last seen Mr. Sauter. "Oh, yes," he said. "I
very much wanted to ask how you had got on. But I was waiting
until we were out of this fearful traffic. Can you manage to talk
and drive at the same time? Well, good. You don't seem as impatient as I am. I always want to get through the noise and bustle,
the industry, quickly." We talked of his cousins and publishers,
and he told me that his cousin Hubert, when in command of the
minesweeper during the Second World War, had really been
quite defiant in defending his crew against Admiralty red tape
and arguing constantly for better conditions for the men. He,
the theoretical Tory turned mildly radical insurgent in practice,
would even have been officially reprimanded had his minesweep-
ing not been so successful. We were soon out of traffic, heading
south on the quiet and well-cultivated roads through the villages
of southern Surrey and, then, western Sussex. As we passed
through almost every village, through Ockley, Billingshurst, and
Pullborough, Mr. Sauter would sit upright and look around,
craning his neck to find and recall various landmarks. Buildings
seemed to have changed less than he had anticipated, and
thatched roofs became more plentiful the closer we got to Bury.
"It's more than forty years since I've last driven along this road,"
he explained. "Living either in Kent or Gloucestershire, I've always approached Bury from either east or west, almost along the
coast. Maybe the last time I took this road was with my uncle
on that long, miserable drive to London to see his doctors. He
didn't want to go. I think he knew, knew what no one would say
and what we didn't even think, that he'd never come back to
Bury again . . . No, no, that wasn't the last time. A few years
later, just before she gave up Bury, Ada had a number of guests

for the weekend. A sort of farewell to the house. James Barrie became ill in the middle of the night, wanted to see his own doctor. I drove him up to London, along this road, an eerie night, lots of wind. He died a few days later." Mr. Sauter paused, leaned back, and the lines running downward from his mouth deepened. A few moments later, he sat up, smiled warmly, and said, "Little wonder I haven't taken this road very often."

As we approached the tiny village of Bury and turned off the A 29, Mr. Sauter leaned forward more intently, trying to make sure he could place each cottage and each of the few crossroads. We decided to have our own early lunch first and pulled into the car park of the local pub, the "Black Dog and Duck." The inside of the pub was simple and comfortable, cushioned benches lining the walls, small tables, an armchair or two, none of the horse-brasses, large Edwardian advertising mirrors, or elaborate scrollwork that characterize pubs as simultaneously tourist and suburban. As we ordered drinks and looked about, Mr. Sauter whispered that he did not know the two or three people in the pub and that the owner wasn't there. The middle-aged woman tending bar and two customers were talking about the Derby, to be run that afternoon. They all seemed to think the favorite likely to win, though far from certain. Neither Mr. Sauter nor I knew enough about the Derby to join the conversation, but we exchanged a smile of recognition when the woman behind the bar told the others "I don't much fancy that horse with the foreign name that's 4 or 5 to 1." Neither of us said the horse's name was Giacommetti, though we both had given some recent newspaper's sporting page enough attention to recognize the fact. We collected our sandwiches and drinks, bringing them out to the slightly elevated triangular green, alongside the pub, set with chairs and tables, directly across the road from a handsome, newly-thatched cottage. As we sat down, moving our chairs into the shade provided by a huge elm, Mr. Sauter said, "JG, of course, would have been much more into that than we. Not quite so much when I knew him as in his 'depraved' Oxford days, but even in the later years he cared about the Derby, had opinions. He went to meetings, sometimes to Doncaster, always to Goodwood, which is close by. He knew the handicapper of the Jockey Club, Bathurst his name was, pretty well. As time went on, he did, I suppose, become less interested in the betting, the gambling side, more interested in the horse as the animal, and he cared very much about his morning ride. But he still kept in touch with the racing, still knew about it."

Since we were early for the first appointment Mr. Sauter had made, having allowed more time than necessary for London traffic, he suggested that we drive south of the village, up the last ridge of the South Downs, where Galsworthy frequently took his morning ride, to look both back down at the village and across the other way toward the English Channel six or eight miles to the south. The road up Bury Hill never quite reached the top of the Downs and, although we tried stopping at several of the paved lay-bys generously scattered along the road, we realized that we would have to stop the car and climb further by foot in order to get the views we wanted. Mr. Sauter, leading the way, scaled the last stretch of steep hill with considerable agility. I stumbled. On the level top of the undulating Down, we noticed that the haze had thickened, not enough to obscure the still blue sky or blot the outline of the village church and buildings nestled in the trees below, but just enough to unify the scene, to make it look as if all the curves of the Down joined in confluence at the clump of village below. Toward the coast the haze was even thicker and we could not see the Channel at all. "It's not quite what it was when we rode here," Mr. Sauter explained. "You see the stubble here—and over there. During the Second War, a lot of the Down was plowed up and planted. Food. Tried to grow as much of what they needed as they could. The Down hasn't been quite the same since. Before the war, it was like a vast elevated lawn, and we often stopped here to look about. The road, of course, was much more narrow then. Same outline, but it was more like a track. And my uncle could ride all the way to Goodwood without crossing a road. He often did. Couldn't do that now, not for years and years back, I should think."

We turned toward the village. The haze seemed to be thickening so we thought we had best try to get the pictures we wanted before it became worse. We paced back and forth on the level summit trying to get the best possible angle toward Bury House, Galsworthy's large home that was partially concealed by trees and foliage from whatever angle we could find. We talked of light and composition as we each tried to define pictures for each other. My own words sounded a bit hollow and pretentious to me as, with my Instamatic, I amateurishly took a few quick snaps that couldn't justify my words. I stood aside and watched Mr. Sauter, leaning on a tree trunk a few feet down the steep ridge, white hair blown out full by the wind that had suddenly come up, moving his hands quickly and intently to read the light meter, fetch and put on glasses to check the setting, put away glasses and meter to hold his camera in position securely as he clicked the shutter. He was the professional, the artist, I the intruder. And, as we scrambled down the hill to the car, I thought that Bury House and Galsworthy might be more difficult to assimilate than I had hoped. We stopped the car several times on the way down the hill, and walked off a few feet into the stubble surrounding the lay-bys. We both found that we could get better angles and views from a halfway point, from the mediate distance, than we could from the summit.

As we drove, silently, back toward the village, I wondered what had led me, back before any visits to England or any interest in English literature, to a perhaps unconscious focus on what Galsworthy at Bury represented. I thought quickly of those stereotyped depictions of the English in the Hollywood movies of the thirties, men in tweeds and plus fours, large spacious houses, grunted syllables of politeness, but, as we turned into the village and caught a fuller glimpse of Bury House, my attraction to this seemed to go back further, back before any knowledge of or memory about films. Characteristically, I used dates to trigger memory. I could recall myself as a child, interested in the arrival of the *New York Times* each morning to scan the baseball box scores in season and the obituaries all year round. I remembered, standing in the hall on the second floor, our only floor, of the narrow wood-frame house we rented in a cluttered area of Perth Amboy, New Jersey, to read the obituary of Calvin Coolidge in early January of 1933. Within the next few weeks, we moved, for my father, an energetic and skillful young dentist, anxious to erase his own childhood in the Williamsburg slums of Brooklyn and prospering even in those early days of the depression, had rented, for what was then the large sum of $85 per month, not including heat, a large Tudor house on Raritan Bay that faced directly out toward the Atlantic Ocean (he could have bought the house, a few years later, for $6,200). I remembered reading Galsworthy's obituary on one of the first days of February, on a grey, foggy, unseasonably mild morning, standing on the spacious porch of our new house, looking across the street at our fifty yards or so of fenced-in lawn and bushes that ended in a dock perched over the bay. I had looked at maps enough to recognize that a straight line from Perth Amboy across the ocean would bring one to Portugal (my childhood imagination assumed a flat earth no matter what I had been told in school), but I fancied that our porch faced just far enough toward the northeast so that a straight line at that angle, even though the southernmost tip of Staten Island was in the way, could carry me directly to England. The large Tudor house, brick and half-timber, built before the First World War, rooms scaled unevenly with dark hallways, odd hiding places, and small unexpected porches, remained my ideal, even though we lived in the house only three and a half years. My parents soon built their own ideal, a miniature replica of George Washington's Mount Vernon, fastidious and symmetrical, tulips lining the front walk in two military rows, on rising ground a block or so further north along the bay. I was interested in the building of the new Colonial house, fascinated with the three modern bathrooms, each designed in a different ensemble of matching colored tiles, but it never held my imagination as the spacious Tudor did.

Stories about the site of the new house had interested me more than the house itself, especially after my father flourished a chipped Colonial coin at dinner one evening, clearly dated 1732 and displaying a likeness of King George II. Workmen digging the foundation for the new house had found the coin and given it to him. I listened eagerly to stories claiming that the old house on the site (which I could dimly remember as an abandoned and collapsing frame) had sheltered Aaron Burr on his escape route after killing Alexander Hamilton. The occupants of the house had been British Tory sympathizers throughout the Revolutionary War, apparently not at all unusual in the town. A cluster of inhabitants loyal to the crown was perhaps one reason for the fact that Perth Amboy never again achieved the prominence it had had, and lost, when it was the Colonial capital of East Jersey in the middle of the eighteenth century. My early interest in England, I realized, might have origins that were local as well as pesonal. I recalled the day in December, 1936, when our sixth-grade teacher, Miss Ruth Emmons, brought a small portable radio into our classroom in Public School #7, announcing that this had never been done before but was justified by the importance of the public occasion. As I stood on the teacher's desk, unscrewing the bare light bulb above, the only electrical outlet in the room, to put in a socket for the radio's cord, one boy grumbled, "Why couldn't we have done this for the World Series?" Yet we all listened carefully, huddled around the radio, hearing the high clipped voice of King Edward VIII, occasionally above the almost impenetrable static, saying something about his throne and the woman he loved. In retrospect, I thought it strange that English royalty should be so distinguished in a city that, by the nineteen thirties, was quartered into Little Dublin, Little Warsaw, Little Budapest, and Little Palestine. These unofficial designations, however, omitted the fairly large number of Scandinavian immigrants, a population large enough so that when the late King Frederick IX of Denmark, then Crown Prince, toured America with his wife, a Swedish Princess, in the spring of 1939, Perth Amboy was one of his official visits. No Memorial Day or Fourth of July that I could recall attracted crowds at all comparable to those that clustered around the large Danish Reformed Lutheran Church, across the street from the High School, to gaze at the two tall, handsome figures and hear him say a few words. Perth Amboy had retained something of its fictions.

As Mr. Sauter and I parked the car in front of Bury House, I was surprised to see that the front door was set back only a few feet from the road and that one side of the front was not far from the small shop and post office, a kind of general store, that still served many of the villagers' needs. Yet, despite its lack of a spacious porch or a gracious approach, despite the fact that I saw it as immediately different from the fantasies that would connect it with my past, Bury House was imposing. It was built in 1909 of brownstone in a rather heavy Edwardian baronial style, the wide classical front with a deep portico in the center and heavy gabled protrusions at each end, small lead-paned windows with their individual Gothic suggestions multiplied with sufficient frequency and regularity to create a simulacrum of classic symmetry. The style suggested a mansion that had since been bought by British Rails or Canadian Pacific and converted into a luxury hotel. In fact, I had, with my wife and children, spent a few days at such a hotel, owned by British Rails, in Devon during our Easter holiday. As I looked at Bury House more closely, I recalled that holiday. We had found the hotel comfortable and formal, had both enjoyed it and felt a bit uneasy. The days, with drives and walks over the Devon moors, pony riding lessons for the children, and excursions to pubs, villages, and steep sea-coast views, had been splendid; but evenings back at the hotel (Devon's roads and the desolate quality of Dartmoor at night did not encourage touring after dinner) had given rise to much more equivocal emotions. We would usually have a few drinks and some talk with other guests. I particularly recalled two successive evenings with a group of businessmen, a group of friends from various parts of England, who met annually for a golfing holiday in Devon. Off without their wives, they were gregarious and friendly, but, with each successive drink, they seemed more bitter underneath: "Of course, I like places like this. But my workmen are undercutting my business, and I don't know how much longer I'll be able to take holidays at all. Was in the south of France last summer, took my family skiing in Switzerland this winter. Now, here. But next year?" "Standards are really going to hell. Workmen don't give a damn. State schools are useless, and this damn new government's out to smash the public schools." "Nixon's only taking the rap for what everybody does. All government's worked that way for years. Has to. He's just been unlucky enough to be caught." "Communists really do dominate our unions. Subversives you chaps rightly call them. They don't want agreements or better

conditions. They're just dedicated to tearing the system down."
And with the confidential lowered voice and thickened speech of
2:00 A.M.: "Now, the place to go is South Africa. The only place
left where values and order still hold up. No, you Americans are
sentimental, sentimental about us. What this country needs is a
strong hand, maybe even the military if that's the only way. Of
course, Hitler went too far in some respects, but he had a lot of
the right ideas. A lot of them. And a sense of order. He saw it
coming." Even in retrospect, I shuddered at this debased contemporary version of the Cliveden set of the thirties. The accommodating Toryism of British business in the fifties seemed to
have disappeared, and the word "Communist" assumed a ma-
cabre and sinister quality I had not heard in America in the last
twenty years or in Britain, at all, since the Second World War.

As we rang the bell of Bury House and waited for admission,
Mr. Sauter and I looked at each other and smiled, a smile in
which each seemed to respect the silence and distance of the
other, in which each of us seemed to know how far we were
from Galsworthy and the past. I did not tell him about Perth
Amboy or the businessmen in Devon, and he did not share whatever he had been remembering or reflecting on with me. Our
smiles, however, brought us back to the present, and he repeated
his earlier statements that Bury House is now an old people's
home, that he had phoned for permission for us to look around,
and that the new matron (unlike an earlier one who had retired
a few years ago) was not very much interested in Galsworthy
and his connection with the house. An assistant matron answered
the door, and we discovered that the matron, not in at the moment, had mixed things up and expected us on the following
day. Nevertheless, we were free to walk round the ground floor,
anywhere we liked although we must excuse her if she couldn't
accompany us. Mr. Sauter brought me through the central hall
that stretched along the central front of the house, far wider
than it was deep, then into the library which had large bay windows looking out to the deep back garden. It was now rather
bare, containing three desks in the corner for the matron and
her two assistants. In Galsworthy's day, the center of the room

had been occupied by a large billiard table. Galsworthy had, in bad weather, worked in a large armchair, drawn closer to the window than to the fire, writing on pads of paper attached to a clipboard, dog or dogs at his feet; in good weather, he sat out in the garden. We moved to the dining room, now a large room painted white with small formica tables that seated four each. The bare room could well have used the painted panels of African scenes that, Mr. Sauter told me, he had done in South Africa on their trip the winter after they had all moved into Bury, and that he still had stored carefully in the house at Stroud. We went quickly through the servants' hall and peeked into the large institutional kitchen in one of the gabled wings; only the arrangement of the bells to call the servants triggered any reminiscence for Mr. Sauter. We returned to the wide front hall, where the assistant matron was helping a few of the old residents prepare for a walk, and crossed to the other wing, a large, light room with a huge bay window at the back and an entry into a greenhouse behind the fireplace on the far side. This had been the music room or drawing room, the setting for tea and for conversation and music after dinner, and had once held a grand piano and deep sofas; now, about twenty or thirty old people were sitting on small chairs arranged in straight rows. A large color television set, in front of the fireplace, was tuned to a soap opera, but few of the old people seemed to be watching. One or two, talking to each other, stopped to watch us pass, Mr. Sauter nodding pleasantly to anyone he thought might respond to a greeting. Most of the people, however, seemed transfixed inside themselves. As we walked out through the greenhouse, Mr. Sauter said, "In one way, this would have made JG happy, knowing his house was useful, doing good for people who couldn't afford it. And the place runs almost entirely on charity. But, in another way, he couldn't have stood it, couldn't have walked through that room as we did just now. Just too sensitive. It would have depressed him for weeks." Out in the garden, considerably reduced in size from the time when it had given way to open fields that swept all the way up Bury Hill and now bounded by a tall chain-link fence, Mr. Sauter showed me where the paddock had been, the beds of flowers, and the favorite spots to sit. We took some more pictures, although the fence prevented us moving back far enough to get the whole house in a single snapshot.

The haze seemed to have lifted slightly, although the day was still warm and close, as we walked from Bury House past the village shop and down another road to the cottage at the end of a terrace of four or five, in which Joan Dean lives with her husband and two of her three children. Joan Dean, who was expecting us and had arranged for me to meet a series of people, is the youngest and most articulate of four sisters whose maiden name had been Souter (no relation), all of whom worked for the Galsworthys at one time or another. Then sixty-five, with a round, rather cherubic face and a constant enthusiasm, Joan Dean looked about twenty years younger and she welcomed us effusively saying that she was so pleased to have the chance to talk about the Galsworthys. She led us into a room with a bed, covered with a pink bedspread, against one wall, and a sofa and several chairs grouped around the electric fire on the other side. Seated in one armchair was a village woman of eighty-eight, who had not seen Mr. Sauter for forty years and had wanted to look at him again and listen to recollections about the Galsworthys. "My sisters will be along in a little while," Joan Dean explained, "though, if you'd like to see my husband, you're more than welcome to come back this evening, any time after six. He's on a job over in the next village. My son, David, too. Do we really need the fire on today? I just started remembering the Galsworthys, and Mrs. Galsworthy always needing to be warm. Fires in all the bedrooms—hot-water bottles—unusual around here in those days. And I must have turned on the fire without thinking." Joan Dean had always felt particularly connected with Bury House because, she told us, she grew up hearing about its great fire in which the original Elizabethan thatched structure had burned to the ground on a night in April, 1909, when she was only two days old. The house was rebuilt, employing half the village for several years. In late 1926, when she was working as a parlormaid in a large house in a neighbouring village, finding the job not very congenial and the employers a bit severe, she saw an advertisement in the *West Sussex Gazette* for a parlormaid at Bury House. Even before she answered the ad, or knew who the new owners of Bury House were (and it would not have mattered if she had, for she had never heard the name of Galsworthy), she felt that would be the job for her. One by one, as places fell vacant within the next few years, her sisters joined her working at Bury House—Dorothy, the oldest, as cook, Addie and Gladys as other maids. "Three of us were still working there when Mr. Galsworthy died. One, Gladys, had left to marry a little earlier. She married Henley, one of the gardeners. He's still there, you know, Mr. Sauter. He'd love to see you both. Well, we knew we'd never have another place like that. After Mrs. Galsworthy had to break up Bury, we didn't want to go into service anywhere else. All three of us were married within eight months."

Two of Joan Dean's sisters, Dorothy and Addie came in (the third, Gladys, had had to work late and would try to see us the next day) and began immediately to confirm the role of the Galsworthys as exceptionally kind and generous employers. "Why, when all of us were working there, Mr. Galsworthy found out that my father had trouble paying his rent," Joan Dean continued. "It was only one shilling, eleven pence a week, but he was out of work and a number of children still at home. Mr. Galsworthy just gave him an allowance of ten shillings a week. It was a lot in those days. Father would have done anything for him. When Mr. Galsworthy died, father didn't say a word. And died himself just two days after we'd heard the news." "The shock," Dorothy added, "I always think the shock killed him." Joan then shifted the conversation to Mrs. Galsworthy: "And she was just as generous. Maybe not in public. The village didn't worship her the way it did him, but she was just marvelous to us girls. She looked just like Queen Mary, the hair and everything. And such beautiful clothes. She often gave them to us when they were a year or two out of fashion. And she was never snob-bish. Made sure we got off early when there was a dance or something. Mr. Galsworthy would give us an extra three or five pounds for holidays. And we always had steady board wages, unusual then when most places supplied either room and board or wages. But it was Mrs. Galsworthy who said we could have our young men in when our work was done. My last job at night was to bring the ten o'clock tray into the drawing room. Lemon tea or whisky and soda. Then our young men could come in. That was a wonderful thing in those days." Addie, a quiet, fair woman, poked her, and they both giggled. Joan Dean leaned forward and covered her laughter with her hand. "Yes," she said, "and ours all *married* us." Addie whispered, "Not like some others."

Mr. Sauter asked Joan Dean if she remembered the guests who came for weekends, and she exhibited what must be almost total recall as she reeled off the list of relatives, fellow writers like Hugh Walpole and Arnold Bennett, theatrical connections like Granville-Barker and Leon Lion, other friends. Her favorite, she said, was James Barrie. "I used to dart suddenly into his room. After knocking, of course. And then jump and say I was Peter Pan. Oh," she giggled again, "I was cheeky in those days." She was also fond of Leon Schalit, the Viennese writer who translated Galsworthy's novels into German and later wrote a critical appraisal of Galsworthy's work (Ada Galsworthy vouched for him with the Home Office when he was trying to leave Austria as a refugee late in 1937): "Mr. Schalit was very methodical. I used to pack his clothes for him, and he always wanted his suits on top, the jackets over the trousers." The three sisters agreed that they enjoyed the guests, never minded the extra work. "It was all so exciting and lovely," Joan Dean explained. "We'd been so poor, and the meals and the life and the clothes all seemed so lovely. Like one big party that lasted six years. We never minded doing anything. We were so excited by dances, even by an occasional ride in a car. Now, just the last five years, my husband and I have a car. I never thought I would. But, then, just to ride in a car was such a treat. Those were good times, good days." Addie broke in to say that her favorite event had been the annual cricket match with Heinemann's. "Oh, yes," said Joan. "What a spread. We prepared for days. Lunch on picnic board tables in the garden. All the players. The whole village. Everybody. Then tea, almost as many, homemade cakes and homemade ice cream. Dorothy was so good at that. Made it all herself. Oh, we enjoyed that. We really did. We never thought of the work then. But, if you want to know more about the cricket itself, ask my husband when you see him later. He was on the village side from the very beginning. Never missed a match."

I asked the sisters to describe a typical quiet day at Bury, one without guests, and, for the next hour or so, I just sat back listening while Joan carried most of the narrative, interrupted by one or another of the sisters who added details. She described the day's routine meticulously from waking at 6:00 A.M. to do the downstairs and get breakfast ready until, taking the 10:00 P.M. tray into the drawing room, she hoped to find Mr. and Mrs. Sauter dancing the tango while Mrs. Galsworthy played. She talked of taking Galsworthy his tea at 7:00 A.M. so that he could get out for his early morning ride, of pretending not to notice Mrs. Galsworthy's first daily appearance at the hall window overlooking the paddock, watching her husband bring his horse in and end his ride with a series of jumps. It was Mrs. Galsworthy who first spotted the fact that one of his legs had begun to drag after he dismounted in the paddock. Joan Dean still recalled how punctual both Galsworthys were—letters had to be answered early because the post was collected at 10:00 A.M., Galsworthy was never to be disturbed in the morning or between tea and dinner, dinner was always served precisely at eight. She and her sisters were delighted to describe the meals: tea consisting of tomato sandwiches on thin brown bread, hot scones under a muffin dish, and homemade cake; Galsworthy's favorite dinner (always served on his birthday) of homemade soup, fish, grouse, asparagus on toast, and apple charlotte. "Everything around the meals was always just right, too," Joan Dean continued. "Always bowls of any fresh fruit in season. And we could take what we wanted. Chocolates from Lasseter's in London. The serviettes folded into shapes. And, of course, everyone dressed for dinner." As the three sisters talked, I noticed another theme emerging from underneath their fascination with the Galsworthys' style, opulence, and graciousness: their fear of the Galsworthys' many dogs. Visitors were often frightened. The Bedlington was notorious in the village as a cat-killer. One of the Irish setters jumped at and scratched Mrs. Philip Guedalla's face badly. "Yes," Mr. Sauter chimed in. "She was a great beauty, and her face was permanently marked. Both the Galsworthys felt just terrible about that. Would have done anything they could." Dorothy, in particular, feared the dogs. Since Galsworthy wanted to see each of his servants every day, and saw least of his cook, Dorothy had the job of bringing him a fresh orange or some orange juice at eleven in the morning while he was working. When the dog at his feet growled at her, as he frequently did, she would hastily leave the small tray and run. She also made sure to be out in the kitchen garden smoking a cigaret at six every evening when Mrs. Galsworthy brought all the dogs into the kitchen to feed them. The laundryman and the postman had to be protected. Even Joan Dean, usually able to handle the dogs almost as well as the Galsworthys could, was once bitten rather badly on the leg just as she was preparing to go out to a dance. "But Mrs. Galsworthy was wonderful. Put something on it and bandaged it for me. Then gave me one of her dresses with a long skirt so it wouldn't show. I was a little late, but I didn't miss the dance. The poor dog, some time later, had to be put away. The Galsworthys just loved animals so much. The dogs. And the horses, too. Mr. Galsworthy had to have everything right for the horses. He always carried cubes of sugar in his pockets. Almost the only time he came into the kitchen. To get sugar cubes. And he had the inside of the stables painted a restful blue because he thought it was better for the horses' nerves." We had stayed a long time, and each of the sisters had one chore or another to do, so, making arrangements to see them again, we walked into the now very heavy and rumbling afternoon and saw the rain clouds beginning to pile on the western horizon.

We went back to Bury House and crossed the road, walking through a gate with a metal-worked sign reading "Forsyte's" and up the drive to the low, modern stone house of Mr. Edward Grinstead. Mr. Grinstead, in his early seventies, had recently retired and sold the village shop he had inherited from his father and kept for many years. A tall, thin, agile man, he brought us into his L-shaped living room lined with windows. Five or six armchairs, the kind with dark plastic seat and back and light wooden arms frequently found in hotel lounges, ringed the television set. Some friends had been over to watch the running of the Derby and had just left. A rank outsider had won, and the favorite finished far back. Giacommetti was third, and Mr. Sauter and I smiled at each other as if we'd always known that's where he belonged. Mr. Grinstead plunged right into the subject of sport: "Galsworthy really did make the local cricket club. It had existed before, but the grounds were in bad shape, almost no equipment. Galsworthy set it up, got the mowers, practice nets, had us order bats, pads, the like. And it became a real club. Henley, the gardener, was captain for many years. The Bury/ Heinemann match continued until the start of the Second World War. Heinemann won the cup the last time, and kept it, I think, though the village cricket team still goes on. We often talk about those days. I played tennis with the Galsworthys. Since I was in the store next door, they called me when they needed a fourth. The first time, when they'd just moved in, I was about to refuse. I was young, and had strong feelings against truckling to the people in the big house. But my father told me I'd better get on over there, and young men obeyed their fathers in those days . . . Galsworthy changed the whole village. His unobtrusive generosity—that's the phrase for it, 'unobtrusive generosity,'—the way he would come out of his house and stall or pick up some grass just to wait until some old villager would pass by and he could ask how the old man was. Galsworthy as a tennis player was something else." Mr. Grinstead laughed and smoothed his grey hair back with his hand. "He was a cunning player, conserved his energy and made others run. He always looked as if he would hit the ball harder than he did."

Mr. Grinstead got up and said he would find his wife and she would get us some tea. She had been ill and was probably resting. When we heard this, we urged him not to bother about the tea, but he insisted that she would feel much worse had she not the opportunity to serve us something. Mrs. Grinstead soon came in, a heavy, grey-haired woman, with the grey pallor and deliberate movements of one who had suffered a coronary not long ago. As soon as he saw what she was carrying, Mr. Sauter leaped up to take the heavy tea tray from her and place it on the table. As we were drinking tea, Mr. Grinstead went back into the past: "I still remember the people at Bury House before the Galsworthys. No contact with the village. The old servant/ master thing. Different meals for the servants. Orders written for the shop. That's the kind of thing Galsworthy changed. The shop had everything in those days. Food. Clothes. I remember once when John Drinkwater came for a weekend, and had no trousers for tennis. A huge, huge man. But we found a pair of oversized white flannels. Drinkwater kept asking were they proper tennis flannels. Galsworthy knew all the time that our tennis flannels and our cricket flannels were one and the same, but he never said a word. I remember, too, the annual village concert that my mother used to organize. Local talent. Singing, sketches. Galsworthy always took the front seats in the village hall," Mr. Grinstead laughed. "He couldn't have thought us very talented, but he never showed it. He gave my father a gorgeous silver teapot. Gave my sister and me tennis rackets one Christmas." Mr. Grinstead got up and paced the room, "I wish I had more things to show you. Our tennis pavilion out back there burned down three years ago. A lot of old photographs and papers I kept in a cabinet there are gone. I've only one letter left." He went into the back part of the L, opened a drawer, and brought back the letter. "I'm sorry about this, too. When we got married, in 1930, Galsworthy asked my father what I would want. My father, quite accurately, said I'd want money, and Galsworthy sent me a check with this." He handed me the letter, a short paragraph that conveyed good wishes and apologized for the fact that the gift "takes this crude form." Mr. Grinstead continued, "Now, of course, I wish we had something more tangible. Some article. We didn't respect the past enough then. It's like people not realizing how much Galsworthy had done until he died. The cottages he had built and, in his will, left to the occupants. But things seem to be changing now. Just the last five or six years. Much more interest in Galsworthy and the past than there had been for a long time. Lots to do with the television series, I suspect. As you probably know, the times of church services here in the village were altered so that people could watch *The Forsyte Saga*. They've not been altered back either. I just wish I had more to say."

Mr. Grinstead collected the tea things and brought them back to the kitchen. While he was gone, Mr. Sauter expressed concern about Mrs. Grinstead's health. "Oh, don't bother, please," she said very slowly and calmly. "I've had two coronaries now. And I'm ready. I've had a good life. A kind and wonderful husband. Children grown and settled. And I've enjoyed this house and garden for more than ten years. I'm ready. We never expected so much in the old days." Mr. Grinstead came back and walked us to the door with his quiet, springy step. His last words urged me to come back sometime when he would try to remember more.

As we walked down the drive, hearing thunder, seeing the dark clouds overhead and feeling the strong, suddenly cool wind, Mr. Sauter and I decided that, since it was almost six o'clock, we had better drive the four miles to Arundel, check on the hotel rooms Joan Dean had booked for us, and find out how late we could have dinner. When we got to the road, Mr. Sauter stopped to get a few pictures of the black clouds looming over Bury House, a composition he had noticed but never photographed before. While he was checking his light meter and adjusting his camera, a young woman in a small, sporty car drove by, turned around and drove back, stopping in front of me. "Pardon me for interrupting," she said. "But are you photographers for one of the magazines or Sunday supplements?" I introduced myself and Mr. Sauter. "Oh," she said, as she shook Mr. Sauter's hand, "I'm so very pleased to meet you. We just moved to the village two years ago. We didn't know a thing about Galsworthy then. But we're so interested in him now. Won't you stop by for a drink? It's about to rain." We politely declined, and, as she drove off, we dashed across the road to our car, reaching it just as the first heavy drops began to fall.

We drove up Bury Hill in the downpour, landscape sealed in by the heavy dark, then down to Arundel through a wood, the road arched by the heavy trees. In the center of town, on a steep hill, not more than a few hundred yards from the medieval Arundel Castle (which has long been the major tourist attraction of the area), we found the Norfolk Arms Hotel, pulled in to the

old inn courtyard, studded with tubs of flowers, and parked in
the garage beyond. Since it was still pouring, we grabbed our
suitcases and ran back across the courtyard to the hotel entrance.
We were led through cross-beamed passages, up and down landings, through corridors decorated with horse brasses and old pictures by imitators of Stubbs and Canaletto, past numbers of
highly polished antique chests and chairs, to our very comfortable and pleasant rooms. We also discovered that we could begin
dinner as late as ten o'clock, "a real change for this part of the
world," Mr. Sauter remarked. Since the rain was already easing,
we stayed only a few moments before driving back to Bury.
Even as we reached the tree-arched road, a few scattered shafts
of sunlight began to filter through the leaves, looking as if they
carried atoms of movement and color. We drove slowly down
Bury Hill, looking for the tiny cottage, half-hidden by a bluff,
near the edge of the village, where we had promised Dorothy we
would stop briefly to meet her husband, Bill. After missing it
the first time, we found the cottage and walked around to the
back, through a market garden in which cabbage leaves and car-
rot stalks were glistening with the recent rain, following a brick
path to the cottage door. We went through the kitchen to a
small room, crowded with a dark double bed, a heavy breakfront, and an old horsehair sofa with wooden scrollwork. The
floor was covered with a worn, green and red patterned lino-
leum. Dorothy introduced us to Bill, a short, white-haired man,
nearly eighty, with soft heavy-lidded eyes and the soft, thick
voice that suggests origins further to the west, in Somerset or
Devon. He wore a striped, long-sleeved shirt and worn, heavy
braces holding up a pair of grey trousers that looked several
sizes too large. He has been a market gardener in Bury for more
than sixty years. He wanted to show us what Dorothy said she
thought was the only remaining picture of Bury House just after
the 1909 fire. He got up slowly and walked to the breakfront,
rummaging through a drawer filled with twine, old accounts,
and a few engraved invitations or announcements, finally pulling
out the postcard photograph he wanted. "My father gave me
that," he said, handing us the card. It showed, in black and
white, the smouldering ruins of the old Bury House after the

fire, only large chimneys standing at each end of the foundation, several dark-suited and bowler-hatted figures poking through the charred ruins. When we returned the card, he held it by the edges and looked at it for a while before placing it carefully back in the drawer. Bill pointed out a picture of his father hanging in a heavy, dark wood frame on the wall above the bed. The farmer's striped shirt was starched, but had no collar, the circular band at the neck, where the collar could have been attached, standing out stiffly; his father had the same heavy-lidded eyes. Bill walked out through the garden with us, becoming more animated as he showed us his vegetables and his roses. "The roses are slow this year," he said. "Too dry. That rain we just had. Wasn't nearly enough. And now, look." He pointed toward the west, the sun, and a rising patch of deep, clear blue. "That's no more rain, at least for this evening. We need a steady two or three days. But it'll come right. We'll get it later in the summer. This is a year that'll take some time." He turned to pick up a few leaves that the rain had beaten down and to fix a wobbly stake on a tomato plant, then waved with a broad smile as we walked down the path to the car.

The outlines of the terraced cottages were much more clear, and we felt the fresh breeze, as we knocked again on the door at Joan Dean's. She welcomed us and brought us into the room we'd been in earlier. Her sister Addie was there, her husband, and her son, David. Jack Dean, like his wife, looked twenty years younger than his sixty-five, a short, sturdy, compact man with a quick, intelligent manner and thinning black hair. David seemed to have his mother's cherubic face and light brown hair, but his father's compressed strength. Primed by his wife, Jack Dean immediately began to talk about the cricket team: "Just before you came in, I was thinking about the cricket. The village team is still going. Matches with other villages. We've built a pavilion, kept it going, do all the work ourselves. But I went through, in my mind, the eleven that played against Heinemann's in 1931. Except for Mr. Galsworthy himself, every one of them is still alive. The second oldest was the village postman, and he's still here. In his mid-nineties now. Yes, the team existed before Mr. Galsworthy's day, but it wasn't much of a team. No proper pitch. But he used the mowers from Bury House to fix the pitch, put up the practice nets, so the young men, like me, learned the game well. He wanted us to concentrate on the proper strokes. We had a local married men vs. single men match." Joan and Addie poked each other and giggled, recalling some incident on the sidelines of the married vs. singles match. Jack went on, "And the Heinemann match was home and home, though not equally. What, no one has told you that? Well, twice, I think, we all went up to London to play Heinemann's there. Mr. Galsworthy chartered a bus to take the team, including wives and sweethearts. But they didn't feed us quite as well as our girls always fed them. They must still have the cup. Do you know any of those chaps at Heinemann's? If you see them, do please tell them we challenge for the cup. This summer. Anytime," he laughed. "Our side, though, is getting on a bit. Not many youngsters. David here, for one, plays in a dance band on the weekends. Doesn't much like cricket." David nodded and said to me, "When they start talking about the cricket, all the anecdotes end up being about the parties and the feasts anyhow."

Jack Dean, who has lived in Bury all his life, is now the leading local builder and keeps three crews working, one of them managed by David. "This village," he said, "wasn't originally anything special. The Duke of Norfolk owned most of it, absentee landlord, back before my time. But it began to break up. There only ever were two big industries, farming and building. And the twenties were a bad time. Agricultural depression, again, after the brief need for homegrown food in the First War. No money to build. Secondary trades, like wheelwrights and blacksmiths, could no longer support people. And the people at the big house didn't care. We were really poor, the worst time I've known. Then Galsworthy came in and changed things. He really did. The village had never known generosity before. I think it started just a few weeks after he moved in. A local man who had seven children was killed in a motorbike smash. His widow didn't know what to do. Galsworthy bought her cottage and let her live there rent free. That started him thinking. He bought other good cottages and lowered the rents. He had houses built for his workmen, his gardeners, the district nurse, and charged them only small rents he knew they could pay. This started the local building industry again. Lots of people, my brother-in-law Henley for one, still live in the cottages Galsworthy had built for them. Henley'd been in building, lost his job in the early twenties. Galsworthy hired him to make a paving walk at Bury House, then kept him on as a gardener. Henley liked it better and he's still there. I know, I've read all about the thirties as the slump, terrible times. I'm sure it was true most places. But not here. The thirties was a *good* time. Not much money, but people did work, and the village had a strong community spirit for the first time ever. Mr. Galsworthy really started that, made it. And it's held, it's still here."

As the history of Bury moved to the Second World War, we all noted the fact that the evening was the thirtieth anniversary of the eve of D day. "Yes," Jack Dean recalled. "I remember every moment of thirty years ago this evening. I was in a landing craft off Southampton, ready to go, looking at the sky and not knowing whether to hope it would clear or not. No bright twilight like this evening's. Then, unexpectedly, someone came aboard with orders for me to get off and hurry to Kent to man ack-ack defenses. The first of the buzz bombs had fallen a few days before and they needed everyone they could find from the Home Guard, where I'd been for three years. By the time my mates landed in Normandy I'd shot down one of the first buzz bombs over the Kentish coast." Mr. Sauter, who had been sitting quietly in the corner during the conversations about cricket and agricultural poverty, leaned forward rapidly and asked, "Where in Kent were you?" "Out in the Romney marshes," replied Jack Dean. "Why so was I," laughed Mr. Sauter. We were living in Wittersham, a small Kentish village, then, and my wartime job was to inspect the ack-ack defenses, the guns and the searchlights, make sure they were in working order. We probably crawled through the same mucky reeds." Everyone laughed, and drew together, and, for a moment, it seemed to me as if I was watching a scene at one of the cricket teas on the lawn at Bury House.

David was particularly interested in American education, its opportunities and problems, how the system that professes a belief in universal education actually works. Jack Dean brought the subject back to Bury. "Bury never did have much of a school. We had a village band, way back, but no tradition at all concerning education. I had practically none. And the Galsworthys weren't much interested in the village school, not in their line. Even for David, born just after the Second War, school in Bury wasn't very much better. But they had a regional system by then. And he went to school in another village. Passed his 11+ and on to a pretty fair grammar school. Yes," he smiled warmly at his son, and Joan Dean ruffled David's hair, "he could have done lots of other things. David's a villager by choice." They wanted to know all about my children. They were particularly pleased when I told them that my son, born in England and then nine, wanted to go to a boarding school and play cricket. Before we left, Joan Dean asked us to meet her oldest daughter, Valerie, about whom, in reply to Mr. Sauter's question, she had told us earlier during the day. Valerie has cerebral palsy. A second daughter, married, with three children, lives in another village. As his wife left to get Valerie, Jack Dean explained, "For her first eight years she never walked or talked. We just didn't know what to do. Then, one day, I was home on leave during the war, and we were sitting here in this room, tired and fed up, and we said, 'Walk, Val, walk, you can do it,' and she did, a few steps. But we still didn't know how to train her, how to do anything but love her and take care of her. Until just the last eight or ten years. Now, there's a school in Pullborough. She goes for three or four hours every day. Takes the bus herself. And she walks a bit, talks a bit." Joan Dean came back with Valerie, a tiny, dark-haired woman, who limped up to each of us, steadying her right hand with her left in order to shake hands, smiled widely, and managed to get out a word or two. When she had finished greeting both Mr. Sauter and me, she rushed to her brother, stretched to throw her arms around his neck, and lapsed into laughter. Joan Dean said, "Yes, she loves seeing visitors. Don't you, Val?" and put an arm around each of her children. They all accompanied us to the door and crammed in the tiny hallway, covered with a wallpaper of pink roses, as they urged us both to return to Bury soon.

The long June evening had finally turned toward darkness, the sky a deep, rich, very dark blue, the breeze cool and fresh, as we drove quickly to Arundel for dinner. Our table was ready in a darkened alcove, and most of the others dining in the hotel had almost finished when we began. We ate our fish and drank our wine, Mr. Sauter lightly offering a running commentary comparing the food we were eating to the food at Bury over forty years ago that we had heard so much about during the day. He knew of the several friends and acquaintances who had written for publication that the hospitality at Bury was far more impressive than the cuisine, and he did not dispute their judgment. Both he and I agreed that we were rather relieved that grouse was out of season, lest allegiance to the past tempt us to order it. When the waiter cleared our plates and asked if we wanted anything else, Mr. Sauter noticed that the menu listed Irish coffee. He turned to me: "Shall we give the Irish coffee a try?" When I nodded, he turned to the waiter. "I'm sorry, sir," the waiter replied, "all coffee is served in the lounge. You'll have to ask the porter." We went out to the lounge and found two comfortable, deep armchairs in the corner. The porter, however, said, "We don't do Irish coffee. I don't think I know how." Instantaneously, Mr. Sauter's usual gentle smile vanished and his eyes narrowed, as if he had momentarily taken up the monocle his uncle used, effectively by all contemporary accounts, on such occasions in his younger years. "But," he said with quiet force, "the menu lists Irish coffee and the waiter told us to ask you." The porter grumbled "Yes, sir" and went off, returning only a few moments later with two huge and delicious Irish coffees. When the porter left, Mr. Sauter smiled a bit guiltily and asked if he had sounded too demanding to the porter. I said I wondered if he hadn't, perhaps because of all our talks that day, been imitating his uncle and the manners of an earlier time and place without even thinking about it. "Yes," he said, his gentle smile returning, "quite likely. More my grandfather, really, than my uncle, you know. I hope the porter isn't offended."

As we settled back to drink, we talked about the various people we'd spoken to during the day and their veneration of Galsworthy. "I suppose," Mr. Sauter said, "that in those last years at Bury he was feudal without ever demanding feudal allegiances. And I can see why they, apart from the girls who saw her every day, really preferred my uncle to my aunt, really made a distinction between the two of them. My aunt was more rigid, more distant from the villagers, not at all the kind of woman who could go in for church committees or charity bazaars. And I think, in later years, she thought some of his kindness was sentimental, some of the people he helped—not all of them by any means—just not worth it. And she said so to him. I know that because I heard it. As a consequence, some of his kindnesses were under the counter. That's why you heard people say they never realized quite how kind he was until after he died." I wondered if the relationship between the two was changing toward the end. Mr. Sauter thought for a while and took a long sip of his drink. "Yes," he said. "I hadn't thought of it in this way before. Bury was much more his place than hers. You know, of course, the story of how he bought Bury House. They had had to leave Wingstone in 1923, and he missed having a country place. And Vi and I were rather at loose ends. I wanted a country place to work, didn't much want to see people after the First War, and Freelands, the place my mother had left me, was too small to accommodate JG and Ada. Before they left the country for the winter of '25-'26, they asked us to look around for a place near the south coast, a fairly modest house in which we could live year round and they could always have two or three rooms whenever they wanted them. We turned up several suggestions, though none with any great enthusiasm. When they returned, in the spring of '26, we drove them round to see our choices. None of them would suit, for one reason or another. We were just about to give up on the second day and stopped for lunch in Pullborough. Vi thought she'd give an agent she'd spoken to one last ring. She came back to the table saying, 'There's only a mansion in a little village called Bury,' expecting us to leave, but JG said, 'Oh, let's have a look.' He and I just stayed outside in the front when Ada and Vi went in. He walked over toward the greenhouse, went around its outside, and saw Bury Hill rising into the Down beyond. 'We'll have this one,' he told me. He never even went inside the house. But you were asking how the relationship changed. He was content to stay at Bury. Had he lived longer, as we all expected him to, I'm sure he would have stayed there more and more, almost all the time, gone to London less and less. He was really happy there; he wanted to talk about wheelwrights and blacksmiths. And Ada was always more interested in town, in that kind of life and entertaining. Not that she resented his interest in the village. She was pleased that he was happy there. But she couldn't feel part of the village, couldn't do more than just *appear* at a village cricket match."

The porter was just about to close the bar for the night when I ordered a last round of drinks. When I returned to our chairs, Mr. Sauter and I talked further about marriages, the Galsworthys' and each of our own. "Yes," he said, "we're the lucky ones. I had a marvelous marriage, forty-eight years of it. I've seen others, each in his own province, no meeting of the minds, the ones in which each partner doesn't blue-pencil and create the ideas of the other. What's the point in marrying if you're going to live that way? My uncle knew that, too. Ada was a part of everything he did and thought, as Vi was to me. That was why all four of us could live together at Bury House. Each of us knew marriage was primary and valued it." Since it was well after midnight and Mr. Sauter had been up since 6:00 A.M., we left the now empty lounge and walked up the stairs to our rooms. Alone in my room, I realized that it was also very late for the Norfolk Arms Hotel. The night porter had to unlock the switchboard so that I could telephone my wife before I went to bed.

After the phone call, I turned out the lights and stretched out on the bed, but it was a long time before I fell asleep, before I assuaged all the moments of uneasiness during the day, of wondering what kind of intruder I was imposing on another life, one over forty years gone, that had never been mine. I recalled that at one point, in the hotel lounge after dinner, Mr. Sauter had delicately asked about my surname, saying that he and some of the other relatives had been wondering about the origins of the name Gindin, "not, of course, that it makes any difference." His curiosity was both like and unlike that of the harassed headmaster of a new Secondary Modern School near Sheffield to whom I had been talking almost ten years earlier (my Fulbright in Sheffield had been split between the departments of English and Education—for the latter, I visited practice teachers in slum schools to dispense sympathy and learn something about the schools). The headmaster had interrupted his tirade against long-haired students who played guitars and ungrateful toughs who vandalized the school to bark at me: "Gindin? What kind of name is that? I never heard it around here." I told Mr. Sauter that the name was Russian, the family Russian-Jewish, in Moscow in the 1870s and 1880s, although I didn't know from where in Russia they had migrated before my grandfather was born in Moscow in 1869. He responded by talking of Galsworthy's visit to Russia in the early 1890s, a visit that engendered a life-long respect and sympathy for Russians and Poles, people living in empty, flat, desolate wastes who, in Galsworthy's terms, never had the kinds of civilized and humane governments they deserved. Mr. Sauter thought that his uncle had well understood why such people had migrated westward as soon as possible. Back in my bed alone, I realized that my grandfather, a talented but unsuccessful tailor and a radical atheist socialist pacifist whose American hero was Eugene V. Debs, could never have seen someone like Galsworthy as Mr. Sauter described him or as I felt him. For my grandfather, the English symbolized the enemy, aristocratic, religious, complacent, the civilized mask of worldwide repression. Even my father, far more attuned than his father to social mobility in America, had little respect for the English during the time I was a child. An enthusiastic reader of H. L. Mencken in the 1920s, he equated the English with bankers, Republicans, and stuffed shirts. Both my grandfather and my father had been pacifists during the First World War; they later confessed that they even shared, in so far as they had any feelings apart from a strict neutrality, a slight preference for Germany until some considerable time after the sinking of the Lusitania. By 1940, they both, particularly my grandfather, were amazed to find England representing the one country holding out against European Fascism. For my grandfather, it was a massive irony, one he always wanted to attribute to concealed infusions of the French or the Celtic or the emigré Russian into English culture. Although, by the early forties, both my grandfather and my father certainly sympathized with my growing Anglophilia in political terms, they still laughed rather tolerantly at my preference for Tudor architecture, my enthusiastic reading (tears running down my face) of sentimental popular novels like Eric Knight's *This Above All*, and the form my phase of teenage asceticism took in refusing to eat for twenty-four hours so that I could contribute the cost of one day's food ration to "Bundles for Britain." When I first visited England in 1948, arriving only a few days before Parliament voted to establish the National Health Service, I could easily reconcile my emotional Anglophilia to my own past, to my family's anti-Nazism and my grandfather's socialism, could dwell on a "new" England trying, after centuries, to change itself and eradicate the divisions of class and manners. Yet, as I lay thinking on the bed in the hotel room in Arundel, that reconciliation was too easy, too momentary a phenomenon in history (although a moment that had significantly coincided with my own). In trying to understand and assimilate what Galsworthy was, there was not only southern England, but also an older England, an England very different from the more obvious origins and sources of my own past, that I would have to take straight.

When the maid came to awaken me with tea the next morning, I saw rain pounding against the window. As I dressed, I thought of D day thirty years before. I had heard the news of the Allied landings at breakfast in the dining room of a Yale college on a hot, still morning. Six or eight of us, all finishing our first year at Yale because we had been too young to enter the services when we graduated from high school, were talking casually, half-humorously, about the morning's news. The Yale swimming coach, in his fifties then, sleepy-eyed and becoming paunchy, brought his tray to our table and joined us. He told us further news of the landings, patiently ignored our easy Battle-of-Britain cynicism, and asked each of us, in turn, what our plans were when the term ended in a few weeks. Each of us responded by saying what service or training program he had already enlisted to join. As the coach left for his early morning class, his eyes widened with unspoken emotion as he simply wished each one of us good luck. Two of the boys, one of whom I knew well and one I hardly knew at all, never returned, killed about six months later in the Battle of the Bulge.

I met Mr. Sauter and we went down to breakfast. The morning waiter, much more cheerful than the waiter the night before, placed us in the main portion of the dining room, at a table underneath a mural depicting the Battle of Hastings, one of a series on English military history. As he brought our bacon and tomatoes, the waiter talked of the anniversary of D day, recalling the crowds of troops, British, Canadian, American, all along the south coast thirty years earlier. He told several stories about trivial national misunderstandings clarified by great good humor. The rain had stopped, and, as we drove to Bury, the sun broke through heavy clouds pushed quickly across the sky by the fresh westerly wind. We had arranged to stop back at Bury House to see Henley and to enable Mr. Sauter to check that some Galsworthy mementoes he'd once given the home were still there: "Nothing very much. A picture, an inkstand, a framed poem in manuscript, I think. But I thought the house should have something of JG's. And the former matron, the charming one who's retired, was really interested. I just forgot all about them yesterday."

Another assistant matron, the one we had not met before, admitted us and brought us to the library where the Galsworthy mementoes were intact, clustered on top of a small cabinet in a corner. The assistant matron was a stolid, middle-aged Dutch lady, and she began to talk of the German invasion of Holland in 1940. She had then lived with her parents in a large house in Arnheim, and they had thought themselves lucky when the original invasion that decimated Rotterdam and captured all the coastal ports in May, 1940, had bypassed them. "But the Germans came back in September. Took over our house for officers' quarters. It was such a lovely place, large rooms and gardens, but they ruined it. Bullied us, too. Kicked my poor father. Things could never be the same. I couldn't go back even if someone gave me the house. I've been in England now it's more than twenty-seven years." She also told us that the old people in the home were to have a celebration that day for the ninety-ninth birthday of the oldest resident. "She's still very cheerful and alert, although she can't get out of her wheelchair anymore." As we left to see Henley out in the hall, Mr. Sauter pressed a 50p. piece into her palm and asked her to get some extra little gift for the woman who was ninety-nine.

Henley was a large burly man, then nearly eighty, with white hair, a sunburned face, and an easy grin. He was no longer working as a gardener. "No, it wasn't that *I* retired. When they sold off most of the back, they just couldn't use all five of us gardeners any more. So I took the job of shaving and bathing the old people. I like it, I like the work and I like the old people." Mr. Sauter recalled Henley's strength, his skill with a gun (he once shot over sixty clay pigeons in a tournament) and his capacity to work endless hours at very heavy jobs. "Not so much now," he replied. "I've slowed down the last five years, though I can still play a bit of cricket. But five years ago, an old man, sixteen stone, slipped while I was supporting him and pulled me into the bath with him. Hurt my back a bit, not the same since." We then talked of the Galsworthys and their days at Bury House. Henley was particularly fond of the musical evenings. "I used to listen from out in the garden, you know. Wonderful it was. Mrs. Galsworthy's piano playing was so lovely. The best *I* ever heard." Then he laughed and clapped Mr. Sauter on the shoulder. "And *you* on the flute. Do you still play the flute? Wonderful it was. Seemed to me just what a summer evening should be." He then turned and winked at me. "But good as she was at the piano, you should have seen Mrs. Galsworthy play billiards. Could beat any of the men when she was on her game. All business, she was, sharp, clear shots and no nonsense. Mr. Galsworthy, now, played games soft, soft and thoughtful. But Mrs. Galsworthy played them hard," and he clapped his hands together with a resounding thud, "or she didn't play at all."

Mr. Sauter looked at his watch, for, he told me, we ought to be precisely on time for our appointment to see his old studio, now owned and lived in by Mrs. Walters. She had six or eight dogs, some of whom would not take kindly to strangers, that she needed to get out of the way in preparation for our visit. We walked across the street at an angle, to a path with a posted sign that read "Jolyon's" next door to Mr. Grinstead's "Forsyte's." We could hear a cacophony of barking as we walked up the long path, winding among several apple trees, to the large frame structure with half its gabled roof one vast window facing north. Mrs. Walters greeted us quietly at the door on the south side that was also a half-landing in a staircase leading to a kind of concrete bunker below, and she asked us please to wait a moment so that she could lock up a few of the dogs. As we waited, Mr. Sauter told me that he had designed the studio himself, built the large fireplace brick by brick, and done all the interior woodwork, but he had not built the exterior frame nor, and he laughed, could he have managed the window without considerable help. "Yes, after all, it took me three years to build and to set up my etching press in the bunker. So I had used it in its finished form for only about two years when JG died." Mrs. Walters returned and brought us into the vast, bright, cheerful studio where all her furniture was carefully polished. She was very proud of the way she kept the ashy finish (a compound of charcoal and white paint) that Mr. Sauter had devised and given to all the large spaces of interior wood. She showed us how she had kept all the cabinets, adapted for domestic use the spaces designed for displaying canvases and storing materials, and added a modern kitchen in the corner. Mr. Sauter pointed particularly to the brick two-story fireplace that rose toward the back wall and the minstrel's gallery behind it—a wooden gallery with a design of repeated, carved, elongated S's or rectilinear curves, that he had made for possible concerts and never used. As Mrs. Walters showed us around and called attention to her meticulously aligned tubs of plants, we caught a glimpse or two of Addie, one of the sisters I had met the day before, cleaning the bedrooms at back under the gallery. We had known that Addie worked there, but she acknowledged us only with a shy, quick smile and wave when Mrs. Walters' back was temporarily turned. As we left, dark clouds suddenly piling up again in the west, Mrs. Walters brought us around the outside of the back showing us the small exterior gables that she had added to the bedrooms behind the studio, as if a picture-book cottage had been grafted onto the structure. Mr. Sauter and I stayed among the apple trees for a few moments while he finished explaining the delight and the problems he had found in the original construction of the studio, how he had angled the structure so the roof window could catch the north light squarely, until the first drops of another rainstorm propelled us down the rest of the path to the car.

We had no one further to see in Bury, and we spent a few moments in the car deciding whether to visit the castle at Arundel or to drive about six or eight miles farther west to have lunch and see the cathedral at Chichester. When I said I'd never seen Chichester (I'd never seen Arundel Castle either), Mr. Sauter said, "Good. Let's save the Castle for another time. I've never been there, nor I think did JG ever go there. He always felt a little disappointed if a guest mentioned it, almost as if they were saying his house was only the stopping point for a tour. But then I'm sure the Castle wasn't nearly so interesting then as it must be now. They take so much more trouble to do such things right these days." Still, we opted for Chichester and drove through a quick shower, finding a small restaurant open almost under the shadow of the cathedral tower. As we ate, Mr. Sauter continued talking of his studio. "Yes, only two years. And, ironically enough, it was the last real studio I've ever had—the first and the last." I asked him about other places he'd lived and worked. "Well, you know," he smiled hesitantly, "with all our talk today of D Day and the Second War, I've been thinking a lot of the place we lived after Bury. As you know, after JG died, we had to move on. We had our own life, and Ada, fond as we all were, wasn't easy then. We hadn't much money of our own, but we found an old mill in a Kentish village, Wittersham. Fixed it up. I had a studio, a makeshift one, nothing like the one in Bury. But I did have the etching press moved—I did a lot of etching in those years—and installed it in the well under the old mill wheel. During the war, I was out in the marshes a lot at night, inspecting the ack-ack defenses and searchlights. There was a special constable about, an older man, not native, doing his bit replacing policemen in the active forces. A strange man. At any rate, he came by suddenly one day and told us we must leave the village within twenty-four hours. He accused me of sending secret radio messages to the Germans about planes and bombing patterns, and he was sure my etching press concealed a radio. He also charged me with sneaking around the marshes near Rye at night to plot the best routes for possible invasions . . . Oh, he had the power all right. The special constabulary during wartime can often act on its own. Well, we were in chaos. Vi phoned a Lady, Lady literally and figuratively, who worked with her in First Aid. She helped, got on to county officials, people in London, told them the charge was nonsense. At first, we only received a reprieve for a few days. Then, it was all straightened out. But we had a sticky few days. This special constable had found out all about my German birth and my First War internment, and he really was convinced I was dangerous." Mr. Sauter smiled, rather more shyly and more to himself than he usually did, and leaned back in his chair. "Funny thing. A year or so after that the special constable was ill. Some sort of nervous breakdown. He was sent away for a rest, then came back to the village, and, a short time later, smashed himself on his motorbike in the blackout. Vi was on duty at First Aid when he was brought in, and she helped bandage his head and fix him up. He came round after he recovered and apologized. Very graciously. He said the knock on his head had knocked out all the silliness. And he really was sorry. No, it wasn't like the First War at all. Of course, there was xenophobia and jingoism, but nothing nearly so virulent as it was in the First War. Even at the height of that little thing in Kent, people were kind, sympathetic, curious, of course, too. But back in the First War they wouldn't speak to us. Friends of years and years cut my mother dead. A world of difference. Even so, when the war was over, in fact a few months before the end, Vi and I realized we'd had enough of village life, needed the city again, and we moved up to London. No room for a studio there."

We took a long time to look around Chichester cathedral, watching the alternating bright sunlight and dark clouds reveal and conceal different patterns in the soft stone and hard tracery of the nave. After showing me his favorite stone carvings in the crypt and the bell tower, Mr. Sauter wanted to find what had been added to the cathedral since he had last visited it more than forty years ago. Neither of us spent more than a moment before the new cast aluminum pulpit, but we were impressed with the large, colorful reredos, seven panels of modern tapestry in bright reds, deep blues, and rich golds, at the far end of the choir. "It's hard color," Mr. Sauter said. "Color in cathedrals can become murky, weak, sentimental. But not this." His hands moved as he traced the patterns of the color. We walked out through the cathedral close, a series of small buildings of stone painted in a softly blending variety of colors. "Yes, it's charming," Mr. Sauter said. "But it is a little weak. That's what I mean. The colors blend too easily, not the strength and the sharpness of those colors in the tapestries. Oh, it's all right for houses, for the close as well. It's just the *inside* of the cathedral that shouldn't have color like that." Mr. Sauter, like many others of his generation, regarded "sentimental" as the most damning judgment that can be delivered against a work of art. He was eager to defend his uncle's work against possible charges of sentimentality, pointing out that Galsworthy was genuinely sensitive, did not fake feelings, and, therefore, cannot justly be castigated as "sentimental." When I tried, as I did on this occasion as we were walking through the close to the car park, to reply that I sometimes do find parts of Galsworthy "sentimental," that feeling no matter how deeply genuine can be seen as excessive or applied indiscriminately, but that this seems to me no crucially serious failure, no reason to dismiss or ignore the work, he was apt to look at me sharply as if I had just abrogated all artistic standards. He did so, momentarily, as we reached the car. Then he smiled suddenly, reached to put his hand on my shoulder, and said, "Yes, maybe you're closer to JG on this than I am. The JG that's in the novels. I just don't know whether or not he would have thought there are things about feelings that go beyond the question of sentimentality."

We began to drive back toward London. During one of the intervals of bright warm sunshine, for the rushing west wind continued to alternate showers and sunlight all day, we decided that, since we would pass only a mile or two from Guildford, we would stop to look at its new cathedral which neither of us had seen. As we drove through dramatic changes in light and weather and their effect on landscape, Mr. Sauter kept pointing to patterns along the hills or the darkened cluster of a village. And we returned, in a circuitous way, to one of our first conversations about Galsworthy, to his sense of landscape. Suddenly, Mr. Sauter looked at me and smiled: "You know, maybe we've tamed my uncle a bit too much. We've talked of Bury and his landscape and his novels, all his balance and judgment. But we haven't really talked very much about his plays, his *drama*. That's what I found so exciting when I was young. He could make the stage seem electric, the moments in *Justice* or in *Strife* when everything comes to a head. I still remember the first time I saw *Justice*, the way a door opened and everyone in the audience was on the edge of his seat." He smiled more broadly, "Yes, another cathedral will help us both get things right."

Our first look at the outside of Guildford cathedral was slightly disappointing, nothing of the old stone or spire seen rising out of close leafy trees that made Chichester seem so warm, just a vast structure of suburban-looking red brick, high and isolated on a windswept plain above the city. Guildford cathedral, begun in the thirties, not worked on at all for over ten years because of the shortage of building materials during and after the war, was consecrated only in 1961, and still seems something of a raw impingement inflicted on the edge of a city. But, inside, the cathedral soars in a dignity and austerity of white stone, tempered by thousands of needlework chair cushions and a deep blue woven carpet that runs up to the altar. Numerous smaller chapels have been done with a recurring motif of white stags on a deep blue background, a civic symbol, which gives the cathedral a sense of richness and depth to balance the pure white of the soaring elevations. We walked, and talked of dramatic distances and elevations, Mr. Sauter extending both arms as he traced the vertical thrusts of the cathedral. On our way out, we saw that the wind was fiercely blowing up another storm cloud, but Mr. Sauter thought there was still enough light to enable him to get a picture of the carved glass angels on the door of the cathedral porch, that, in fact, the heavy dark light might bring out the glass on film more sharply. He stood on the porch in gusts of wind severe enough so that several others passing temporarily lost hats or were thrown off balance, his feet planted wide apart, white hair blown out at a right angle from his head, carefully adjusting his meter, setting his camera, holding it firmly, momentarily intent on the picture. As I walked a slight distance away from him and looked back, he seemed the one firm and unyielding point in the darkness and wind that surrounded him. He, himself, seemed to represent a dramatic moment.

As we drove toward London, Mr. Sauter continued talking of cathedrals and of his taste for searing, dramatic, and un-English scenery, his love for the Grand Canyon and Alpine peaks. I ventured the suggestion that, from my external point of view, he seemed more English than he might acknowledge. He laughed, "Yes, yes, you might have a point. Oh, of course, you're quite right. I talk about the Grand Canyon and the Alps from the safety of England. Of course, I do really love them. But I might not have been any more comfortable living with them than my uncle would have been. I just don't want to be a patriot—but, then, neither did JG, not toward the end, though I suppose he always was more of one than I. Still, of course, you're right. I *have* lived here all my life, and I suppose that must say something. I could have gone to the Continent with my father after the First War. But I didn't, wouldn't have. Yes, I must be more a part of all this," as he gestured toward the rain and hills outside, "than I like to think I am." He smiled again and turned toward me. "And I'm not contemplating any sudden moves now." He leaned back and became more pensive, speaking more slowly, as if not certain he wanted to express what was on his mind. "But, you know, there's the other side of it, too. After the First War, things weren't going very well for me. My mother had died and my father had gone back to Germany before that. JG took me aside one day, and asked if I would like to take the name Galsworthy by deed poll. I knew that I was already, after Ada of course, his literary executor, but he wanted me legally to become his son. The son he never had. He told me to take my time about responding, think it over. But I knew all the time that I couldn't do it, couldn't change my name. My father was still alive, but I don't think that was the only reason. JG understood perfectly, never mentioned it again."

We soon became involved in London early evening traffic, but, since we managed to enter London from the southwest and head for Paddington while still avoiding Hammersmith, we arrived in time for Mr. Sauter's train. As we walked through the station, he told me how much he had enjoyed the two days, and he hoped that I had found enough in Bury to justify my time. I started to reply, but just then the whistle blew announcing the imminent departure of his train for Stroud. We clasped hands warmly. I watched him, a neat, wiry figure still, stride rapidly down the platform carrying his suitcase, with his camera and light meter bouncing against his jacket on the other side.

Within the next few days back in London the westerlies died down and were succeeded by an anticyclonic shift to the east, a spell of about ten days of clear, hot weather. For the first time all year, we began to feel that some of the gloomy newspaper prognostications about the future of Britain, which we had laughed away during the winter's "energy crisis," might be accurate. A higher intensity seemed to characterize pieces in the more intelligent journals that labelled Britain's economic problems insoluble or wondered if some kind of military or far-right takeover might be the inevitable response to another Labour government failure and increasing militancy within the unions. One evening we went out to Wimbledon for dinner with Simon, whom I had known since he was reading law at Oxford in the early fifties and my wife had known since the year we lived in Cambridge, when he worked as a young lawyer in the Foreign Office, wearing his bowler hat only to and from work on the Underground, hiding it deep in a closet when he came home. He, his French mistress at the time, my wife, Joan, and I had spent many weekends together that year, driving to country pubs and going to plays (including the third or fourth night of John Osborne's *Look Back In Anger*, during which a tall, distinguished, elderly gentleman actually did rise in the middle, his face turning red, splutter, "Damn it. He can't say that," and walk quickly out of the theatre). I could recall Simon, later that year, shortly before we were to leave, having drinks in the bar of the American officers' club in London, confiding to us his skepticism about the policies that would, in just a month or so, lead to Suez. He explained that Anthony Eden was simply applying old policies inflexibly, establishing a colonial imperative, with no understanding of all the forces and issues operating in the Middle East or the third world. And I could also recall, two years before that, Simon, on a graduate student year in America, in a wooden-boothed bar in a small town in upstate New York, calmly and rationally deflating a rabid McCarthyite, while I, seeing more sense of menace in the man than Simon did, could only mutter into my beer. Simon's politics had always seemed so knowledgeable, sane, and comprehensive, so little limited by his class or background or various occupations. Now, in Wimbledon, in 1974, as we were eating salmon trout on a hot evening, he, just back with his wife and children from working two years in Iran as a lawyer for one of the large oil companies, began to berate the unions, to say that they were responsible for Britain's economic difficulties, and to speculate that Communist influence was responsible. When I protested, he replied: "One can't ignore the Communist party. And it isn't entirely true that it's not like the Soviet model in Western countries. Of course, there are struggles within it, but it all feeds on the British workman's notorious laziness, his refusal to do anything he doesn't have to when the state will take care of him. Just a few years ago, when I took a trip to Germany, I went through some of the refining plants. Efficient, hard-working men. You should see the difference." Joan interrupted in a heavy mock-German accent, "You mean the trains run on time." Simon stopped and laughed, his wife telling him that he was being pompous, and said, "No doubt I'm exaggerating a good deal." Then he laughed at himself more heartily, and said, looking at our empty plates, "Let's have coffee in the other room. Shall we? I'll put on some music. Would you like Vivaldi, or a rather good rock concert the children taped last week?" After we returned home, I was still slightly bothered by the note of excessive respect for efficiency in his conversation. Talking with my wife, I said I thought that Simon's point of view was probably only temporary, a mild colonial aberration, the result of the two years in Iran and an earlier stint in Libya, which he had described to us two years before, when he had some difficulty with the secret police in Libya, leaving the country just as nationalization of oil forced out the oil companies. Joan wasn't so sure about my explanation. "Besides," she added, "maybe he's right about Communist influence. He didn't imply anything about plots or international conspiracy. Just English Communists. Maybe they really do want to disrupt the Labour party, to make its compromises impossible. How do you know?"

The next few days brought further assaults on the England I wanted to see preserve itself. The IRA planted a bomb in the Houses of Parliament. A boiler exploded, ripping out some walls and most of the windows, in the neglected house Miss Beattie had left only two weeks earlier. Our architect friend next door, remarking that the basic cost of building had gone from eight pounds to twenty pounds per square foot in just two years, told us that he quite suddenly had no commissions at all and was planning to move to Portugal at the end of the summer to build condominiums along the Algarve coast. One night, at our favorite Chelsea pub, which had both a dart board and French food, where we often had an excellent roast beef sandwich or curry or the best Brie we had found in London, a drunken man began to scream insults at the girl behind the food counter just because she was Australian and all Australian women were "fucking cows." At another pub, I saw a customer and the barman almost come to blows because the customer had leaned over the bar himself to spear a sausage from the grill behind, leaving his 10p. piece on the counter. Neither would yield the rightness of his position. The still suspension of heat made London seem angry and intense.

The heat wave broke, however, and, for our last five days in London, the westerlies returned in a deluge, more rain, I think, than we had seen all year. For one of our last evenings, Mrs. Watts had arranged a dinner party so that we could meet some of her friends. Before we went, my wife and I played with the stereotypes of what she might wear to a Hampstead dinner party on a cool, rainy night, a party given by a woman who had often dined with Galsworthy. Should it be the kind of peasant blouse and skirt connected with ceramics, heavy silver jewelry, and the Hampstead of the thirties? Or the plain wool dress, preferably grey, that is invariably safe in an atmosphere of academic high-mindedness? But we both knew that it would be an evening for long dresses and, as we immediately confirmed when we walked up the stairs and entered the already crowded room, one of formal patterns for seating and movement as well. Mrs. Watts also orchestrated conversations carefully, making sure everyone had his or her "innings" with almost everyone else. Conversations jumped quickly about politics and places and art: Sissinghurst, Chicago, the social services, Watergate, open-air Shakespeare at Regents Park. It all sounded liberal and benevolent and interested on the surface, with another note, a note, as one woman spoke to my wife of "our sort of people," of a cultivated smugness, sounding just underneath. At dinner, I was seated next to Mrs. Watts, my wife at the other end of the table next to Mrs. Watts's daughter, a woman taller and softer than her mother, who illustrates children's books. As everyone was appropriately disposed around the table, Mrs. Watts, sitting down, whispered to me, "I'm so pleased my daughter could get here. She only managed to sort out her domestic problem and get to me at the last moment." Mrs. Watts turned to look down the table and announce, "Yes, we must have soup," smiling widely, "Pavel always says that a meal can't begin properly without soup." Pavel was a courtly-looking Russian gentleman whose English wife has written a biography of Turgenev. Mrs. Watts asked me to open the wine, and I ineptly crumbled the cork and had to push some of it down into the bottle. Pavel rescued me and opened the second bottle deftly. After she had collected the soup plates and carved and served the roast, Mrs. Watts turned to me to tell me one or two anecdotes about Galsworthy that she had not told before. The man across from me, on her other side, a young theatre director who had been frowning, looking like a bald version of Mischa Auer in 1940 films, interrupted to ask her if she modelled her dinner parties after Galsworthy's. "Oh, no," she responded, smiling widely and pausing pointedly to let us listen to the word "criminal" coming from one conversation down the table and "damn Tory" from another, "I *hope* one says what one likes at my dinners. One didn't really at the Galsworthys. One had to mind his p's and q's, at least I always felt I did. Oh, they tried to listen or encourage any talk. But I was afraid to put a foot wrong, always felt there were unspoken rules that I didn't quite understand just underneath the gracious surface." We opened, in a joint venture, another bottle of wine, and the conversation became quick and diffuse again.

After dinner, Mrs. Watts, rearranging our positions and partners on the sofa and chairs around the fire, perched herself on a small, straight chair, and clapped her hand against her thigh. "Now I heard Ronnie down the table at dinner talking about the social services. I didn't quite catch all of it. Did you talk of the battered-baby issue? Let's all talk about battered babies." The room was suddenly silent. My wife, who had been in the middle of a conversation she was enjoying, winked at me when no one was looking. I turned to the woman next to me, who had written about Turgenev, to continue talking about biography, while others around the room resumed their conversations. Mrs. Watts shrugged her shoulders, then briefly joined in conversations, about books and music and children and education, as she passed coffee around the room. Later, when we left, wishing each other luck, Mrs. Watts clasped my hands warmly and said she wondered whether she would finish her biography of her mother before I finished my book. I almost thought she wanted to make a good-natured bet. The woman with whom my wife had talked for a long while after dinner and her husband, Ronnie, who lived in South London, drove us home, explaining something of the Probation Service, its connection with an old system of court missionaries established by the church and its relation with magistrates, as we rode through an almost deserted London in a steady rain. I felt comfortable in the back seat of the closed car, listening to the warmth and interest of voices, looking out at the shafts from street lights or traffic lights that glistened on the wet asphalt pavements.

At home, my wife and I stayed up late, still talking, the usual result of lots of wine and coffee at a dinner party. We began talking of the party and the people there. I said how much

I enjoyed the rapid shifts in conversation, the range of topics; Joan said, "But didn't you notice all the little bursts of hostility, the way, under the polite surface, a number of those people were after each other?" "Mild hostility," I replied, "mostly just talk. At least we didn't hear any long tirades or monologues, no extended advertisements for the self." I went on to compare the party favorably to some academic American dinner parties, claiming that, at least at this and at parties like it, hostility was quick and individual, did not emerge as assertive opportunism or careerism. I added an old, worn theme of mine, that those most dedicated to selling themselves, to using any social occasion to advance their careers, were the British migrants to American academic society, willing captives to the trap under the brain drain. "I like my Englishwomen and Englishmen so much better in England, not striving for anything, not full of challenge." Joan looked at me wearily and smiled, "There you go again. Romanticizing England as if it were some special paradise, ignoring all the references to class that are used as social weapons. You're always going to parties and places looking for the quintessence of Englishness—at the last six parties we've been to I've talked about post-partum depression or career vs. marriage, things I could talk of anywhere. Yes, England's fine, and it's civilized, and people are nice to you because you're a stranger. But really, Jim, people are alike anywhere. They all hurt, have pain and anger. Only the forms it takes are different." I realized the force of her point, and thought of one of the earliest classes that I, as a graduate student, had taught. Analyzing an essay, a long since forgotten treatment of some series of national differences, and, referring to the scheme of organization of the essay, I asked the class, "Now, what's the basic difference between the English and the French?" An engineer in the back row drawled, "The English live in England and the French live in France." Joan, I knew, didn't intend to carry common sense quite that far.

We talked further, trying to isolate what it was that we both found unique in England. It was not just the politeness, the manner, we agreed; rather, a deeper respect for individuals, a quiet willingness to let others be what they were, an acceptance that didn't seem to strain or challenge, although it could have indolence or indifference as its other side. We talked of the verbal agility of so many of the English we knew, all the various forms of expressing yet moderating hostility, in both conversation and in fiction, that might do less damage than other forms of assault would. We talked, too, of our travels that year, of Devon and Wiltshire and Kent, of the green hills and rolling weather and clustered villages we had wandered through all year. We knew that air and earth and water were common to all places, but we felt that, more tangibly and more thoroughly than during other years in England, we had worked through the initial sense of euphoria we always felt rediscovering plays and pubs and galleries on our arrival, had lived through the grey industrial sameness of the early December dusk, and had come to understand and appreciate a little of the particular climate and geography of England. Not always easily, sometimes too protected by our role as alien visitors, and occasionally too abrasively, we had accommodated ourselves to the space around us. We felt, talking of space and accommodation, that we didn't need, for the moment at any rate, to challenge or assert. We realized as we went to bed, that we had, vicariously at least, painted ourselves into the landscape. And I felt, momentarily, in a better position to understand Galsworthy than I had before.

The next morning, a cool wind pushing gusts of rain against the windows, I assembled all my notes and papers to pack and wrote a few final letters. I saved the one to Mr. Sauter for last. As I sat smoking, thinking of what I wanted to say to him, I recalled his statement that Galsworthy might well have been "shattered" by the Second World War, that his acute sensitivity might not have been able to survive the horrors of another war or the horrors that followed it. I realized that he had seen all the implications of Fascism, abroad and at home, all the impending dogma and the inhumane attempts to paste theories on men and make them live or die by them. And he was frightened, severely so. But England, despite all the competing dogmas and indecisive governments and inadequate response to social, class, and economic issues, had not gone Fascist in the thirties, not lived or died for an apocalypse, not created scapegoats or succumbed to an abstract version of its own virtues. Something in the climate, in the succession of various westerlies that we had seen all year, that still blew gently, stalled, billowed high and fresh, closed in, stopped, and reasserted themselves in inconsistent patterns, had qualified, moderated, kept the country from explosion. I did not know whether the westerlies would keep coming and changing, just as I did not know how long the England I saw and felt might remain or whether or not Galsworthy really would have been "shattered" by the Second World War. A small part of me was almost eager to get back to America before I could feel, incontrovertibly, that the climate of England and Galsworthy were part of a finished past; the myth that it still existed, if it really was just myth, might be easier to sustain from a distance. I did not write all this to Mr. Sauter. Instead, I wrote of my impending journey to America, my work, his work, and my plans, beginning to congeal with greater certainty, to return to see him the following summer. I had, for him and for others, further questions to ask.

John Galsworthy senior with his grandson, Rudolf Sauter. Painted by Géorg Sauter in 1899-1900.

Blanche Bartelot Galsworthy

Reproduced by permission of Miss Muriel Galsworthy

John Galsworthy as a student at New College, Oxford, between 1886 and 1889

Reproduced from the Galsworthy Papers by permission of the University of Birmingham (on behalf of the Galsworthy Estate)

John Galsworthy

Ada Galsworthy

Photographs by E. O. Hoppé
appeared in *The Bookman* of
November, 1913.

*Reproduced by permission of Mr. Frank Hoppé,
Hodder and Stoughton, and the Mansell
Collection.*

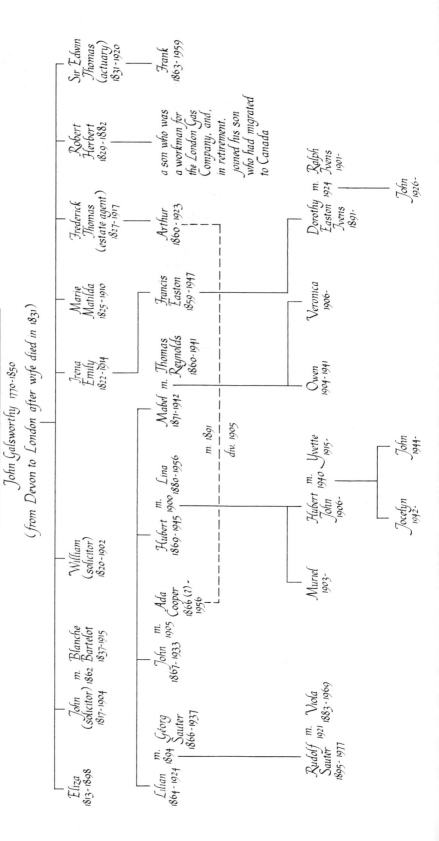

Galsworthy Family Tree

John Galsworthy 1770-1850
(from Devon to London after wife died in 1831)

Eliza 1813-1898

John (solicitor) 1817-1904 m. 1862 Blanche Bartelot 1837-1915

William (solicitor) 1820-1902

Irene Emily 1822-1914

Marie Matilda 1825-1910

Frederick Thomas (estate agent) 1827-1917

Robert Herbert 1829-1882

Sir Edwin Thomas (actuary) 1831-1920

Lilian 1864-1924 m. 1894 Georg Sauter 1866-1937

John 1867-1933 m. 1905 Ada Cooper 1866 (?) - 1956

Hubert 1869-1945 m. Lina 1900 1880-1956

Mabel 1871-1942 m. Thomas Reynolds 1860-1941

Francis Easton 1859-1947

Arthur 1860-1923

a son who was a workman for the London Gas Company, and, in retirement, joined his son who had migrated to Canada

Frank 1863-1959

m. 1891
div. 1905

Dorothy 1891- m. 1924 Ralph Ivens 1901-

Rudolf Sauter 1895-1977 m. 1921 Viola Sauter 1883-1969

Muriel 1903-

Hubert John 1906- m. 1940 Yvette 1915-

Owen 1904-1941

Veronica 1906-

John 1926-

Jocelyn 1942-

John 1944-

PART II

July–August
1975

A
S WE LANDED at London airport and walked through the terminal, a year almost to the day from the one on which we had left London at the end of June, we could feel the heat, the continental anticyclonic mass of warm thick air suspended over England. Knowing that both time and money would be limited that summer, we had, uncharacteristically, planned ahead and rented a cottage in Devon for a few weeks, assuming that the new motorway, announced for completion in November, 1974, would be ready enough by the summer of 1975 to allow quick driving visits to the Galsworthy relatives in the West Country. But I learned, on the hot, crowded drive to Devon, that the motorway was far from finished, had only two or three more miles open than when we last had driven the road well over a year earlier. Stalled in a traffic jam on a dusty, dirt-tracked detour leading off the motorway, I realized that I should have known better. I recalled, almost twenty years earlier, driving daily from our house in Cambridge to the Huntingdon Air Force base where we had jobs, that workmen had taken almost a year to dig up the road for sewer repairs in the town of Godmanchester. Each day, we had taken a half-hour to go the two blocks along the narrow street with cramped terraces of dirty red brick houses squatting along the road, before crossing the single-lane, humped-backed bridge, each direction signalled alternately by traffic light, over the Ouse into Huntingdon. Workmen were visible drinking tea in litttle shelters at intersections or cheerfully directing traffic. I also remembered the year in Sheffield, living at the top of the hill, watching workmen, at the rate of two or three feet a day, always willing to stop for a chat or a smoke or a cup of tea, inch their heavy resurfacing machinery up the steep and rutted incline of Crimicar Lane. And now, even in 1975, with all the news of shortages and diminishing industry and pleasantly indolent workmen, I had

foolishly trusted English deadlines. I, too, could be irritated by trains that didn't run on time.

Finally in Devon, we found the little village along the Dart where we had rented the cottage. But our advance information, several duplicated pages that read more like an advertising brochure than like a description, had not included the fact that, just at the point of the picturesque village, the Dart widens into a shallow lake, the shores smelling septic with litter and dead fish in the heat. We had to break into the cottage by climbing through a tiny transom, to the laconic enjoyment of the village postman who had given us the key the landlady left. He had known the doors were double-locked and the key useless and then disappeared to go fishing, chuckling that *he'd* not be an accomplice to housebreaking. And, once inside, we found the cottage itself far from what we had anticipated. Dank, humid, a sunken basement, and cramped, four of us trying to sort out the best arrangements for sleeping in three tiny, built-in box beds, the cottage's modern conveniences were all patio gimcracks on the outside. In addition, my wife wasn't feeling well so that leaving her there with the children, as I went off to visit people for two or three days at a time, would have been impossible. We managed, driving or walking the two miles up a steep hill to the village's single public telephone several times each day, to shorten our stay in the cottage to a week. The landlady in London was, we discovered, a transplanted American. Carefully formulated plans, for me, were obviously not the way; forethought and human engineering, at least in my "soft" hands, were doomed. I had more sympathy with the laconic village postman than I could ever let myself acknowledge.

The week in Devon was, however, far from totally wasted. We happily wandered the streets and hilly shoreline of nearby Dartmouth and other villages along the coast. We visited several castles and an old abbey where the children climbed and wandered. My daughter joined me on a boat trip up the Dart to Totnes, and the accommodating boatman stopped long enough for me to see slowly the vast yew that Galsworthy had once stopped to measure, a thick, obtrusive bulwark that seemed to flatten the surrounding landscape. On the blisteringly hot Saturday, I took my children to swim in the English Channel, choosing a beach I had read about that was scooped in a semicircle out of the high cliff, with a thick, fine sand bottom. Just as, carrying our towels down the steep path, we set foot on the beach, we heard a loud roar of delight emerge from among the many transistor radios and reverberate along the walls of the cliff, and we knew that Arthur Ashe had beaten Jimmy Connors in the final at Wimbledon. Later, after my children had joined a half-splashing, half-swimming game in the shallows of the Channel, first a French tourist couple and then an Englishman asked me if I had been disappointed that Connors hadn't won. When I said, "No, I was pleased," each grasped my hand warmly, smiling as if, momentarily at least, America had been redeemed.

Two days later, we temporarily settled in Salisbury, a city from which we really could visit the Galsworthy relatives with ease. Leaving our children to wander the cathedral themselves, to draw what windows or traceries they would, my wife joined me for the drive across Wiltshire villages to Warminster to see Miss Muriel Galsworthy. Since I had had to change the date for our meeting and Miss Galsworthy had other guests for lunch, she had asked us to come about three and stay on through tea and later. After she opened the door, Miss Galsworthy, looking cool and trim in a blue dress with a wide, white collar (in spite of shielding her eyes from the shaft of bright, hot sunlight our entrance had brought into the polished wood hall), kept us in the hall a few minutes to greet my wife and to explain that her other guests were her nephew, John Galsworthy, Hubert's son, whose marriage had broken up a few years earlier, and the girl-friend he was now taking around to meet the family. Miss Galsworthy puffed out her lips in an exaggerated mock-frown as she said, "And I believe she's called 'The Bouncer.'" We entered the drawing room and were introduced. John stood up, tall and thin, dressed in a modish light-colored suit with wide lapels; his thin face, dark mustache, and square chin seemed to bear some resemblance to the photographs taken in the 1890s that I had seen of his great-uncle until I noticed that John, like his mother, had large dark eyes. "The Bouncer," a straightforward and square-shouldered young woman, dressed casually, stood to shake our hands and greeted us with a direct and open smile.

As she showed us photographs and the picture she had drawn of her grandmother and of one of the early Galsworthy houses built in Surrey on what is now Kingston Hill, Miss Galsworthy, in part for our benefit and in part for her nephew and his friend, began to talk of the distant past. She talked of her Galsworthy grandmother, "finicky" and highly principled, insisting her children arrange the cushions on the sofa exactly and, herself deeply religious and the sister of a Church of England clergyman, able to accept graciously the fact that all four of her children were "free thinkers." "I still think, you know," Miss Galsworthy said, smiling at me, "that my uncle got his tolerance, his respect for other people's beliefs, from his mother. She was quite different from all those Galsworthys who gathered almost every Sunday at the old Aunt's. More international, more ethereal, too. She had a box of shells, arranged in carefully graded colors, that she always kept. When I was a child I thought it the most beautiful thing I'd ever seen." I asked Miss Galsworthy if she knew of a book on her grandmother's family, the Bartelots (or Bartletts or Bartleets in various other branches), that had been written by a clergyman member of the family during the Second World War and printed privately, that dealt only with genealogy and the family crest (containing three moons crescent, a sign that members of the family had taken part in the Crusades), and told her of the copy I had seen in the Galsworthy collection at the University of Birmingham. Miss Galsworthy had not known of the book and was excited at the possibility of getting hold of a copy: "I've always wanted to know more of the Bartelots. It seems just a little unfair to have heard chronicles of Galsworthys all my life."

John Galsworthy, however, leaning forward in his chair and offering cigarets, wanted to hear more about distant Galsworthys. Miss Galsworthy obliged by talking of the novelist's favorite cousin, Frank Galsworthy, a small, dapper man who lived to the age of ninety-five, never married, "was always surrounded by ladies," and achieved some fame painting pictures of flowers.

He had a large home in Scunthorpe, in Lincolnshire, with fields of variously shaded tulips. She knew where several of his paintings were, paintings done for the Chelsea Flower Show, one of them, of striped tulips, in honor of Ada. Miss Galsworthy also talked of Arthur Galsworthy, whom she had never known, and of his son, a child of his second wife, who she understood was still, or had recently been, in the diplomatic service in Ireland. Shifting to closer relatives, Miss Galsworthy talked of her cousins whom I, like her nephew, had never met, the children of Mabel Reynolds. She spoke fondly of Owen who, early in the Second World War, knowing that he had leukemia, had insisted on taking part in the Commando raids, instituted mostly for purposes of morale, on the Norwegian coast. He survived the raids, dying of leukemia soon after. "He had the most lovely wedding, before the War. They were both so handsome, Joyce was an artist. He left a daughter. Oh, yes. Joyce is still in touch with the family. She remarried, and is now a widow again." Miss Galsworthy spoke less fondly of Mabel's daughter, Veronica. "Oh, Ronnie was attractive and clever—like all the Reynolds, bigger and blonder than the rest of us—but she was always the family rebel. Wanted nothing to do with us. She married a Swiss man, beefy; it didn't last. Married again, I think. I very much doubt your trying to see her would do any good. I wouldn't know how to find her, but I'm sure she'd want nothing to do with Galsworthy. Mabel, you know, was killed going to see her. It was during the blackout, and Ronnie had just had a baby. Mabel stepped into the Kensington High Street, thinking it was the small road nearby on which Ronnie lived, and was killed by a bus."

Miss Galsworthy shuddered and excused herself to bring in the tea, refusing any offers of help. While she was gone, John told of his year or so in America about 1967. He had worked in hotels, as a waiter and desk clerk, at Bear Mountain in the summer and in Florida during the winter. He had wanted to make his career in the United States, but soon realized that serving in the U.S. Army in Vietnam was too high a price for permanent migration, "though I liked the States a lot. Thought the future might be better for me there." He now works at a hotel, the bar and the desk, near Winchester. When I, feeling in advance that the question would probably elicit little response but determined to satisfy my curiosity anyhow, asked him if his name had meant very much to the people he met in America, he smiled shyly, looked at "The Bouncer," whose name, we learned, was Cecilia, and replied, "Not really. That was one of the things I rather liked. Maybe after the TV series it would have been different." Miss Galsworthy returned with an elaborate tea, large delicious strawberries and fresh cream, and several different kinds of cake. As we ate, we talked of various recent productions of Galsworthy's work, Miss Galsworthy having liked a recent television version of *Strife* and thinking that television has generally done better by Galsworthy than did some of the earlier films, like one of *Escape* that "was too much fox hunt." She finds she remembers the plays best, the "moving, upsetting" quality of *Justice*, the theatrical force of *Loyalties*, the performances of Sybil Thorndike's daughters, as children, playing cats in *The Roof*, Galsworthy's last play, which was not well received or, he thought, well presented. "It's the excitement of the plays I remember best. The way I was always moved by sudden changes, almost like explosions. He took trouble as a playwright, went to rehearsals, cared how it was done. St. John Ervine, who saw him on the London Underground at 5:30 one morning, going to a slaughterhouse to get material for his campaign against methods of slaughtering animals, once said that his plays were so good because the 'exits and entrances were so perfect.'" Talk of the plays led us back to Galsworthy's internationalism and translations, and I asked Miss Galsworthy how skillful a linguist her uncle had been. She laughed, and said, "He was *not* a linguist. A Bartelot in sympathies, but a pure English Galsworthy in speech. His Spanish was no good, his French was laborious. When he had to speak at P.E.N. in French, Ada did most of it. Knew what he wanted to say and wrote it out for him. Ada really was talented." Ada's French was good, as I knew. She published her own translation of some Maupassant short stories, with an appreciative introduction by Joseph Conrad. As so often happened, when one of the relatives or others brought Ada into the conversation, I found myself asking further questions about her. I asked if Miss Galsworthy had seen very much of her aunt after her uncle had died. "No," she said, "not really. She was still very kind. She gave me money for a godchild of mine who badly needed it and those Regency chairs, there, the ones alongside the secretary were hers. She left them to me. She bought the house in Torquay, kept the London staff, and left the house itself to the staff. But I didn't see much of her. After Uncle Jack died, particularly after the war, she became more and more remote, almost a recluse, blind, with a bad chest, trouble breathing. The heat in that house was just terrible. Fires everywhere. She needed them, of course, but for anyone else it was suffocating. She might have missed children, yes she might have. Uncle Jack once told my mother that they didn't want to have children because of her age when they married. But she, so far as I know, never said a word."

John Galsworthy insisted that it was his job to help his aunt with the washing up; as a hotel man, he had lots of experience and the rest of us were guests. When they left the room, my wife and I began to talk with Cecilia, who had been silent through most of the conversation on the family and Galsworthy's plays, about her work for the British Social Services. She was a specialist in postinstitutional care, a visiting supervisor of the halfway houses in which people who have been in institutions or are mentally retarded live together in the attempt to ease adjustment into ordinary society. Cecilia (whose nickname seemed less and less appropriate to us the longer we talked) discussed the problems of her clients with considerable sensitivity and judgment, recognizing with an understated sympathy both the difficulties of her clients and the difficulties others had in accepting them. The discussion moved to the issues inherent in state schools, the diverse population, the numbers of West Indian and Pakistani pupils, the long tradition of English schools in enforcing a rigid discipline. I recalled my experiences visiting schools in the slums in and around Sheffield: the children sent out in the halls so that the headmaster, circulating every hour or so, could collect and cane them; the sometimes black-gowned headmasters who sneered at pupils for not meeting standards they could never understand; the designations by class and occupation which became labels that seemed to mark the children for life. "Yes," Cecilia said. "In spite of some good new programs, a fairly progressive ministry, and more and more sensitive and well-trained teachers, it all still goes on. All too often." As she and my wife continued the conversation about education, I found myself bothered by the fact that Galsworthy, even at the height of his Liberal interest in ameliorating other forms of injustice, had expressed, so far as I could discover, no interest in reforming education at all. Neither at Bury nor elsewhere, so far as I could tell, had he any interests in the schools; no one had ever reported a conversation with him about state education. Perhaps, I thought, I was being naively American, too easily assuming that educational changes are central to social reform, although the assumption was often British as well. I also realized that not everyone could take up every cause, even one as fortunate and capacious as Galsworthy could not include every issue in his humanitarian concern. Still, the apparent absence in Galsworthy gnawed at me, and I felt suddenly that there is something more fundamental about the education of children than about methods of slaughtering animals or campaigning against egret plumes.

Miss Galsworthy and John returned, she asking if I would like to see her garden, recalling that I had been unable to see much in the cold dusk of my visit the year before. In the hot sun, now slanting strongly as the day passed toward evening, the garden was resplendent with phlox and cannas. I took her picture using the last of her peonies as a background. As we walked around the garden, she told me that her cousin Rudolf had also worked for social welfare agencies during the Second World War, had divided his time between that and inspecting the ack-ack defenses, leaving no time at all for his painting. We returned to the others in the drawing room, Miss Galsworthy still standing as she told us that, for Rudolf's eightieth birthday, two months earlier, Mrs. Scrivens had invited a number of his friends and booked the afternoon at a small flying club near Stroud, arranging that he, with his friends watching, spend an hour or so flying in a glider, which he had always wanted to do. The birthday surprise was apparently a great success. Miss Galsworthy, waving her arms in the air, then swooping them down, said, "Yes, I heard all about it. I was invited, and was so disappointed that I couldn't go that day." She then smiled rather shyly to herself, "You know, I think some of the things Rudo does or wants to do are a little crazy. But not the gliding. I can understand that. It must make one feel very free. I think maybe I should like to try it some time." And then she laughed, as if she had been saying something outrageous. She sat down and we continued to talk about the family. She told me that Rudolf had finished most of the woodwork at Bury in the same silvery charcoal he had used for his studio, that the whole house had had an aura of lightness to counteract the size and heaviness of its structure. I asked her if some of her uncle's internationalism, some of what she called the "continental outlook" attributable to the Bartelots, might also be attributed to Rudolf's father, Géorg Sauter, the Bavarian painter. She thought for a moment, and then replied, "No. I don't really think so. Uncle Gé was a bear of a man. Very difficult. My father, you know, was really rather frightened of him. Didn't like to meet him. When they were in the same room, they always argued within ten minutes. Only Aunt Lily or Uncle Jack could mediate. They were the only ones who didn't have to take one side or the other. Oh, I suppose it was mostly that my father was so very English and Uncle Gé was so very, very German. You know, after the First War when he was interned, he was bitter, quite understandably. He went back to Germany, stayed there, and became famous as a painter of the aristocracy. Hitler sent a wreath to his funeral. No, I don't really think Uncle Gé had much influence on Uncle Jack." We talked further about the Nazis and the Second World War. "Of course, Hitler went much too far," Miss Galsworthy said at one point, "incarcerating Jews, brutally moving people away from families. But he did have a problem. The Jews in Germany weren't entirely guiltless and had contributed to the situation." My wife and I looked at each other, silently deciding not to pursue that particular aspect of the conversation further.

We talked further of Galsworthy's houses and the films made from his work, until we realized how long we had left our children alone in Salisbury. As she accompanied us to the door, Miss Galsworthy repeated how pleased she was to see us and how much she enjoyed talking about the past, feeling that both times I had visited I had caused her to recall things pleasurable she thought she had forgotten. She gave me a picture of her grandmother to have copied and return; she hoped she could think of more drawings that I might like to have or copy. As my wife and I drove back to Salisbury in the fading light of the hot, still evening, we talked of how kind Miss Galsworthy was, how generous and sharp and interested and eager to be helpful. She also seemed to exude, more than she had when I had first met her a year before, something of the past, but it was a past in which I was not entirely comfortable. Once again, I felt that reaching a fuller sense of what Galsworthy was might be more difficult than I had anticipated. Luckily, when we reached Salisbury, it was dark and a fresh breeze, cooler than any we had felt that summer, began to sweep across the plain.

Since the drive to Stroud was considerably longer than the drive to Warminster, I left, by myself, early the next morning, crossing the military encampments on Salisbury Plain on a bright day a good deal cooler than the days before. Threading my way on B-roads across country, through unfamiliar villages with placid market squares (although twice I noticed that I was only a mile or so from a major motorway I did not take), I realized, as I approached Stroud, that, having been too chastened by the traffic congestion in Devon, I had allowed far more time than I needed and would arrive about an hour early for my meeting with Mr. Sauter. I stalled by stopping for coffee, then petrol, before driving up the steep hill to Mr. Sauter's. He welcomed me effusively, saying, "I'm glad you arrived early. I've so many things to show you downstairs and the light is perfect just now." As we walked downstairs, Mr. Sauter talked of the thunderstorms over Stroud that had cleared the air the night before and of his attempt to sort out all his paintings and books since, within a few weeks, he would have to evacuate his house for several days to have it treated for woodworm. He walked into one of the large downstairs rooms, arranging the curtains to filter out a slanting shaft of direct sunlight, and, like an impressario held up a large and beautiful painting of a woman shrouded in various shades of grey, Whistler-like on the surface, but far more tactile and sensual the longer one looked at it. I expressed considerable enthusiasm. "Yes," he said, "it is marvelous. One of my father's late paintings, after he went back to Germany. I've just been sent a number of his paintings from his German inheritors—you know, he married again, after my mother had died, back in Germany—I've been trying to buy the paintings for years. Now, I'm preparing a retrospective show of his work, in England, next spring perhaps." He showed me other paintings, portraits, stark abstractions, all evidence, in a diversity of styles, of a talent executed with strength and richness. He then led me along to the other downstairs room in which a bowl of flowers had been placed on a table in front of the large window. Alongside the table, a painting of the flowers, almost finished, was set on an easel. Other paintings of similar flowers, in different lights at different seasons, stood against the wall on one side of the room. I liked them very much, and said so. Mr. Sauter continued, "I've been working on flowers all this past winter and spring. More painting than I've done in six or seven years. Trying different lights. Both the seen and the unseen, the way light influences objects even when it can't be seen or painted directly. Yet more representational, more naturalistic if you like, than any of the work I'd done in a long time." Mr. Sauter paused, and then smiled broadly as he turned from looking at his paintings to looking directly at me. "I know you're really not very fond of some of my abstractions. Sun and mountains and ice. My paintings of the sixties. I'm not so fond of them now either. Yes, these new things really are better. Smaller, less grand, but more of me, I think."

We went back upstairs and Mr. Sauter began to rummage through some cabinets in the kitchen to find a gin and tonic for me and some Dubonnet for himself. As he searched, he apologized, claiming that "old widowers" were not very handy in finding things to eat and drink. I said that I thought him a good deal handier than my own father, now a recent widower in his mid-seventies, who had suggested, when I had visited him not long before, that we go out to get just a cup of coffee, almost never having, so far as I knew, made coffee for himself. As I said this, I was conscious of my own deliberateness in bringing myself into closer contact with the Galsworthys. Mr. Sauter accepted this and asked more about my father, recalling, too, my talk of my Russian grandfather the year before. As we sat and drank, I asked him about the play he had been finishing the year before, an abstract postapocalyptic fantasy of a group of young people climbing a mountain to satisfy *The Fifth Hunger*, which is universal love. I had read the play and we had exchanged letters about it. An amateur group in Stroud had performed it recently, quite well he thought, but no more professional theatre or television producer had expressed any interest. "I think it's about run its course. That's behind me, too. This has been more my year for painting than for plays or poetry. Would it be all right, do you think, if we went down into the center of town for lunch?"

After parking in the Stroud railway station car park, we crossed the busy street to an old stone structure, now owned by a popular chain of restaurants. In their format, the building was divided into three or four restaurants at different levels, like the "Snack Bar" and the "Businessman's Special," each advertised with brightly painted signboards of the menu at the entrance. We chose the most expensive because Mr. Sauter said, smiling widely, "I've been told they do a fine Irish coffee here." As we were eating our steaks and drinking our wine, welcoming the uncrowded room and the quiet dark imitation leather furnishings among which we sat, the hostess, an ample friendly woman with bleached blond hair, approached our table and asked, "Aren't you Mr. Sauter, Pat Scrivens' friend?" When he said that he was, she said, "It's so nice to see you here. May I send over another drink, some more wine?" We settled for complimentary Irish coffees, which arrived in huge mugs, richly topped with whipped cream and laced with thrice the normal amount of whiskey. Most of our conversation still revolved around painting. Mr. Sauter had gone to London four separate times during the winter, each time spending the whole day at the Royal Academy Exhibition of Turner's painting in honor of the bicentenary of his birth. "You'll still be able to see the water colors. They're at the British Museum all summer. At the Academy, I kept going round, looking at the paintings over and over. The seen and the unseen. More and more, each time, I noticed the unseen light, the light of the mind. Last year, when we talked so much about landscape and JG, we compared him to Constable. And Constable's fine. Very good, dense and alive, all the shadings of color. But it still misses something that Turner saw." We agreed that Constable might be too simple a metaphor for the range of Galsworthy's work, and Mr. Sauter, laughing at himself, said, "Something of Whistler in his work." "Something of Gainsborough, too," I countered, "the tension between the people and the backgrounds." "Yes, yes," he replied, "although nothing of Reynolds, not that stiff portraiture, although that's just what some accused him of. Still," Mr. Sauter added, lowering his voice into a more serious tone, "perhaps too little of Turner, too little of the unseen, except in the poetry. Although he tried very hard, always worked at it, at the craft and at trying to see." On our way out, we stopped at the hostess' desk to thank her again. As he was talking with her, I thought of our game of trading painting metaphors about Galsworthy's work. For me, it was much more strained than it was for Mr. Sauter, much more self-conscious. Yet, that strain in itself, that effort to capture the tone of the unfamiliar, might be an analogue for the process of consciousness Galsworthy himself went through, the distance he had to travel, in becoming a writer.

We drove by a roundabout route, up and down different hills, one so steep that I had to shift back into first going down to keep control of the car, so that Mr. Sauter could show me various local views I had not seen before. A few minutes after we returned to his house, still trying, each with deference to the other, to decide whether to sit in the shade of the house or outside in the sun, Mrs. Scrivens arrived. She opted for the sun, and, as Mr. Sauter arranged the chairs, she told me how sorry she was that I had not been in England two months earlier so that I could have joined the party for Mr. Sauter's eightieth birthday watching him ride in the glider. "I enjoyed it a great deal," he cut in. "The draughts weren't very good that day, a pilot told me. A bit too still. I'm planning to go up again when the draughts are better. More exciting." When I told him that just the day before his cousin had said that she might like to go up in a glider herself, he said, "Thank you for telling me that. Now I know what to do for Muriel's eightieth birthday." As we settled into chairs, I began to ask some questions I had thought about over the winter, some of them stimulated by retrospective thought about past conversations, some by further reading, and some by examining a very full correspondence between Galsworthy and his American editors in the Scribner Archives, now donated to the Princeton Library. I learned that Mr. Sauter had been so pleased that Scribner's had accepted Galsworthy's suggestion to include a series of Mr. Sauter's drawings, some of houses, some of characters, in the publication of the then complete works in the Manaton edition of 1923, that he would have done them for nothing. I had previously regarded his remuneration as small pay for a lot of excellent work, even by what I guessed were the standards of 1923, but he thought Scribner's had been more than generous. I realized that, unlike his cousin Muriel, he had little recollection of the various films and television dramas made from Galsworthy's plays. As my questions moved more and more into the past, his answers increased my skepticism about some of the information contained in Marrot's official biography. In addition to Marrot's understandable reticence, I found, increasingly, a kind of distortion that no closeness to the family could explain in his treatment of the works and in his discussion of some events and customs. For example, he claimed that the Galsworthys' permanent renting of a set of rooms in the farmhouse at Manaton was "unusual," although the practice (as Mr. Sauter confirmed) was frequent at the time. I asked Mr. Sauter why Ada Galsworthy had chosen Marrot as the "official" biographer, and what kind of man he had been. His first comments expressed sorrow that poor Marrot drank too much, never "sorted out" his private life, had died too young, never having had the kind of literary career his talents seemed to promise. Then, Mr. Sauter paused, "But that's not really what you want to know. Why would Ada have picked him? In the first place, she trusted him, got on with him, and thought he knew more about them than most. But, as you say, Ralph Mottram certainly knew as much, was as close, and was a far better literary critic and writer than Marrot was. Why not

Mottram? I really don't know." When I pointed out that the last volume of short stories, *On Forsyte 'Change*, published in 1930, had been dedicated to Marrot, a preface stating that he had suggested the idea of supplying earlier backgrounds for some of the Forsytes that constitute the stories in the volume, Mr. Sauter responded with more certainty: "Yes, that would have been his sort of thing. A quick comment, brilliant in a way, like 'just tell us more.' He was a good talker, charming, always quick and entertaining, in and out all the time in those last years. He could do the *Times* crossword in ten minutes, good on words. He wrote poems, always very quickly. You know he first introduced himself to JG and Ada when he was an undergraduate, in the early twenties, compiling the first full bibliography of all JG's works. That must have been attractive to them, too. Ada probably thought of him as a good assembler. I'm sure they both knew he wasn't a good literary critic. But I agree, I'm still a bit baffled about the choice." He talked further about Ada and how distracted and difficult she seemed after Galsworthy died. I asked him about the two Galsworthy death masks he had worked through two days and nights to finish immediately, that had been photographed and included in the first English edition of Marrot's biography, although cut, at Ada's last minute request, from the first American edition. "Yes," he said, slowly and sadly, "she had just as soon I hadn't done them. But I felt they *had* to be done. I couldn't see any objection. In fact, I still can't. What I saw and tried to show was the peace in his face when he died, peace after all the ravages of illness, all the pain of the last months. Oh, I suppose Ada just didn't want to think about death."

We got up and shifted our chairs to avoid the direct rays of the sun, now becoming a good deal warmer. Mrs. Scrivens decided not to move, leaning back, closing her eyes, and keeping her face toward the sun. I asked more questions about Wingstone and Manaton, wondering particularly about a few entries in Galsworthy's diary in 1910 that mentioned Rudolf's "sudden fit of depression." Mr. Sauter laughed, "JG always did take my moods seriously. Just general weltschmerz. I was always having fits of it in those days. I loved going to Manaton, then, either with my mother or by myself—my father only went once that I can recall. We would take the train to Bovey Tracy, having changed at Newton Abbot, and be met by the dog cart. About three quarters of an hour's ride, and then the welcome, the dogs rushing out, the lovely smell of wood smoke. It was quite a place. The household was always relaxed, informal. Only an outside toilet. And Mrs. Endacott or her niece would bring a tin bath to the bedroom. Then, there was the dripping candle grease. I can't forget that." He leaned in his chair, toward the sun, as if lost in recollection for a moment. Then, he sat upright and leaned forward. "I was thinking of our talks and our visit to Bury last year. Maybe a bit too much about the food. What I remember most is how much fun the evenings were." When I asked him to describe how he recalled a typical evening at Bury, he leaned back in the chair again, covered his eyes with his hands, and began to talk, slowly at first: "Dinner at eight. We'd all dress. But we didn't feel formal. The talk, like the color of the rooms, was light. Afterwards, billiards. Then, to the music room. Ada playing the piano. I, on the flute. Duets sometimes. JG might fall asleep listening, or he might read. He and Vi might read 'bloods,' mysteries, compete in a friendly way to see who got the murderer first. Sometimes, having revised between tea and dinner, JG would read aloud what he'd written to get our comments. Oh, yes, he'd take them seriously, especially Ada's of course. He'd consider everything we said. He had a warm, direct reading voice, lots of skill in using it. He could do every character in Pickwick, really convey the feeling and the nuances. He could take off Devonshire dialect better than anyone I ever heard. Endacott spoke broad Devon, and, once when Mrs. Endacott, herself Yorkshire but moderated by education and reading, overheard, she laughed heartily. JG felt guilty, though everyone knew there was no harm in it. JG and Ada often did dialects in conversation, back and forth, their own private language that no one else could quite penetrate. No, Ada's voice wasn't as rich or as full. Carefully articulated. More like Muriel's, I think, although Muriel bubbles more than Ada did. Always composure in Ada's voice." I noticed that, often, when Mr. Sauter started reflecting about Bury, a chain of association in his own mind would lead him back to Wingstone. "Yes," he said, "though evenings at Bury and at Wingstone were much the same. In the last few years, of course, JG was growing more silent, more withdrawn. Perhaps I just remember Manaton as more fun, perhaps just because I was younger then and it was so different from school. More talk, at Manaton, I suppose, of what was going on in the world. Shaw came to Manaton often, and one had to move rapidly from light to serious and back again with Shaw. Gilbert Murray, too, although he was often on the floor, doing tricks and inventing games. JG's sense of fun, his sense of warmth, was more in his voice than in anything he did."

We all decided that we had had enough of the sun for the afternoon and that it would be more comfortable to have our tea in the cool of the sitting room, now entirely out of range of the sun. As Mr. Sauter went inside to put on the kettle, Mrs. Scrivens told me that she had read a good deal more of Galsworthy's novels than she had when we had last met. She was particularly fond of *The Dark Flower*, Galsworthy's 1913 novel that tells the story of a man and his three passionate loves (in youth with an older woman, in maturity with a woman married to someone else, in middle age with a younger girl), each of whom, in one way or another, he destroys. Mrs. Scrivens found it his "most passionate, most feeling" novel, his sexiest, and wanted to know if I shared her reaction. I answered honestly that I didn't. When she asked me why, I said that my own crabbed reticence caused me to prefer some of the under-rated novels of feeling and social density held together, novels like *The Country House*, *The Patrician*, *Fraternity*, and *The Freelands*, to what I thought was a rather too desperate search for emotional intensity in *The Dark Flower*, a too heavily transcendental quality that I found resembled that of the long portions of undigested "soul" in *Beyond* and *Saint's Progress*. She smiled warmly and knowingly, and said, "Oh, you intelligent men. You're all alike. . . . But, I wonder, don't you really find that the more you know the more you sympathize with JG and picture Ada as rather cold and forbidding, rather keeping him from things?" I said "No," that I didn't see things that way, and I talked of her close involvement in his work. I talked, too, of my sense of his dependence on her emotionally, and recalled the ornately scripted, round-topped notations of "A" at the bottom of his diary entries irregularly, sometimes two or three times a week, very occasionally doubled on one day. These notations of "A" could be correlated with how Ada was feeling, absent sometimes for several weeks when other parts of the diary entry showed she had not been well, present with greater frequency when life was otherwise quiet and she was healthy. I had made the assumption that these recorded the nights on which they made love. "Oh, how wonderful. How lovely," Mrs. Scrivens exclaimed. "Yes, I'd heard something like that before, but I wasn't sure." And, with delight, she repeated what I had said to Mr. Sauter, as he came out to tell us the water for tea was boiling, and asked him if he had known about the diary notations. He smiled broadly and said, "Yes, it doesn't surprise me. JG could be like that. Always noting anniversaries and things." Then he turned to me and said, "You know I was thinking, when I was out in the kitchen, that I'd not really answered when you asked if Ada like to read 'bloods' as JG and Vi did. She didn't. With serious fiction, she was always very much with JG. She shared his ideas and they talked them over. Lots of talk, I remember, about D. H. Lawrence as each novel came out. But she only laughed tolerantly at his partiality for P. G. Wodehouse." I realized, as we were going back into the house to have tea and I was alone for a few moments, that I would have to work out my own position toward Ada more consciously and carefully than I had. Immediately, I thought of my own wife, her once having told me that she knew she wanted to marry me when she realized that my voice belied the apparent reticence and distance which made her rather apprehensive of me. But, I thought immediately, I can't read us so closely into the Galsworthys. She likes "bloods" far better than I do—and both of us have, at times, found even Delderfield more absorbing than P. G. Wodehouse.

As we were eating honey sandwiches and drinking tea, I brought the conversation around to an old subject that, especially since some of the talk at Miss Galsworthy's the day before, I still felt uncertain about, Galsworthy's sense of politics and social issues in the years after the First World War. I was still bothered by some of the things I heard and read, a sense communicated by other commentators that Galsworthy was stuffy and remote, mired in a feudal dream at Bury, a perspective that was close to the one J. B. Priestley, in both his publications and his letters to me, had demonstrated. I had, over the intervening winter, seen this perspective in its most extreme form in George Orwell's opinion that Galsworthy was a sentimentalist who was troubled about pit-ponies though not about miners, and that, if he had lived ten years longer, he "would quite probably have arrived at some genteel version of Fascism." Mr. Sauter and I talked of Galsworthy as a possible member of the establishment, Mr. Sauter pointing out that, since he lived with the Galsworthys only in the country and not in London, his memories might well be distorted by his lack of close knowledge of his uncle's town life. Still, he did not see his uncle as an establishment figure at all. He explained Galsworthy's refusal of a knighthood in 1918, followed by his acceptance of the O.M. in 1929 and the Nobel Prize in 1932, not as a change in his attitudes but, rather, as a valid difference in the meaning of the awards themselves. "The knighthood, especially in 1918, would have been the mark of the establishment, accepting it would, for him, have meant his approval of the government. The later awards were just recognition of his work, his independence as an artist. And he welcomed that." I tried another tack in asking about some of the people I knew were close to the Galsworthys in the twenties and early thirties, people who visited often. I knew that Marrot and Henry Williamson, the novelist, were politically far to the right, Williamson even having, for a time, supported Oswald Mosley and his English blackshirts, although other close friends of the Galsworthys, H. W. Massingham, the editor of *The Nation*, Gilbert Murray, and H. W. Nevinson, shaded, in various degrees, toward the left and were all strongly anti-Fascist. I asked particularly about Williamson. "Yes," said Mr. Sauter. "He was there often enough. Both JG and Ada thought highly of his work, particularly his best known work on animals and nature. Did JG write the publisher's introduction to *Tarka, The Otter*? No, no, I suppose not. But he certainly approved of the book. Like W. H. Hudson earlier, Williamson used to talk with JG and Ada about nature and dogs. He knew a lot. He was very free and easy. He once came to Wittersham to see Vi and me later, but, you know, as I think back on it, I really didn't know him at all well. I've no memory of his politics at all. But, there, you realize what you're getting is my lack of interest in politics in those days. I just paid so little attention to it between the wars. Twenty years of trying to ignore politics and London as best I could."

The three of us agreed, as we talked further, that books and paintings and people were more important than politics or religion, and I had to let some of my questions lapse and withdraw to the back of my mind. A fresh breeze swept through the sitting room, as Mr. Sauter told me of the various talks he had given for the Galsworthy centenary in 1967, one with Ralph Mottram and others for the BBC, another in Bristol, one in German for the British Overseas Broadcast Service. "I don't think I said anything that's not in the book I did. I need questions to stimulate my memory, and I didn't get many on the broadcasts." I said that I wished he had written more about his reactions to the novels and plays now. He smiled widely, and said, "You know I like to talk about them. But I think I need to know that someone else is interested as well." He leaned back, comfortably in his armchair, relaxing more than I'd ever seen him relax, "I see the plays when I can. Tele, too. But I don't really remember the recent productions for long. I *think* much more about the novels." He looked up at me, and smiled warmly, "I remember what I said last year, that we might, in our talk, be neglecting the plays and the poems. But that was because I thought *you* needed, and *I* needed, a bit of that point of view. The novels really are more personally human; the plays all had purposes, messages. And JG knew the difference between the two, always wrote and said that drama was the more propagandistic form, the one more molded by ideas." We talked further about particular novels, both agreeing that *The Freelands* was one of our favorites, *Saint's Progress* perhaps the one we liked least. "He didn't really concentrate on *Saint's Progress*. Written in 1918, the very worst time for him, so busy, with all the work for rehabilitation of men from the services, and so depressed." Then Mr. Sauter turned to Pat, and said, with rather a pixyish glint in his eye, "But I don't really agree with Jim about *The Dark Flower*. Not his very best, perhaps, but it really rather grows on one."

The July sky was already darkening as Mrs. Scrivens and Mr. Sauter walked me out the gate to my car. Mrs. Scrivens told me of a road that would avoid Stroud and cut at least fifteen minutes from the drive; I had only to climb the hill further, through some of the steep hills I had shifted on early that afternoon, to a point well south of Stroud where five roads met and signs proclaimed the fact that, now including the newly constituted county of Avon, five counties could be seen. We parted affectionately, all three of us mixing politeness with the difficulty of separating ourselves from conversations we enjoyed until we laughed at ourselves. They asked me to promise to bring my wife and children for a long visit in a few weeks. I drove up the hills and found the bare plateau with the confluence of the five roads, black asphalt strips in the deepening blue twilight. I stopped the car near the junction. It was much too dark to see five counties, but, as I stood there, lights switched on on each of the roads, a five-pointed star radiating out over England. The alternatives seemed clear enough, but I still wasn't very sure about my direction. I soon found the wooden signpost pointing toward Wiltshire, and, as a strong wind rushed up from the west, returned to the car and drove quickly back to Salisbury.

The next day we drove up to London, steamier and dirtier than it had seemed the year before, houses in need of paint peeling from the heat. After a few days in a comfortable hotel, we found an almost affordable flat in Knightsbridge, a small one centering on a "garden" that was principally a concrete well, sheltered at most hours of the long day from the sun. We went to plays and galleries, and the children began, almost daily, to swim in the Serpentine in Hyde Park. We realized that, because of the change in our plans, we would have to give up the car, but we kept it long enough to drive out to Wimbledon to spend Sunday with our friend Simon and his family, drinking Pym's Cup in his back yard while grilling Wall's sausages on a hibachi. As his children

and ours competed in a variety of games, soccer, a form of court-
less tennis, spelling bees with no allowance given for Anglo-
American differences, we talked of England and what Simon
had said the year before about "Communist destructiveness."
"No," he said calmly, looking at the trees around him, "I don't
see it that way now. In spite of the shrinking pound and infla-
tion and the infuriating slowness of industry, England really isn't
altogether different. Even Wedgewood Benn is quite sane and
moderate when he's not facing a large crowd or a television
camera. I shouldn't say this, working for an oil company, but I
rather like this indecisive government. Of course, some things
are changing. Particularly economically. We won't be able to afford the way we live much longer—children in school, holidays
on the Continent. And I'll miss it. But I don't see it as the disaster I did when I came back from Persia a year ago. The country
doesn't seem as divided, class feeling's not so hostile or stupid.
It would be nice, though," he finished smiling widely, "just to
find a little bit of American-like interest in a gross national product." We shifted conversation to other friends and other days,
to his attempt to organize a company that rented boats to tour
the English canals for holidays, and to books we'd read and
plays we'd seen.

A few days later, I took a local train to Windsor to meet
Donald Wilson, the man who, as originator, director, casting
director, and principal writer, had been, far more than anyone
else, responsible for the BBC twenty-six part television series of
The Forsyte Saga that first appeared to celebrate the centenary
of Galsworthy's birth. Now retired from the BBC where he
worked for about thirty years, traveling frequently, and writing
on independent projects, Mr. Wilson lives in the country in
Oxfordshire and had suggested that we meet for lunch at the
Old House Hotel in Windsor, since he dislikes venturing into the
center of London when he can avoid it. As I waited for him on
the hotel terrace, paved with flagstones and dotted with tables
protected by large, brightly colored umbrellas, jutting in a semicircle out to the crowded Thames alongside the bridge that leads
from Windsor to Eton, I watched a party of French tourists
meeting for lunch. They talked about their tour through Windsor

Castle that morning, describing, with exaggerated gestures for each other, the uniforms of the Eton schoolboys. The French tourists went inside for lunch, just as I noticed the heavy clouds of an approaching thunderstorm rising over the Thames from the west. I went inside to wait in the wood-panelled reception room, designed, like the front of the original structure, by Sir Christopher Wren, looking like a miniature version of a cubed anteroom in a late seventeenth-century country house. I thought of the richness and profusion of the baroque, of the conflicts in English literary and social history of the seventeenth century, which, as a graduate student, had been my "period." It was the chaotic time, I had thought far too simply and periodically then, before English literature settled into cosmic order and the heroic couplet. A few moments later, seeing a tall, loose-jointed man rush in from the rain, putting his car keys in his pocket and wiping his large-framed tortoise-shell glasses with his handkerchief, I realized that this man, with a mustache, loose jacket, thinning grey hair, and a rushed, shambling walk, must be Mr. Wilson. He seemed, as he peered about the room for a moment and then immediately approached me, far more like an American academic than like the thin, compact, wiry Galsworthys I had been talking with. As we went toward the dining room, speaking rapidly to get our arrangements for the rest of the day out of the way of conversation, I felt I would welcome speaking with someone knowledgeable who was not part of the Galsworthy family, talking with someone else who had had to develop and question his own interest.

Over lunch, at a table along an inner wall, at the opposite end of the dining room from the French tourists who sat at long tables set up in the bay window overlooking the terrace, Mr. Wilson gave me an account of the history of filming the series. He had worked for MGM and the Rank film organization in the thirties and forties, and had, in the back of his mind, always had the idea of filming *The Forsyte Saga* and *A Modern Comedy*. He had acquired the rights to the Galsworthy material in the early fifties, by then having moved to the BBC, but he wanted to wait until he had worked in the organization long enough to be able to exercise "close control" over all aspects of the production. By the mid-sixties, he was head of the Script Department for drama in the BBC, and could exercise the kind of authority over production that he thought his knowledge and long-time dedication to Galsworthy merited: "The idea was approved in October of '65, filming to begin in May '66, with the series to start running in January '67, the start of the centenary. A great rush, tremendous amounts to do. No, mostly the timing with the centenary was a happy accident. More that I was ready then, in my own mind, and in my position in the organization. I wrote a good many of the episodes, even some not under my name. One writer's credit is Laurie Gregg, a *nom de plume* for me that I used when another writer couldn't deliver his material on time. And I had charge of casting, final approval on all sets and costumes, really the good luck to have complete control of the whole production. I don't think anyone could do that in the BBC now. Too highly organized and people specialized; corporate structure has grown so just in the past ten years. I couldn't have done it in America even then. Maybe it was almost the last chance for essentially one-man productions." We talked of other serialized multiple novels on television, both of us registering our disappointment with the series of Trollope's Palliser novels that had been telecast over a year earlier. Mr. Wilson, rearranging his fork and knife on the finished plate, sat back and said, "I agree that Simon Raven's point of view, as writer, was shallow, more shallowly satirical than I'd like to see. But, you know, it wasn't all his fault—there were producers and directors who knew less of Trollope than he. I'm sure he had to compromise everywhere along the line." We returned to discussion of the Galsworthy series, Mr. Wilson reminiscing about the pressure on all concerned to get each episode ready on time. "When the series began to show in January, we had only half the episodes filmed, so we had to film fortnightly in winter weather. Just luck that it was a mild one, and we could get out of doors. The greatest rush was when Eric Porter came down with appendicitis near the end, two episodes left to film. We had to shoot around him, the doctors assuring me that he would be back in three weeks. And he was. Everyone cooperated marvelously. We all had this sense that nothing like this length had ever been attempted on television, and it held us together."

The French tourists had long since gone, the dining room was almost empty, and the rainstorm was over, a bright sun now flooding the terrace. Mr. Wilson and I decided to have our coffee outside, beneath one of the umbrellas, overlooking the Thames. As we looked at the boats, tarpaulins being removed, he said, "But I'm sure that other issues must interest you more than production reminiscences. They don't tell very much about Galsworthy." Realizing that he, now in his mid-sixties, would have some political sense of the thirties, I asked him what he thought of the Orwell opinion that Galsworthy, had he lived longer, might have become some sort of "genteel Fascist." Mr. Wilson reacted immediately, "No, no. That's all wrong. Just name-calling. The committed left of the thirties could never understand Galsworthy. That was their trouble, they could never understand the ideas of others as well as Galsworthy could. He could always understand what he didn't agree with, or share. Soames, for example. No name-calling in Galsworthy. Not ever." Mr. Wilson thought that he himself shared Galsworthy's sense of politics. "Moderately left, at least he was so for his time. Moderately left in the twenties wouldn't necessarily include strong support for the strikers in the General Strike of 1926 from people in the middle class, though it would in a similar situation now. In 1926, I was at school, just fifteen and full of admiration for the older boys who ran off to man buses and stoke train engines. Just what I think Galsworthy showed, but it wouldn't be the same at such a school now." We talked further about Michael Mont, the central character in *A Modern Comedy*. "That's the best example of what I mean about changes in time," said Mr. Wilson, stopping to light his pipe, which kept going out in the breeze fluttering the umbrella. "He's a perfect characterization of the time, the twenties. Entirely sincere, involved, not really brilliant, and he can't entirely make up his mind about the strike. By the mid-thirties, or the late thirties, after Galsworthy was dead, a character like Michael would have been quite different. By that time he'd have joined the Communist party."

I told Mr. Wilson that I had, in watching the television series, very much liked the device of voice-overs, young Jolyon in *The Forsyte Saga*, Michael in *A Modern Comedy*, that I thought the device had kept an accurate interpretation of the material carefully focused, had prevented people from what I thought was the critical error of assuming that Soames grew into a kind of hero. "Yes," Mr. Wilson agreed, puffing on his pipe. "But you know, in television, voice-over is really a confession of failure. If the work is dramatic enough, and I think Galsworthy's is, one ought to be able to keep the point of view right without it. Still, it was necessary for me in the Galsworthy. In fact, I'm relying on it more, making it habitual in a series of *Anna Karenina* I'm doing now." We talked about class, about changes in class feeling that make dramatizations of novels from the past difficult to do well, Mr. Wilson echoing the comment that Edward Garnett, the editor, friend, and prepublications reader of all of Galsworthy's early work, once made that Galsworthy, reflecting the upper middle classes of his time, really did not understand the aristocracy he had depicted in *The Patrician*. Mr. Wilson also thought, as the matter came into our conversation peripherally, that Galsworthy had been strongly dependent on Ada, that she had made him, hitherto uncommitted, a writer, and that the recently publicized charges of her hypochondria impeding him or his work were silly echoes of trivial conflicts from the past. Talking further of class and trilogies and Galsworthy's perspective, I asked Mr. Wilson why he had stopped with the end of *A Modern Comedy*, why he had not gone on to dramatize the third trilogy, *End of the Chapter*, in which I found the fullest realization of Galsworthy's complicated point of view toward society. He smiled and placed his long arms out across the table, looking out into the river, and replied, "Yes. A number of people would agree with you. Some of the BBC people wanted me to do the third. Not enough time for one thing. We were so rushed as it was. But I'm also skeptical about the third trilogy. Not only not the same characters, but no real characters, not dramatic enough for television, more thematic as if Galsworthy then was more entirely inside himself, though I agree it's interesting. Besides, he used the aristocracy again, and I don't think he had any real knowledge of it, not the way he knew lawyers and estate agents. For me, a kind of slight falling off begins with the middle novel of *A Modern Comedy*, *The Silver Spoon*. All that business chicanery is a bore, and I compressed it as much as I could. But the trial scenes are fine, and the last novel of the trilogy, *Swan Song*, recovers fully. Everything on the General Strike is good, very good. His sympathy for everyone, people of whatever class, people like Bicket, infuses the whole work. Occasionally, there's slush, like 'Awakening,' the second of the long sections making the transition from one novel to the next, the one that concerns young Jon's idyllic boyhood. That's the worst of Galsworthy. But the best is fully part of the way he saw social class. No real politics, ever, just the sympathetic ability to see what people's lives in different classes were like."

As we continued to discuss interpretations of Galsworthy's fiction, we left the terrace and began to walk the wide footbridge from Windsor across the Thames to Eton. Mr. Wilson wanted to see his tailor in Eton who was making several pairs of trousers for him to take on his autumn trip to Russia to work on the filming of *Anna Karenina*. As we crossed the bridge, Mr. Wilson laughingly explained that it was now a very peaceful and pleasant footbridge only because of the strains and petty arguments of local politics. Some years before, engineers had reported that the old bridge was no longer safe for heavy vehicular traffic. Neither county council (Windsor is in Berkshire, Eton, across the river, in Buckinghamshire) would assume any responsibility, each claiming that its county had not built the bridge in the first place. Both were right—the bridge had been built by a direct grant from Queen Victoria. "So it's still not repaired for heavy traffic, though most people are happy that it's now a footbridge. You have to go miles around to drive from Windsor to Eton." At the tailor's, while Mr. Wilson's trousers were being fitted, I looked at the dingy, once elegant, pattern books from the thirties, pictures of creased trousers that looked like patent leather and figures with pencil-thin mustaches. I also talked with one of the tailors, a small, thin dapper man, over seventy, who had migrated from Russia more than sixty years ago. "I don't see why a fine man like Mr. Wilson wants to go to Russia. Nothing there now. This, Eton, was a lovely place in the thirties. Lots of gentlemen who cared about clothes. Less and less now, every year; I'm not sure how much longer we can stay open. Yes,

yes. Everything custom-made. I couldn't work any other way."
When Mr. Wilson had finished being fitted by a more cheerfully
loquacious, but equally old, tailor, and was promised that his
trousers of heavy twill for a Moscow autumn would be ready in
a few weeks, we walked back through the main street of Eton,
its shops seeming smaller than I had remembered them being
and Russian emigré tailors seeming more tired, to the car park
of the Old House Hotel.

We drove around to several villages, looking for a place to
have tea. At several quaint-looking, white-washed and half-
timbered inns or tea shops, we discovered that they either no
longer did teas or did them only for touring coach parties, arrangements in advance. "This used to be a lovely place to live.
We had a house in Datchet, the next village, for years, most of
the time I worked for the BBC. A lovely place until Heathrow
expanded and jets became so loud. As I'm sure you've noticed
we're right in the principal path of landing, or takeoff, or something." I suddenly realized that our conversation all afternoon
had been punctuated by searing aircraft noises. As we drove,
Mr. Wilson talked of his plans for future adaptations after he
finished work on *Anna Karenina*. He thought he would probably
not do any more of Galsworthy, although some of the short
stories like "The First and The Last," provided good and sufficiently dramatic material. He had the rights for, and wanted
someday soon to adapt Hervey Allen's *Anthony Adverse*. We
were driving in Windsor Great Park, coming near the Castle,
then turning around and heading away from it. Mr. Wilson suggested we stop and stretch our legs, since the Great Park seemed
uncrowded, saying "Most of the tourists must have done a better
job than we did in finding tea." We stopped and sat under a
large oak, Mr. Wilson stretching out his legs and lighting his pipe.
I said that, in the television series, I had been most impressed by
the first three episodes, the background for the characters, not
in the novels, that Mr. Wilson had supplied himself. He smiled
warmly, and said, "Yes, although, you know, the hints are all
there. In the novels, or in other stories. The themes and the past
grow out of the characters Galsworthy presented; the strong
story lines are implicit. It wasn't really hard. But I am proudest

of the things I did that weren't in the text, the dialogue between Irene and Bosinney for example, whereas Galsworthy seemed almost afraid to give them any dialogue. Galsworthy created Bosinney, saw the type, the truculent artist, beginning to develop, but didn't really understand him as well as we do. Changes in time and history. Oh, yes, I was criticized heavily for the things I added or left out. I kept out Annette's bed, the physical side of the affair with Prosper Profond. No real point in it. It's clear enough anyhow that sex impels most of Galsworthy's characters a good deal of the time. But I was criticized for not being more explicit. More often, I was criticized for adding things, like the dialogue between Bosinney and Irene, or showing why Irene had originally accepted Soames. I also wanted to show the violence of young Jolyon's first wife's death, and the schizoid illness of his second wife, Helene. There are hints of all this in the novels, but a television audience demands more filling out, more dramatizing in explicit terms, more connection between past and present. I think all my additions fit Galsworthy's concept, and, on television, you must *show* it."

As our talk became more desultory, under the tree in the late afternoon sun, I asked Mr. Wilson what had started his interest in Galsworthy in the first place. He told me that when he left school, in 1928, his parents decided that it would be a good idea if he learned German and sent him to Freiburg for a year. This was a minor version of the shift in sensibility that sent Auden, Spender, Isherwood, and others to Germany rather than to France for a year of unstructured postgraduate educational wandering. "I hated it," Mr. Wilson said suddenly. "Hated Germany. Hated the family I lived with. So I began to read Galsworthy in the Tauchnitz edition. I could honestly tell myself that I was practicing my German, and I did. But the material was all English. And I lived every bit of it. I was so lonely that I lived entirely in the Galsworthy I read and reread. His world became the England I missed." As I told Mr. Wilson, when, a year and a half earlier, I had lectured on Galsworthy in Sheffield to a group taking a Worker's Education extension course, a lecture arranged so that I could visit old friends at Sheffield and show my son his birthplace, a small heavy woman with a thick Germanic accent had come up to me after the lecture. She told me that, in the thirties, when she was young and unhappy, wondering if she would ever get out of Austria in time, she had read all of Galsworthy again and again, assuming that what Galsworthy wrote about was what England was, that he was the quintessential English writer. I asked her if living in England had disillusioned her. "Ach," she said. "Thirty-five years I have lived here. Too long for illusions or perfection. But Galsworthy was more right than wrong, more right than anyone else. I have only wanted to stay here," she concluded, looking around at the basement lecture hall with a grimace that seemed to express resignation.

Both Mr. Wilson and I said that, regretfully, we had to get back to our homes and families. As he drove me through the Great Park to the Windsor railway station, he continued talking about the effects of his German reading of Galsworthy. "I think it had something to do with shaping my life. If one ever knows that. I became young Jolyon. My parents became his. My art became his, a minor art like his water colors. Never intense or brilliantly original, but with its own imperatives, its own sense of getting things right." As he left me off at the station, just in time for a train, he got out of his car to shake hands firmly and bid me goodbye. I realized suddenly, as I stepped onto the train, that Mr. Wilson had talked of his "parents," not separated father from mother in any of his own biographical recollections. Yet Galsworthy, in *The Forsyte Saga*, never presents the mother. Old Jolyon is a widower long before the action begins, and, even in retrospect, the mother is barely mentioned. As the train carried me quickly back through suburbs of increasing density to Paddington, I wondered whether or not Mr. Wilson, in supplying past characters and events for the Forsytes for the television audience, had ever been tempted to create the memory of a mother for young Jolyon.

During the next few days, back in London, taking my children to the London Zoo and, with my wife, to the exhibition of Turner water colors at the British Museum and a production of D'Oyly Carte's *The Yeoman of the Guard* at the Royal Festival Hall, I kept thinking, at odd moments, of my talk with Mr.

Wilson, of the problems of creating a past for characters known only in a fictional present, of Galsworthy and his parents. I had, the year before, realized that it could not have been as simple as veneration for the kind and generous father, the Victorian patriarch with almost unlimited sympathy and tolerance for those who do not act on the strict principles he does, existing along with a circumspect but almost complete denial of the existence of the mother. Although most of the relatives continued to idolize, from a distance, Galsworthy's father, I knew that the mother must also have been important, that the circumspection must have covered a combination of hostility and attraction that Galsworthy had never worked out. Beyond the few recollections of her fastidiousness, her distance, her child-bearing years spent reclining on a sofa, and her lack of interest in money, I had little information to go on, and I realized that much of her influence on Galsworthy must remain undemonstrable speculation. I felt that my speculations had a somewhat firmer basis in regard to the father, for the drama, and particularly the fiction, when read carefully, reveal far more ambivalence toward the father than most of the biographical information or recollection suggests. Invariably, in *The Forsyte Saga* and in other novels, like *The Country House*, that deal with fathers and sons, the son is suffused with guilt, feels that he can never measure up to or find the strength to rebel more forcefully against the kind and gentle Victorian patriarch. The father is stronger, more coherent, more a presence than the son; the son is more sensitive, artistic, able to perceive more, yet far less able to express the contradictions he feels, to break through his own veil of circumspect and well-behaved silence. In Galsworthy's plays, where characterization is generally more one-sided, more simplified, the representation of the father never budges, never changes, remains the immovable capitalist, principled but ultimately destructive in *Strife*, or the stoical tyrant in *Old English*. In the novels, and particularly in *The Forsyte Saga*, the far more complicated characterization of the father is sometimes transposed into a heavily dramatic wish fulfillment. The novels show sunderings and reconciliations, reconciliations in which all is made clear and forgiven. Still, in the son's sensitive conscience, guilt lingers, perhaps because, in his own life, Galsworthy had not apparently told all, had not revealed the affair with Ada to his father, and, consequently, could not have felt fully accepted. For me, the most extreme example is that long, fulsome link between the first two novels in *The Forsyte Saga*, "The Indian Summer of a Forsyte" (which some sensitive readers among Galsworthy's contemporaries, readers like Professor William Lyon Phelps, found the most moving and effective prose Galsworthy ever wrote). It is a chronicle of the reconciliation between the father and the son's love that takes place when the son is not even there, the reconciliation that, biographically, doubtless could not have taken place because the affair, the issue that might have caused permanent disruption or sundering between father and son, had not been confessed. In a way, Galsworthy's fictional image of himself was always looking for a oneness with the father, an acceptance, perhaps a share in the father's omnipotence. It is important, too, that the reconciliation comes through an intelligent and sensitive woman, a woman who understands the son so well that they need not speak about it, a woman who does what the mother was felt never to have done, united the son with his father. The long episode of "The Indian Summer of a Forsyte" is reminiscent of other Romantic fiction written by men who were, or felt themselves to be, left without a mother. In Meredith's *Ordeal of Richard Feverel*, for example, the too harsh and systematic father confesses and repents to the son's loved one, while the son is absent, sparing the son the embarrassment, the ambivalence and the fear his presence at the scene would invariably cause. In Meredith's version, however, the reconciliation comes too late, does not stave off disaster. Galsworthy's is more simply the emotional projection, although structurally the episode provides for young Jolyon, the son, the liberation necessary to become the coherent identity and point of view for the next two novels in the trilogy. In *The Forsyte Saga*, the later novels, *In Chancery* and *To Let*, are far more dense and psychologically complicated although, for some readers, less appealing than the more distant and single-minded satire of the first, *The Man of Property*. Only after the intervening link of "The Indian Summer of a Forsyte," only after his father's acceptance of

Irene and subsequent dignified death, can young Jolyon become
the fully understanding lover and the carefully understated artist
(Galsworthy's kind of artist in trying "to take himself seriously,
yet never bore others by letting them know that he did so").
Still, in the two later novels, young Jolyon doubts himself most,
and is, in fact, least capable in his role as a father. The trans-
mission of qualities through generations is, for Galsworthy, an
issue far more difficult to resolve than is the appropriate or satis-
factory disposition of the self, and it is an issue central to the
fiction. The persona of the trilogy, young Jolyon, is an only
child who sires, by three different wives, four children. John
Galsworthy, crowded with three siblings, had no children.

As I thought of Galsworthy's parents, I also thought of my
own, some few similarities in emotional terms that might be
either an aid or a barrier to understanding Galsworthy. I, too,
was an oldest son of an oldest son of an oldest son, my father,
tall, handsome, gracious, yet gently controlling, seen by others
in the family as a kind of paradigm for the first American-born
generation. And, as a child, I had felt that I would never measure
up to him. Although warm and generous to me, the source of
contact (in addition to my grandfather) when I was a child, I
had never fully confided in him, always felt slightly estranged
between my desires to emulate and my desires to become something entirely different. I could recall his having given me, sometime in the late thirties, a copy of Warwick Deeping's 1925 best
seller, *Sorrell and Son*, and, following my reading, our rather
ponderous and wary talks about the relationships between father and son, the sense of continuity through generations. More
than thirty years later, during the winter in England, rereading
the novel after I had found it on the shelf of the London Library
while looking for something else, I saw Deeping as combining
the high Tory work ethic and male chauvinism, the father slaving
and sacrificing for the grateful son in an idyllic world in which
loyal and hearty male virtue triumphs unless destroyed by the
predatory and levelling female. Not Galsworthy's world at all,
nor mine. My mother seemed, when I was a child, cold and distant, likely to remove herself in tense tight-lipped rage which only
later did I realize originated in frightened love. As she explained

to me long before I understood what she was talking about, she was a conscious and obedient disciple of Watsonian principles of child-rearing, never showing affection, never violating a child by touching it, the antiseptic principles of "advanced" thinking that was another side to the "jazz age" of the twenties. In the fiction I tried to write in my adolescence, I eliminated her entirely. As I sat, scribbling some notes and some questions late one night in the kitchen of our small flat, I realized I was repetitiously reviving old and too simplified speculations about my own psychic past. Lots of it was quite different from Galsworthy's, and I still didn't know whether the few similarities might help me understand him and his perspective better, or might simply show the presumption of my imposing myself on him.

As I made myself some strong black tea, I focused on my interest in Galsworthy as a writer, like any writer the product of his parents only in part, perhaps in small part, for the act of writing, of consciously committing oneself to paper, is an act of discovering and creating the self. And Galsworthy had written a considerable amount, never fully resolving the dilemmas of his childhood, generally silent about what he could not fully assimilate or control, yet able to shape a good deal of his experience consciously, to understand and create enough of himself to transmit a world effectively to generations of readers. I thought of other writers who had known and respected both Galsworthy and his work. Several had commented fairly acidulously on the Philistine qualities of all the Galsworthys except Jack, Lilian, and Mabel. Joseph Conrad had often, in the parts of his letters reserved for polite regards, asked after Galsworthy's father's health and hoped the fine specimen of an old man was thriving; but Conrad expressed a genuine sense of delight when, in 1904, he learned that Galsworthy was abandoning the psychologically transparent pseudonym of John Sinjohn, under which he published his first novels and volumes of stories. Conrad thought both the change in name and the fiction symbolic of Galsworthy's having come into his own. Ford Madox Ford, as a commentator often acute although not always reliable, who was fond of Galsworthy personally and admired his work, did not think the old Victorian patriarch either kind or benevolent.

Between 1898 and 1903, Ford lived at times in Campden Hill close to a small shed that Galsworthy used as a workroom, while Galsworthy's parents, until his father left to live with his daughters in sequence, lived in nearby Campden Hill Square. Ford gave Galsworthy considerable credit for breaking away from a tyrannical family who "jeered" at his writing, regarded the father as a "Tartar," a view he said the servants confirmed, and concluded that there was "something pixy-ish and hard about both those old people, the father ferocious, the mother young for her age, flighty, with bright colored bonnet ribbons . . . It was not usual stock, that from which Galsworthy came." Ford's point of view seemed to have more to recommend it than I had thought when I read it first.

Although, by a slow process, Galsworthy had become a writer, had to some extent created himself, echoes of the past always remained. Echoes of his boyhood worship of his father, the firm and understanding beneficence of the father, the silent guilt of the erring son, appear, unfiltered by the complexity of the treatment in most of *The Forsyte Saga*, as late as one of the stories in *On Forsyte 'Change*, published in 1930. It is a graceful and affecting story, although it seems a naive one. More seriously, I thought, Galsworthy was always limited by his background and his parentage in his difficulties in expressing strong emotion, particularly rage or anger. Almost all his characters, particularly those of whom the authorial perspective most approves, express themselves through understatement, experience strong feelings most of which are held in. Some of the crucial incidents, like Soames's rape of Irene, and important dialogue, like that between Irene and Bosinney that Donald Wilson had had to add for the television production, are left shadowy or omitted entirely, their effects or reverberations hinted at or assumed, their specifically emotional content left out. It was as if Galsworthy had never really overcome, only worked around and through, the barriers against direct emotional expression his early years had established. He had, at his best, in portraits like those of Soames and young Jolyon and Fleur, with all their dense detail and rich variety of qualification, made a virtue out of his incapacities. Yet he never managed to depict strong rage or strong passion that was not destructive. I thought that one of his less successful "causes," the 1911 campaign against aerial bombardment in time of war, might be connected in some way with a fear of rage, of emotional explosion. Certainly, it was a worthy cause, a humane objective, but, as G. B. Shaw had seen so clearly, why, especially in 1911, single out bombardment as the prohibition in the midst of general mayhem and insanity? It was as if, for some part of Galsworthy, at least before he knew its reality in 1914, war could be tolerated if it did not express itself too explosively or aggressively. And, although he soon understood war itself and its radiating catastrophes much more fully, for Galsworthy, even in his later work and his later years, banality or conventionality was often regarded as less sinful than aggression.

The visit of the summer that I was most looking forward to was the one to Scotland to see Mrs. Dorothy Ivens and her husband. Mrs. Ivens, Galsworthy's goddaughter and the only other member of the family who wrote professionally, was the daughter of Francis Easton, one of Galsworthy's first cousins with whom he had been close. As Dorothy Easton, she had written a highly praised first novel, *Tantalus*, more than fifty years ago, followed by several other books, although she had written me that "Personally, I've had no 'career'—a first novel got A 1 reviews—but I married & was busy learning to cook." We had established a correspondence the year before, when I had been unable to get to Scotland, where she lives, with her husband, on a houseboat moored through much of the year not far from Inverness. Throughout the winter, I had welcomed her long letters that revealed a sharply intelligent and gracious woman who remembered almost every conversation with Galsworthy, described him and his wife with pithy and observant reverence, and held opinions that were both strong and acute about all his work. Then eighty-four, she had written that, until the last several years, she and her husband had always cruised for four or five months each summer. But they had recently cut their cruises to a month or six weeks because she could no longer take her turn steering for very long periods of time. Letters defined our summer plans carefully. That summer, she and her husband would take a short trip from Inverness through the Caledonian Canal to the western lochs. They organized their cruise, around a time convenient for me, in order that we might meet at the southernmost point they would reach, Loch Melfort, only about seventy-five miles north and west of Glasgow.

As my son and I ate smoked haddock on the train from Euston to Glasgow, just as we had eaten smoked haddock on the train trip to Sheffield a year and a half before, I recalled the pleasures of breakfast in the gastronomic rhythm of my first visits to Britain, in 1948 and 1951-52. In those days, when post-war shortages still kept food carefully rationed, I had depended on breakfast, that full meal of smoked fish, or porridge, or bacon or sausages with grilled tomatoes and mushrooms, accompanied by strong black tea (I was never hungry enough to include the fried bread). Thus fortified, food for the rest of the day conveniently could be a matter of chance. After breakfast, my son and I returned to our carriage, playing some of the games, a soccer game, a cricket game, a baseball game, that he always carried in a blue canvas satchel. We remembered playing the games on the earlier trip to Sheffield, controlling impatience when a partial railway workers' strike had left us, on a still, grey December morning, stalled on a siding in Nottingham for over an hour. Late as we were at Sheffield, there had still been ample time for my lecture and for old friends. One friend had driven my son, peering through the windscreen in a pouring rain, to see the red brick hospital in which he had been born and the rolling hills and variously dense foliage of the green belt of western Sheffield, partially shrouded in cloud, shading toward the Derbyshire peaks. He saw the green dells, where my wife and I had often picnicked, with white wine and smoked salmon sandwiches, on the warm days before his birth, and the house, in a small curved cul-de-sac near the top of Crimicar Lane, where we had lived. He now recalled the drives up and down hills, the various cats he met, and his rides on the pater-noster, the continuously revolving belt with ledges that serves instead of an elevator for the new high-rise Arts Tower at the university. The visit to Sheffield had worked as part of the parental process of transmitting something of our mutual past to my son's consciousness. I was not at all sure about the visit to Glasgow. The lines of connection, for him, were far more tenuous, and I had not been in Glasgow for twenty-three years.

Arriving at the Central Station, we put on sweaters in immediate acknowledgment of the fact, that, on this grey, windy day, the temperature was twenty degrees lower than it had been all summer, and picked up our rented car. The new arterial roads, nearly empty of traffic, took us quickly, past large tracts of space where tenements had been, from one end of the city to the other, across the crowded Clyde and back, past the square, old cathedral now surrounded by vacancy. I was astounded at the speed with which Glasgow could now be traversed, although I missed the acres of brown tenement (their miseries, I recalled, could not be seen until one went through the gates in the solid stone facades to the dirty courtyards and decaying wooden stairs) and the bells and screeching wires of the electric trams (trams on which, after boarding just one or two stops before, students would be ignored until a fare stage had been passed, the conductresses, "chippies," then running up to say, "Aye, I didna see ya," and saving the student a ha'penny). I told myself to stop sentimentalizing. The tenements had been squalid, much of life there grim and violent. Obviously, people were better off without them. But, then, I wondered where the workers now lived, and I had read that unemployment was particularly high in Glasgow, higher than it was anywhere else in Britain. At least, in the congested early fifties, the memory of joblessness had been, for most, submerged by more than ten years of steady work. I need feel no particular obligation to the present. I drove across Sauchiehall Street that had been, twenty-three years ago, the bustling road full of department stores, offices, and tea rooms, from the University down to the center of the city. It was now a pedestrian mall, sparsely populated, the colored light standards and painted crosswalks in light blue and orange already fading, a conscious municipal gaiety gone sour, stalls set out on the street in front of the shabby stores. I drove up the hill of

Buchanan Street to see again the Glasgow School of Art, an architectural classic of art nouveau designed by Charles Rennie Mackintosh. I found it, almost too quickly, stopped and admired, but it seemed smaller than I had remembered it or than it looks in pictures in architecture books, and the hill down from its perch seemed steeper and emptier than I had recalled. As I drove past streets of Victorian mansions, I found where I had lived—three contiguous terrace houses made into a "hall of residence" for students. Details were familiar but my sense of proportion seemed askew. I told my son about the gas street lamps and my memories of watching an old lamplighter walk by each early winter dusk to light them with his long pole, but, now electrified, the standards seemed stubby, without distinction or elegance. We reached the University, two large quadrangles around paved courtyards, a Victorian design almost exactly like that of St. Pancras Railway Station in London, the losing design in a competition for the nineteenth century rebuilding of the Houses of Parliament. I noticed that my memory had turned both quadrangles ninety degrees awry. The portico that I thought would reveal a view of the deep valley of a park looking across to the domed Art Gallery actually showed a line of grimy and decaying Victorian houses. A cold shower of rain blew across us and we quickly huddled alongside the pillars between the two quads. The classrooms and offices were nearly empty, and a Commissionaire, who seemed hesitant until we worked out that he, having held his job only nineteen years, could not possibly remember me, explained that the city seemed empty because this was right in the middle of the annual fortnight of Glasgow Fair. Glasgow Fair, in spite of its name, is closer to a *fermeture annuel*, a fortnight for which plants close, large stores shut down, even the University's summer session breaks in the middle, and everyone leaves the city to take holidays elsewhere. I later read that the invasion during Glasgow Fair is annually regarded with considerable apprehension by the Blackpool police, something like a workingman's version of the annual Easter invasion of Fort Lauderdale.

My son and I found a comfortable hotel room on the road leading north and west from Glasgow toward the loch on which we were to meet Dorothy Ivens the next day. None of my old friends still living in Glasgow answered their phones—not the man who had introduced me to Lallans poetry and brought me round to pubs in Edinburgh and Aberdeen to meet Scots nationalist poets trying to write in the dialect unused between the days of Burns and the literary revival begun by Hugh MacDiarmid in the twenties; not the woman on the staff who had hoarded her sugar ration coupons to bake a vast chocolate cake for my visit, thinking that was what any American would miss most; not the engineer who was a frequent bridge partner and who had also taken me to meet his then ninety-year-old grandmother in Greenoch who remembered canvasing for Gladstone. After dinner and a walk, forced back into the hotel by another cold shower of rain, I went into the hotel bar, while my son read in our room. I had a pint or two, the bartender explaining the near emptiness of the bar as a result of Glasgow Fair and talking proudly of his two sons, both graduates of the University of Glasgow, one a lawyer, the other an engineer, fully justifying all his years moonlighting tending bar after a full day's work. Galsworthy seemed particularly far away that night.

The last letter from Mrs. Ivens, full of directions and accompanied by a map carefully lined by her husband, had warned me to allow six hours for the drive because of "winding roads, heavy lorries, tourist coaches, and probable bad weather." I allowed about four and a half hours. The roads did wind, as we drove through showers of pouring rain. We slowed down on the crowded road along Loch Lomond to read a billboard advertising Highland Games later in the week. I explained what I could remember about "throwing the caber." Looking at Ben Lomond, I recalled the time some friends of mine and I had climbed the gentle, rather pastoral, mountain in a winter mist so thick we could only see the loch the first third or so of the way up. My son and I paused at Inveraray to drink coffee and walk past the souvenir shops down to the quay along the loch between tourist coachloads. Even so, we were at Loch Melfort in just over three hours, early for our meeting. We stopped at the tiny local post office, one full of shelves lined with stale Hostess cupcakes, cardboard boxes containing assorted pencils, erasers, and plastic toys, and packages of frozen food, to learn that the Ivenses had picked up their mail a day or so earlier, but had spoken to someone not now about. The post-mistress, looking through some scraps of paper on the long spike that served as the message center, could find nothing and suggested that I try a boatyard a few miles further along Loch Melfort. At the boatyard, partially submerged under water from heavy rains that morning and the evening before, I saw only an empty caravan and a few boats moored well out in the loch. I heard sounds of hammering from a distant shed and went off to inquire, while my son went down to the shoreline to see if scaling rocks might attract some attention. At the shed, a man explained that I might return to the caravan, find an aerosol foghorn, assemble it, and call the Ivens, in the large, old houseboat nearest the far shore. He referred to them as the "old ones." After my laborious assembling of the foghorn yielded a few tentative blasts (my son, reading the directions, told me I had ordered all ships to return to port) and no response, the man from the shed appeared, and said, "Look. See that figure just beaching a dinghy on the far shore of the loch. That might be the old guy. Take your car, go out to the road, take the first three successive tracks left, and you might head him off before he reaches the main road." We ran through puddles of water to the car, managed the turns, and met Mr. Ivens, who looked at us knowingly and slowly said, "I thought you'd get here sooner. My wife invariably mixes up dates, distances, and numbers, but otherwise she's completely reliable." We returned to the shore, but knew that all three of us could not get into the dinghy while it was beached. He looked at my thin London shoes and sighed, then sat down, took off his Wellingtons and threw them to me, rolled up his trousers, picked up my son commenting "not much more than seventy pounds," and carried him out to the dinghy he had just pushed into the water. I followed, in the Wellingtons, carrying my shoes as if I were taking out the garbage, as it began to rain heavily again. He rowed us out to the boat where Mrs. Ivens, who as a teenager had regularly sent her diary to Galsworthy, which he would return with extensive comments on the writing and complete reticence about the subject matter, was waiting, a small, thin woman, holding her cane firmly to the narrow, rolling deck.

Mrs. Ivens and I were arranged sitting on a bunk that stretched along one side of the wheelhouse, her feet resting on a shelf that we had pulled out as a ladder, my head back against the porthole so that I would not jam it against the iron ceiling. My son was established in the cabin, three steps down from the wheelhouse, playing the complicated facsimile of cricket, with three dice, which he had invented. Mr. Ivens excused himself, saying he would leave us to talk while he went down into the engine to fix a defective pump. Mrs. Ivens began by talking about her family and Galsworthy. She had met Galsworthy's parents only once and had only once been taken to meet "the terrifying aunts in the Bayswater Road." She could recall that her father, Francis Easton, had great respect for the patriarch that her immediate family called "the family Abraham," but had not cared very much for his wife. Her father had, in their youth, been very close to his cousin Jack, the two of them sharing an interest in natural history and in animals, often going off together on long country tramps. Mrs. Ivens told me a little of her Galsworthy grandmother: "A tiny woman who never said a word or had an opinion. Not at all like the formidable Forsyte one would expect from the novels. She had six sons, five of them, all except my father, over six feet tall. And, then, as if exhausted, said nothing for the rest of her ninety-two years." It was her other grandmother, whom she referred to as Granny Randall, her mother's mother, whom Mrs. Ivens remembers most forcefully, who cared for her, the oldest of three sisters, when her mother was ill and at many other times. Granny Randall was a decisive and determined woman, very much concerned with propriety, and "thoroughly Victorian." She had no interest in literature or any other form of art. Mrs. Ivens recalls keenly that when, in 1910, *The Saturday Westminster Gazette* published two of her short literary sketches that her Uncle Jack had sent them, her first published work, her grandmother saw the copy she had left with silent pride on a table, "seized its greenish papers with the tongs, rammed it onto the coal scuttle and wrathfully commanded me: 'Go to your room, Miss, and if I ever find that filthy Radical rag lying about . . . '" She laughed, and said, "But it only made it more certain that I should go on writing."

Mr. Ivens came into the wheelhouse, having fixed the pump, and said he thought it time for a drink before lunch, asking me if I would join in their usual cocktail of one part Scotch, one part gin, one part dry vermouth, and one part tonic water—"That way we get all the things we like in at once." I agreed. Mrs. Ivens asked if he could fix her hearing aid before he mixed drinks, "Here I am doing all the talking because the blasted thing isn't working very well." Mr. Ivens smiled, rapped the hearing aid sharply on the ledge that held his maps, and handed it back to Mrs. Ivens. She held it to her ear, asked me to talk, and said, "Yes, that's it. It's fine now." Turning to me, she said, "You see, when Ralph fixes something, it works." Mr. Ivens, a tall, lean man, ten years younger than his wife, with a fringe of fine white hair, a long nose, a mournful face, and dark eyes, mixed the drinks, handed each of us one, and then took his own down into the cabin to prepare lunch. As he left, he said, "I don't want to interrupt you two talking. I'll take my time with the lunch." Mrs. Ivens then began talking about her first memories of her Uncle Jack, always her favorite relative, long before she knew he was a writer. She remembered him coming for dinner when she was a child, during the Christmas of "pink accordian pleats," and watching her and her sisters perform a playlet that she had written. "Uncle Jack roared, he really laughed, throwing his head back and forth, so unlike the other relatives. And he gave each of us girls a gold half-sovereign." In later years, while she was growing up, she worshipped her Uncle Jack, looked forward to his visits, valued his sensitivity and his interest in her writing. She spent an adolescent year in Dresden, presumably to combine a healthy climate and musical instruction, and she sent Galsworthy her work and corresponded with him constantly about writing. She thought his advice invariably sound, welcomed the way he talked and wrote to her, as an equal, about craft, and remembers still many of his injunctions, like "the artist should not point a moral in his work: the moral should be there implicitly or else by inversion." When I commented that I found Galsworthy's work itself often very moral, she replied, "Yes, certainly by today's standards. But moral writing then was so very much *more* moral, so very explicit, that Uncle Jack really felt he wasn't moral." We went on, talking of her early work and his advice further. Mrs. Ivens held back her head and laughed as she told me, "I was sometimes so naive. From Dresden, I sent him a long story I'd written, about a young girl who can't express her admiration for an older relative who is a writer. He wrote back a long comment on the technique, not a word about the subject matter, though he must have seen how transparent it was. He talked of it all as work, was never embarrassed. Work and craft were so real to him, to both of us." Banging her hearing aid against the side of the bunk she said that all of her family shared her great affection for Uncle Jack, even Granny Randall. She quoted her grandmother as reflecting the general family opinion: "Poor, dear Jack. He's so handsome and charming, but he will waste his time scribbling when he could have pleased his father so much and been such a success at the bar. The writing's even more pointless than the way he spent his time at Oxford." In defending his "scribbling," she felt she was her Uncle Jack's particular protector: "The family code was dead against expression." Mrs. Ivens continued the theme of Granny Randall's combination of affection for and disapproval of the young novelist and playwright in the family. "After all, she did allow me to visit Addison Road when I was in my teens." Mrs. Ivens began to laugh as she recalled that, at Addison Road, one day when they were both waiting for Ada to return for tea, she met the young Ralph Mottram. They talked of poetry and music, and, later, began to correspond. "Granny Randall wondered at the strange writing on the letters coming to the house. She insisted that I write Uncle Jack for more details, that I 'make inquiries.' Uncle Jack replied: 'Your correspondent is quite grown-up, nearly thirty. He has no prospects and is of good character. Some of his poems you've read—he is a bank clerk at Norwich— and his soul is not simple.'" (For this anecdote, I have quoted, and, for a few of the subsequent anecdotes and descriptions, I shall quote, from a typescript of recollections Mrs. Ivens later gave me. What she said is very close to what she has written; she had reflected on her memories of the Galsworthys long enough so that the forms of memory, especially the memory of physical detail, have a finished quality.)

In response to my question, Mrs. Ivens said that her family, skeptical about her Uncle Jack's career, was not, however, outraged at the scandal of divorce or the earlier hints of the affair with Ada. They had never liked their cousin Arthur ("she only married him because he begged and pestered"), and they sympathized with Ada. Although they talked about the affair among themselves, they did think any indications of it needed to be kept from the family patriarch. As Galsworthy became better known, Mrs. Ivens told me, her family, other than herself, saw somewhat less of him. At times, they were shocked, and Mrs. Ivens's father could not understand how "Jack could put his sister Lily in a book." But, more than that, Mrs. Ivens thought, they were slightly sad that his early novels were not very successful financially (Galsworthy could not, I had learned sometime earlier, have lived as he did on the earnings of his work in England before the publication of *The Forsyte Saga* as a trilogy in 1922) and that his early plays, no matter how well received critically, did not run longer than the five or six conditional matinées at Granville-Barker's Royal Court. "My father would often say, 'if only Jack would write something popular' or 'he's too pessimistic to sell.' Father had a good legal mind, he was fond of poetry, and, when he died, at the age of eighty-eight, we found that the last book he had been reading was a first edition he kept of *The Man of Property*. He couldn't show his emotions very well, was always guarded. He could never be convinced, or convince himself, that making money wasn't the measure of all things."

Mr. Ivens called us down into the cabin for lunch. I helped Mrs. Ivens down the three steps into a small room with two armchairs, a table, bookcases lining the gunnels of the boat, plants and photographs on the tops of the cases. I was given an armchair, the table pushed up against me, and other chairs set around. Mr. Ivens brought in a bowl of steaming soup from the galley just beyond the cabin (there was also a small bedroom beyond the galley), a large ham, and salad. As Mrs. Ivens ladled the soup and Mr. Ivens sliced the ham, he told me that he had watched my son's cricket game with fascination. "He really has a lot of combinations, a lot of possibilities in that game." James ate half a bowl of a kind of thick soup he ordinarily never touches. We talked about cricket a good deal, Mr. and Mrs. Ivens both having closely followed the fortunes of Kent in county cricket during the years between the wars, years in which Kent never won the championship. "It's a good game," Mr. Ivens said, "can be a village game, bring out a feeling of community. And one doesn't need to be an expert to play it reasonably." As we ate, talking of village cricket and Test Matches, universities and Scottish scenery, Mr. Ivens gradually revealed that he had, just after the First War, taken a degree in Classics at Oxford, but, rather than become an academic or a schoolmaster, he had returned to his father's (his father was a professional rose-grower in Kent) to experiment with new strains of edible plants. "I had just reached the point at which I thought I might try to market some of my grains when the Second War came along. The ministry drafted me to go round the country, teaching people to grow their own food, a necessity then. But the food had to be restricted to the most common varieties, marrows, beans, and so on. My experimental strains withered with neglect." He paused, smiled at his wife, and then went on, "After the war, we decided that we'd had twenty years on the land, we might well spend the next twenty on the water. We'd no responsibilities. Our son was grown, going in a direction different from ours. He's an engineer, at Ford's in Dagenham. Has done very well." Mrs. Ivens cut in to say that her son had been fascinated with machinery from the time he was a very small child, then Mr. Ivens continued: "Well, we took all the money we saved. Bought this boat. I didn't know a thing about machinery when we started, but I just borrowed some books from the library and read up on the subject. We always moored near Inverness, far from crowds or people. During the late forties and fifties, we cruised more ambitiously, Scandinavia, France, the Low Countries, even, finally, Germany. The boat people are never provincial or nationalistic, always accept what one is. In more recent years, we've been less ambitious. The islands and the highland lochs.

Still, we try to vary things a bit each year. Dorothy has a book, you know, about living on a boat. Came out ten years ago or so." Mrs. Ivens smiled a bit shyly, and leaned close to me, saying, "It's a very simple book. But I've always had lots of time to write on the boat. My noncareer is mostly a matter of choice, choice and a very small talent. We've been happier on the boat than we would be rooted to land all our lives, though I've still a lovely garden at our mooring in Scaniport. You must see that sometime."

We had long since finished lunch, and Mr. Ivens, standing up, thought that, before the shops on shore closed, he would row James in and they would do some errands and pick up a few things for dinner. I suggested that we all go ashore for dinner later, perhaps, if they liked, at the hotel in a village further north where I knew they had booked a room for me for the night. "We had thought of that," Mrs. Ivens said. "We had wanted to take you. And we had a nice dinner there, eight or nine years ago, when we last moored here. But now I've heard they have music in the dining room. One of those things that plays on a machine while you're eating. I think we'll be more comfortable here. Quieter, and more time to talk. There's so much to say." I went outside on deck, watched Mr. Ivens climb down to the dinghy, and handed James, clutching his blue canvas satchel, down to him; then, for a few moments, I leaned over the rail as they rowed toward the shore. When I came back to the cabin, Mrs. Ivens said, "Now I'll do the washing up. My job. You just stretch out along the bunk in the wheelhouse and have a nap. You must be tired after your drive. Oh, it's a rule of the house, or the boat, if you like. All visitors nap after lunch." Obediently, I climbed on to the bunk and stretched out as far as I could, but I didn't close my eyes. I wasn't tired, and, as I heard sounds from the galley, I watched the dark clouds and the deep green hills, moving visibly, through the porthole.

Mrs. Ivens soon came to the wheelhouse, banged her hearing aid sharply on the ledge holding the maps, held it to her ear and smiled triumphantly, then pulled out the shelf to climb onto the bunk. We arranged ourselves as we had earlier, she pulling a multi-patterned quilted cover over her knees, for the wind was becoming colder. We began to talk of Sybil Carlisle, a young lady with whom Galsworthy was presumably in love from 1886 to 1891. According to some accounts he was sent on the two-year voyage around the world by his father as much to get over the effect of the unhappy relationship with Sybil as to learn about maritime law. Marrot, in the official biography, never mentions Sybil's name, referring only to an "unsuitable" early attraction that his family was anxious he avoid; Dudley Barker, who says little more, refers to her as "Sybil Carr." As I quoted the statements of the other biographers to Mrs. Ivens, in response to her request that I refresh her memory, she leaned back and laughed heartily, "What nonsense. I knew Sybil well in later years. You see, she was Granny Randall's niece, and so some sort of distant cousin by marriage to Uncle Jack. They used to sing duets together and he fell in love with her when they both acted in an amateur theatrical. She was a good actress, with a fine voice. She had something of a career later. Barrie wrote *Peter Pan* for her, and she played Mrs. Darling. 'Unsuitable' really is ridiculous. The plain fact of the matter is that she wouldn't have Uncle Jack. Of course, she had no money, which may be what Marrot meant, but she was just as wellborn, just as charming and talented, as Uncle Jack was. My family, her parents, too, would have encouraged her to marry Uncle Jack—everyone always thought he was 'special.' But she just didn't want to marry him, or anyone. She never married. She was always fond of him, always asked about him later, when I used to take tea with her in London. When he was offered a knighthood, you know the story, when the papers published his name in the list because he'd been away at Wingstone and hadn't been able to wire his refusal in time, Sybil wrote to congratulate him. She couldn't understand his refusal, although I was delighted with it, with the whole error. She would tease me because I worshipped him, but I didn't mind because I knew she cared about him." We talked about why Marrot might have been so needlessly reticent, not only about Sybil Carlisle, but about others as well (he even omitted Mrs. Ivens's name and relationship in mentioning the "young relative" whose writing career Galsworthy helped, although he had mentioned her name in an earlier list of visitors).

Mrs. Ivens had not known Marrot well, had met him only a few times. "He was just a puppet for Ada. No one talented, no real writer, would have spent that much time being a puppet. It's a bad book. The language, the style, it's all such gush. You're wise to be skeptical about Marrot."

Returning to the story of Galsworthy's refusal to be knighted, Mrs. Ivens thought that the rejection of officialdom was characteristic. The presidency of the P.E.N. was, she felt, quite different, for P.E.N. confined its interests to writers and artists, and advocated a not always popular internationalism. "After *Tantalus* was published, he thought I should join, and he even paid for my subscription. For the first dinner I was to attend, Ada sent me a silver frock. Low backs had just come in, which I had not noticed, so I wore it back part front and set out for the dinner with my second cousin—oh, of course, you know Rudo—who was also attending his first P.E.N. dinner. We went by bus. Both of us were very shy, yet we felt we couldn't let Uncle Jack down. Sensitive Rudo got stuck between two lady novelists in corduroy velvet who kept telling him how hungry they were. I found myself sitting by a tall blond gentleman, a writer, celebrated no doubt, and at once every book I had ever read, every literary name or thought, went out of my head. In a panic of blankness I began to talk about cricket. I was lucky because he knew about cricket. Oh, Rudo was so talented and so humble. Suggestions of him, I sometimes think, are in the character of Jon Forsyte, although Rudo had more wit and talent."

At the sound of a sudden squall of heavy rain, I turned to look out the porthole. Mrs. Ivens immediately said, "I'm sure they'll be somewhere fairly dry. Ralph will take care of your boy. He always takes care of things so well." Mixing recollections of her Uncle Jack with stories about her husband, she developed the theme of men who were always sensitive to the needs of others, always willing to efface themselves in their concern for those they live with. "Sometimes, it's hard to know what they want for themselves." Mrs. Ivens talked of their life on the boat, their sharing of all work, until a few years earlier when she had needed an operation on her hip, the operation that had left her a permanent limp that required the use of her cane. "When I was in hospital, and the doctor said I should always be a bit lame, Ralph said we must sell the boat and get a house on land. I agreed, knowing that I could no longer do my share. We'd found a spot, right near the mooring at Scaniport. We advertised for a buyer for the boat, had a lot of inquiries. When Ralph had to go away for a few days, I was on the boat alone and a man came up to look it over. All the way from Glasgow. He liked it and named a good price, a bit more than we'd expected. Although Ralph and I had agreed before he left that I could accept any good offer, I just couldn't say 'yes' on my own, told the man he would have to wait until the weekend when Ralph and I could talk. On the Sunday night, we were sitting here in the cabin, Ralph with his hand under his chin just looking round, and I said to him, 'You don't want to leave the boat.' He said, 'I know. I'm sorry.' And, the next morning, we just rang up Glasgow and apologized. We've never regretted it." I knew, watching her tell the story, that, however many times I might hear the tale repeated and recognize that some of the details of who said what when might be different, I would never be able to tell who had played which part in the decision.

The squall had temporarily passed over, and, a few moments later, we heard the sounds of Mr. Ivens and my son climbing onto the boat deck. Mr. Ivens was carrying some biscuits, some cheese, and a bottle of Scotch; my son had loaded his satchel with a book and a few more games. We went inside to get tea ready, while my son stayed out on the deck, running back and forth, watching clusters of thunder showers come down the loch toward us, pass over the boat, and rush away toward shore. He said he'd never before seen rain look the way it's depicted on a television weather map. As we were putting out bread, cheese, and cakes for tea, we began to talk more of Galsworthy's work. The three of us traded opinions on the various novels. I was delighted to discover that they both shared my preference for *Flowering Wilderness*, the middle novel of the final trilogy, admiring its crisp prose and what Mrs. Ivens called its "humanity, more fully and subtly expressed than he'd ever done before." They did not entirely share my admiration for *The Freelands* and *The Patrician*, Mrs. Ivens thinking that Edward Garnett had probably been right in claiming that Galsworthy could not depict the aristocracy, and Mr. Ivens thinking that the novels conveyed their time, the agricultural and social conditions just before the First War, intelligently enough, but seemed dated now. They both said they enjoyed rereading the very early work: the stories of *A Man of Devon*, the attempt to echo Turgenev in *Villa Rubein*, the dedication to art in *The Island Pharisees*, work that sometimes seems to me too labored and derivative, too simply what the author is trying to be. Mrs. Ivens also praised the depiction of the frustrated minister (a character who is not unlike, although less explicitly sexual than, the central character in her own novel, *Tantalus*) in *Saint's Progress*; agreeing about the character, I said I thought the novel slack and overblown, Mr. Ivens joining my dissent, and Mrs. Ivens adding that "perhaps the two of you are just not as interested in unhappy clergymen as I am." When Mr. Ivens laughed in turn, I realized that I was hearing something of a well-established conversation.

We arranged ourselves for tea; I was again in the armchair boxed in by the table. As we began to eat, Mrs. Ivens told me of the plays she still enjoyed thinking about: *Escape*, which she thought technically the best; *Loyalties*, which she had thought "electric and courageous" at the time, about a phenomenon like anti-Semitism that had existed then which others would not talk about, but she found the play slow and dated now. We talked, too, about the origins of literary characters and ideas, Mrs. Ivens always resisting too easily biographical equivalents. She paused with her knife in the air, just about to cut herself a slice of cheese, saying, "When I was younger I used to assume biographical equivalents in almost anything he wrote. I hadn't enough sense of the work of art. I once asked Uncle Jack how June in *The Man of Property* could be his sister Mabel when she looked so different. Uncle Jack smiled and said, 'The character is June, not in our family.' And he wasn't bothered at all by what others said. He told me, too, that a character just changes, almost of his own accord, as he goes along. The way Soames changes as *The Forsyte Saga* goes on." Since Mrs. Ivens, in talking of particular works, had seemed able to be selectively critical about her uncle's work, I asked her what she thought might be his most serious general limitations. She answered quickly, as if she had thought of the question before: "His ironic eye could get him in trouble, he could rather tend to see urban characters as vulgar. Even a worthy old chap like Gradman is mentioned in conjunction with stout and pickles, when Soames is dying. He never gives a cut of this sort to peasant characters; they keep their dignity. When I think back, the touch of vulgarity he often gave his working class or lower-middle-class urban characters bothers me. It's a satirical touch, a barrier. The greatest novelists, Hardy and D. H. Lawrence, never do that; they respect all their characters more. That was Uncle Jack's limitation."

As we extricated ourselves from the table and went back to the wheelhouse, we noticed that the rain had settled into a steady drizzle. We opened the porthole to get some air. Mr. Ivens, seeming for a moment the Oxford don he almost became, likened our conversation about Galsworthy's "vulgarity" to something in Horace, assuming I would know the reference. I didn't, and I realized that it had been over twenty years, when I was last in Scotland, since I had felt a twinge of embarrassment about my ignorance of the classical authors. He looked out the window, and said, "I think the steady drizzle will hold now. No trouble getting you back to shore," just as Mrs. Ivens came up the three steps, saying, "Yes, we were so worried yesterday. From tea time until early this morning, there was a heavy swell, a minor gale. We couldn't have taken you on or off the boat. No matter now. We can always sleep four here if we have to." She also wanted to make sure that I had not misunderstood her point about Galsworthy's limitation: "I was talking of his art, of the ironic manner that was often there, not of his politics. On politics, in my early years, he was fine, compassionate, could understand others who weren't like he was. He made me a Liberal in the bosom of a Tory family. And he was so sensitive about the War, too, unlike most of my family who were bloodthirsty and xenophobic, especially Granny Randall. After I'd written him about Granny's reaction to something in the news, he wrote back: 'Tell your Granny that if the God of the Old Testament ever gets himself remobilised (which is exactly what the War Lord is after all this time), he'll strike the British and French not only blind but pink, and leave the Germans not only untouched but haloed. He took no stock in humanity or freedom, that barbaric God.' Granny Randall was so upset that she took to her bed and mourned." All three of us laughed. Then, Mr. Ivens said, "Of course that's right about the early years and the War, but he seldom talked of politics at all in the days I knew him." "Yes," said Mrs. Ivens, "after the early twenties, disappointed, I think, that the League of Nations was a failure, he very seldom talked about politics. He became more withdrawn generally, less frequent laughter, but he was particularly silent about politics." Mr. Ivens perched himself halfway up on the ledge on which the boat's steering wheel was mounted, holding the wheel to balance himself, and said, "Well, the twenties were a difficult time politically. Things breaking up, and no one very sure how to go about patching them sensibly." I had noticed earlier two recent copies of *The New Statesman*, open to articles with points underlined in red pencil, under the steering wheel, and I was not surprised that the conversation turned toward more current political issues. "Yes," said Mr. Ivens, "I suppose I would call myself a 'communityist.' My own word, since I've always wanted to distinguish myself from anything Marxist or Stalinist, any form of Communism I know. The Second World War was really the best time, the healthiest politically of any time I've known. Oh, I know it was unity under an external threat, but people really did grow their own food, look after one another, live in groups that were almost entirely independent. Some of the communes today are pretty silly. They don't know enough, haven't thought enough, to live the way they're trying to live, but I admire the spirit and think that that's the way we're all going to have to live. Even my son, an engineer, no longer thinks that Ford's, the international corporation, is a healthy place. Now that little model you're driving," he continued, referring to the small car I had rented, a new model Ford, the cheapest available, in which he had ridden only the half a mile from the point we first met him back down to the shore. "It took the ruts in the path so well this morning. A fine little piece of machinery. My son, who worked on it, says it's the best thing Ford's has designed in fifteen years. The bad time, here and in America, was Macmillan's time. All that confidence in bigness and the corporate world. All that assurance. I've been much less depressed these last few years. Well, I've been doing too much of the talking. Let me fix us all another drink, then go down and have a look at the chickens roasting for our dinner."

After he had passed the drinks around, and gone down to the galley, stopping in the cabin to ask James how Kent was getting on, I asked Mrs. Ivens about Galsworthy and children, about how he, particularly in his later years, related to children. She replied, "I still remember when he came to visit Flowerfield, the little house we built in Kent. We bought the land with the money Uncle Jack had given us as a wedding present. He came to see our son, John, for the first time. I was busy cooking, and I looked out to see Ada on the lawn talking with Ralph. And there was Uncle Jack on his hands and knees going round and round the table and in front of him, on *his* hands and knees, most solemnly crawled John. And John had his first cricket bat at Bury, a gift from Uncle Jack." I had noticed, all during the day, that, whenever Mrs. Ivens mentioned Bury, her voice held a note of sadness, and I asked her about it. "Yes," she said, "we were never really happy at Bury. The routine, the formality, the village—it was all too much. Uncle Jack wanted the shrubs to be older than they were, and he was disappointed when Ralph showed him how to tell that they weren't. And some of the help, not the maids or the cook, cheated him. Ralph had to get him a new gardener to replace one who was dishonest, had to find a new ironworker to help with Rudo's studio. It all seemed a production, not real the way Wingstone was, not cut-rounds and cream near a wood fire but tomato sandwiches—and, in a room like that, if the tomato shoots out of the sandwich you feel such a fool. Dinner was rather more of an observance, and the evening was given to music or billiards rather than to talk." As she recalled other incidents at Bury, another theme seemed to develop to explain what had made the days at Bury less happy for her. She talked of herself at Bury with Ada and Viola Sauter, all three women who had not married the men they loved until they were well into their thirties. Both she and Viola Sauter were married to men ten years, or slightly more, younger than they. And, of the three, only she had had a child. "I always felt something of a strain with Vi, from the moment John was born, during the same year that they moved into Bury. We never talked of it, oh no, not a word. But Vi was a bit jealous, and it made a strain. Not Rudo, he was always gentle and intelligent." Mr. Ivens had come up into the wheelhouse, and was leaning against the wheel sipping his drink. He said, "What Bury missed most was Aunt Lily, Rudo's mother. She was a saint, had perfect understanding. I've never met anyone like her." Mrs. Ivens agreed enthusiastically, "She was never selfish, was unconventional, and really loved people. In the summer of 1924, when I was just deciding to marry Ralph, Auntie Lily invited me to bring him to Freelands, her house. I remember that she and Ralph disappeared up the garden talking Persian poets together. She was the only one who got to know him. She was the one who talked to me about life, her conception of it was selflessness, its true reality was love. After she walked with Ralph, she came up to me and said, 'My child—there is only love.' She died that autumn, just before our wedding. She was ill only one day, although she'd always been frail. Rudo insisted that we go through with the wedding, and he gave me away at the ceremony and gave the wedding breakfast. Vi helped us settle in; she was very kind in those days, before Bury and John."

The two small chickens were set out on the table, ready for carving, as we sorted ourselves into the small space for eating. I was becoming quite snug in my armchair backed up against the wall and held in by the table. As we ate, our conversation—first, about their three grandchildren, and then rambling from the difficulties and possibilities of preparing interesting food on a tiny stove in a tiny galley to interesting meals we had all eaten in unlikely circumstances—gradually focused more and more on Ada. Mrs. Ivens said several times that "Ada had perfect taste," and she tended to depict Ada in terms of the various houses she had decorated. She talked, over dinner, of her visits to the Galsworthy's first house in London, on Addison Road, after they married, a house that expressed Ada's "perfect taste!" "The surface was too civilized, the enchanting drawing room too different. Bare of knicknacks, with no silver photo frames, no floral cretonnes or Dresden china, it had silky cushions faintly gleaming pigeon's breast blue, dark velvet curtains, scarlet Chinese lacquer, books, flowers, and a few pictures." This was quite unlike the "large and white rooms" in "an upper flat above the Thames, such a prospect," in Adelphi Terrace House, where they lived in London during the First World War. She described Grove Lodge, the Hampstead house after 1918, where Constable had once lived, before it became a rectory in the middle of the nineteenth century. Grove Lodge had "an L-shaped drawing room with a deep bay window set round with a blue covered seat, low book shelves and Ada's grand piano. There were pale walls, in off-white paint, Persian rugs, parquet, pictures, Chinese needlework, and cushions conveying the sheen of bird's wings or the blue shade on the combe. There would be one perfect pink azalea or blue hydrangea in a pot." Mrs. Ivens shifted to the music room at Bury: "When we had tea there it seemed so far from the door to the tea tray, the floor so golden, so polished, so slippery, the French brocade on chairs so sharp an emerald green. I missed the wood-smoke tints of Ada's other drawing rooms, particularly the applewood smoke of Wingstone." Yet all of these, for Mrs. Ivens, were Ada, who was always complicated, self-contained, difficult to know. "She could be generous and high-spirited, but she could be cold, too, as I found out when Uncle Jack died and Ada cut what he'd left us in half." Twice, I tried to approach the subject of Ada's possible reasons, and, each time, Mrs. Ivens said, "Something happened. I don't know. I never saw her again after Uncle Jack died." We finished one of the chickens and began on the second. We listened to the rain beating on the cabin roof for a moment, and Mrs. Ivens changed her tone abruptly: "But she was always civilized, gracious, and so very intelligent. She never missed anything, taut but composed. Some of the people who exaggerate the Margaret Morris episode," and Mrs. Ivens stopped for a moment to laugh. "One has to realize that Ada typed that book, *The Dark Flower*, for him and was in it with him. No concealments. He *felt*, but he behaved. And wrote the book. He was, after all, an artist. But, you know, I didn't understand the whole thing when *The Dark Flower* first came out. I loved the book then. It was severely criticized as 'sordid' and 'subversive,' although it had its defenders like Gilbert Murray and Masefield who thought it Uncle Jack's best book. Yes, I loved it, and I fancied there were touches of me in the portrait of Nell, in the descriptions of clothes and gestures. I was entirely devoted to Uncle Jack, but I wasn't what one would call 'in love' with him. I was visiting at the time, and I felt a strain between them, which was unusual. When Ada left the room, he said 'You're not to worry about this. It's not taken from you, I promise you. It's taken from someone else, another person altogether.'"

As we cleared off the empty dishes and folded and put away the table, leaving enough room so that the three of us could sit, legs stretched out, in the cabin, Mrs. Ivens told me that she, like the other relatives, thought Barker's book entirely mistaken in talking of Ada's "hypochondria." She said that Ada had suffered from asthma, bronchitis, and neuralgia, and "really stood up to them all quite bravely. Uncle Jack wouldn't have enjoyed nursing had Ada not been the patient." As we leaned back in our chairs to talk, Mrs. Ivens recalled that her favorite place in the world had been Wingstone, that, every summer, she had waited for an invitation to stay there a week or two. She described "the low gray house front covered with flowering creepers, roses, Clematis montana and wisteria wreathing the bedroom windows. The flat yellow tin bath upstairs, and downstairs French windows open to the lawn. A couple of dogs would be lying half across the sill; one would flop down on his feet when Uncle Jack came to table. White walls and Botticelli prints and, over the sideboard, an engaging St. Cecilia with a halo the size of a plate." She went through a typical day: mornings for work; after lunch a long tramp or climb, sometimes on horseback, sometimes on foot, a mixture of "hot tea and orange juice in a Thermos," often out until tea for "nothing seemed to tire them then"; more work after tea; dinner, with Galsworthy in a black velvet smoking jacket and Ada "always in something charming, lacey yet simple and somehow unique"; after dinner, music and talk over little glasses of the sloe gin Mrs. Endacott made. Mrs. Ivens had always worried that she could not feel quite as close to them as she would have liked to feel. She laughed quietly, almost to herself, as she said: "I remember one night when I was bursting with feeling and shyness. After I'd gone upstairs for the night and closed the door to my room, I heard his footsteps. I blew out my candle, ran out into the dark of the hall, and flung my arm around his neck. I ran back into my room and thought 'now we can talk.' But breakfast the next morning was just as conventional as ever." The happiest time at Wingstone that she could remember was the summer of 1918, the First World War almost over, the flowers blooming with a particular brightness, Ada well and happy, her Uncle Jack particularly energetic and full of ideas as they walked long miles in the sun. Mrs. Ivens spoke of one morning that summer, she having, the night before, read and loved "The Indian Summer of a Forsyte," then still just a story on its own, when she had asked at breakfast, "What became of them all? What happened to young Jolyon? Why not go on with them and give us more Forsytes?" Her Uncle Jack, she recalled, had walked up and down, mused, smiled, and said, "That is something . . . " When I asked her, she could not remember whether her visit was before, during, or after what Galsworthy called the "red letter day of Sunday, July 28th," on which, according to his diary, he conceived the idea of continuing the Forsytes through at least two more novels and realized that it would be the major work of his career.

Mr. Ivens stood up to get us small glasses of whisky. James came down from the wheelhouse where, wrapped in the comforter while lying on the bunk, he had read his book as long as the grey, waning, northern light allowed. Mrs. Ivens talked about Galsworthy's later years, the gradual decline in energy and the increasing silence, which she thought might have been evident as early as 1923, when he wrote her, agreeing with an unfavorable review of his own play, *Captures*, "I have lost fervour." Still, as we both agreed, much of his best fiction was in front of him, the three novels of *A Modern Comedy* and *Flowering Wilderness*. "Part of it, I know," Mrs. Ivens continued, "is in my own view, in the fact that I was never as happy at Bury. He did seem to withdraw more into his work, lived there more completely. And then our last visit to Bury, in 1932, was so very sad. I took John alone, Ralph couldn't go that year, too busy in the nursery. Uncle Jack really was ill by then. He spoke very little. I shall never forget the look on his face, the painful combination of triumph and defeat with which he, shambling into the room, brought Ada his morning's work. It was only half a page." We shifted the conversation to Mrs. Ivens's own work, to Galsworthy's advice (almost all of which she still thought was sound), to her difficulties in organizing and ending her novel. "But I never really had a career," she repeated to me. "The first novel had encouraging reviews, but then I married and I wanted to learn to cook. For years I felt that if I went back to writing more seriously I should forget to cook." I asked if she knew where I might find a copy of the first novel, which I had not been able to find in the London Library or elsewhere the year before. She said she would be pleased if I borrowed her copy, and Mr. Ivens rummaged through the bookshelves in the cabin until he found the book, among many others, slightly mildewed. Mrs. Ivens took it and looked at it before she handed it to me: "Yes, that's what happens on the boat. All my books are damp, have a bit of mildew after a time. But here it is. *Tantalus.* The title, you know, was Ada's suggestion, after we found that the one I'd originally chosen had been used recently by someone else. *Tantalus?* I never liked it. I don't think it fits, even as a metaphor."

Several times during the preceding hour or so, I had stood, more from motives of politeness and not wanting to impose further than from any desire to leave, saying that I thought, perhaps, it might be time to go. I must have been transparent because, each time, Mr. and Mrs. Ivens had both insisted that we continue talking. Now, however, we all knew that the hotel on shore, where they had reserved a room for me, would soon lock its doors. As I stood, Mrs. Ivens went over to a cabinet and brought out a typescript of about one hundred fifty pages, one called *Uncle Jack: A Sketch of a Relationship*, that she had written over the past winter. She told me to use it in whatever way I liked. When I protested that it was hers, and that she should publish it, she replied that one publisher had rejected it already and that she wasn't sure she could make a book out of it. "Besides, Uncle Jack always said I was no good at transitions.

I'm still not." I agreed to take the typescript, read it before I left England, and then return it to her. I would, I knew, want to quote from it, but I would not want simply to appropriate it. She smiled warmly. She asked her husband to find the plastic bag she had been saving and, then, carefully wrapped both the typescript and the copy of *Tantalus* in the bag. Saying goodbye several times and telling James what an exemplary boy he'd been to remain so patient while grownups "nattered" all day and night, she walked out with us to the wet and slippery deck and clasped my hand warmly in both of hers as we said goodbye. I could still feel her fragile strength as I climbed down into the dinghy. It was raining steadily as Mr. Ivens rowed us to shore, silently. James was burrowed under a poncho in the bow; I was seated, with the plastic bag kept dry under my sweater, in the stern. I rolled my trouser legs up beyond the knees. When we were ten or twelve feet from shore, I jumped out of the dinghy into the shallow water to help push it well up on the rocky beach. Mr. Ivens smiled approvingly. After he and James had climbed out of the boat, he said that he wanted to walk with us the hundred yards or so to where we had left the car. As we walked, he said, "You know, you can always come back tomorrow. If you think of anything further you want to ask, just come down to this shore and scream loudly for me. I'll hear you. But not, I think, before early afternoon. She's been so excited about your coming, and so happy today. She'll need a long sleep tonight." He also asked if he might look at the engine in my rented Ford. I opened the bonnet and he took out his torch, muttering a few comments about the economical design as he inspected the engine. We exchanged more thanks and farewells, and then James and I watched a moment as he trudged, his shoulders looking hunched in the dark rain, back to his dinghy on the shore.

We drove, just a few miles north and east, to the village of Kilmelford. The crowd of cars in the narrow car park, and the lights and noise coming from the front door, indicated that the hotel was still open. We parked in a muddy lane leading to a crofter's barn, grabbed our suitcase, and ran through the now heavy rain to the hotel. The bar was jammed with drinkers, full of cheerfully raucous good humor and trading information about various hiking trails through the Highlands, all eager to buy someone else a final drink before the special summer midnight closing time. The friendly crowd spilling over into the reception room violated the old stereotype that Scottish pubs, surrounded by the disapproval of a generally teetotaling society, were grim, unfriendly places, Spartan locales for serious drinking. As I waited for the busy receptionist, I realized that I had never found the stereotype true. The receptionist quickly appeared, promising to rummage through the attic to find a "camp bed" to add to the one already in our reserved room, the last available in the hotel. We waited at the bar. Not long after, as the crowd began to thin out, the receptionist returned to tell us our room was ready. The camp bed was not the stretched canvas I imagined, or even an army cot; rather it was a full, wooden-framed bed with a thick mattress and thin, carved Edwardian-Gothic bedposts.

The next morning, we had thick kippers for breakfast, at the last possible moment, and headed back toward Glasgow in the steady rain. At one point, as the road climbed along Loch Melfort, I could see *Mallard*, the Ivens's boat, square and stubby in the distance, silent, bobbing slightly in the waves and rain. We stopped again at Inveraray, buying a few souvenirs for my wife and daughter, and, since the rain had temporarily slackened, we walked around the outside of the medieval Inveraray Castle. As we neared the suburbs of Glasgow, I wondered if I should try to see Margaret Morris. When I first read her book about Galsworthy, I had thought it probably accurate enough about their relationship: the frequent lunches at Addison Road with both Galsworthy and Ada, her choreographing the dances for Galsworthy's *The Little Dream*, a stage fantasy, his awarding her a fairly large part in his next play, *The Pigeon*, her surprise that Ada no longer seemed so welcoming at lunches, and Galsworthy's assertion, after the single kiss in the taxi, that their friendship must end because Ada would be hurt. I had also found the book full of the "meetings of souls," essays on free love, the elevated nature of giving herself, and a good deal of self-pity. I had wondered if I would learn much more from her than I had from the book, and, consequently, I had not sought to meet her. Now, nearing Glasgow, where I knew she still lived, the widow of a Scots painter she had married in the twenties, J. D. Ferguson, I reconsidered. She might, I thought, be interesting to talk to. I had read in the *Times*, in late 1973, that, in a Parliamentary by-election, she helped an attractive young Scots Nationalist woman win a hitherto safe Labour seat in a working man's district in Glasgow, telling her Galsworthy story again to all the reporters. And others had described her to me as still, two or three years earlier, quite beautiful in velvet dresses with deep décolletage, charming visitors with talk that mixed her advocacy of Scots Nationalism with her old causes of "free love" and women's suffrage. Interesting though it might be, all the stories seemed so similar that I suspected a too carefully rehearsed quality about whatever she might say, even if she could and would see me at such short notice. I doubted that I would be clever or skillful enough to cut through to some "truth" behind her story, some insight or switch that might alter my interpretation. Knowing that I might be making a mistake, might be a less than completely responsible biographer, I decided, once again, not to try to see her. On the points that most interested me about *The Dark Flower*, Galsworthy's fiction itself seemed the surer guide. Later, at a party in London, I met an Eastern European emigré painter who had spent the Second World War in Glasgow, becoming friendly with J. D. Ferguson and his wife. He told me that, sadly, I was a year or two too late for the likelihood of sequential conversation with Margaret Morris. He had been fond of her, heard all her stories, and thought that, now, well into her eighties, she would only repeat the major themes of her life.

As we drove into Glasgow, I parked only a half a block from a telephone box, intending to try to phone again the friend who had introduced me to Lallans poetry. My son decided to wait in the car, examining one of the souvenirs we had bought in Inveraray. When I got to the phone box, I turned and saw that two or three teenage toughs were staring into the car, jeering at my son. I walked back and the toughs scattered. We stopped at a safer phone box, but there was still no response at my friend's.

Glasgow Fair. We drove quickly through the rest of the desolate city toward the center and turned in the rented car. We were just able to catch an Express train that brought us back to London in time for a late dinner with my wife and daughter.

❧

The temporarily cooling breezes had, in our absence, even reached London. The next day, on a grey afternoon, I walked quickly past the antique stalls and the "Wild West" boutiques of the Kings Road, Chelsea, into Glebe Place, where I was to meet Mrs. Watts at the P.E.N. house. Mrs. Watts had invited me to join her at a reception honoring V. S. Pritchett on his seventy-fifth birthday, telling me over the phone that "you might meet a few people who knew Galsworthy—and, besides, there's a portrait of him there I'm sure you would want to see." Just as I approached the address, a taxi stopped and Mrs. Watts, in a long dress and a short fur jacket, stepped out and greeted me. We walked into the house, Mrs. Watts leaving me for a moment in the anteroom to look at the large portrait of Galsworthy, while she checked with some of the other early arrivals about arrangements and refreshments for the reception. The portrait was almost life-size, an official-looking Galsworthy, standing, looking stiff and benign, like the founder of a family firm. Mrs. Watts rushed back to introduce me to several writers, as more guests began to arrive and tight-jacketed waiters passed among us with trays of hors d'oeuvres and glasses of champagne. Most of the people I talked to were slightly older than I, not old enough to have known Galsworthy. They agreed that it was "high time" for a serious revival of interest in Galsworthy, talked of their own fondness for the fiction and their appreciation of all he had done for P.E.N. Several people told me, sadly, that this might be one of the last receptions in this "lovely old house," a series of large-windowed rooms set at right angles to each other, tucked neatly into a large garden behind Glebe Place. The house had been left to the P.E.N. about thirty years before, but the ninety-nine-year lease was due to run out shortly and the house would have to come on the open market. The P.E.N. could not afford it without considerable aid from a wealthy donor who had not yet appeared. Alone for a few moments, as the largest of the rooms filled with members and guests, I told Mrs. Watts that I was really most eager to meet writers who had had some sense of Galsworthy's ideas on politics and society in the twenties, who might challenge or corroborate the attitudes that Priestley or Orwell would express. She said suddenly, "You know the person you really should talk to, Dame Rebecca West. I wish I could help you. But she's very difficult, apt to be very abrupt." I asked if she would be likely to appear at a reception such as this. "Oh, no. I very much doubt it. These days, she's"—Mrs. Watts broke off, suddenly laughing and nodding toward the doorway where a number of people were beginning to cluster around a small, stocky woman holding a cane as firmly as she held their attention.

Gradually, I made my way toward Dame Rebecca, introduced myself, and explained why I wanted to talk with her. She listened closely, looked me directly in the eye, and, when I had finished my justification, turned away to greet someone else, holding out a hand to show that I was not yet dismissed. She turned back to me, planting her cane imperiously in front of her, and said, "Young man, you had better telephone me, some morning around noon. I'm in the book. We'll arrange a lunch to talk about Galsworthy." Then she turned rapidly back to the someone else to continue her conversation. A few moments later, the room was suddenly silent for the presentation to V. S. Pritchett. I was standing on the edges, at a far window, and an old woman, seated on a folding chair, with a cheerful wide face, showed me an empty pot behind a drape where I might get rid of my smoldering cigaret butt without having to stamp it on the worn carpet. The presentation was quick and graceful—a short talk by Rosamond Lehmann, standing tall and elegant, speaking, in a hushed voice, humorously, in perfectly formed phrases; a comic poem, full of references to Pritchett's career, written by a woman who wrote occasional verse for the *New Statesman*, rather in the manner of Frank Sullivan's Christmas Greetings in the *New Yorker*. It was a self-effacing presentation, carefully light, expressing itself as if pomposity or long-windedness would be the most inappropriate of sins. Afterwards, I talked with Rosamond Lehmann, with whom I had already corresponded, both of us half-leaning, half-sitting on the edge of the long table which held the hors d'oeuvres, altering slightly the time for the meeting we had already arranged. When, several evenings later, my wife and I had drinks at Miss Lehmann's—Miss Lehmann has long been my wife's favorite of all novelists—she told us of her delight when, in 1927, Galsworthy, whom she had not known and never did meet, wrote her unexpectedly to proclaim his enthusiasm for her first novel, *Dusty Answer*. She did not know whether or not any of Galsworthy's interest had been influenced by his past acquaintance with her father, the editor of *Punch* and a Liberal M.P. before the First World War, with whom Galsworthy had lunched and talked about divesting the Lord Chamberlain of the power to censor drama and other reforms; she did not even know how well Galsworthy and her father had known each other, for, by the time she was an adolescent, her father had suffered a serious stroke that made communication difficult. Whether or not Galsworthy had known she was her father's daughter, he had not mentioned it in the letter.

I drifted about the reception, talking with a number of writers. Because the question, although not really relevant to Galsworthy and his wife, had gnawed intermittently in the back of my mind, I asked several older people if they knew anything of Leon Schalit, the Austrian Jew, translator, and writer of a book on Galsworthy with a heavy emphasis on the soulful and passionate, *The Dark Flower* side, for whom Ada Galsworthy had vouched to the Home Office. I knew that Schalit had been a loyal member of P.E.N., fully sharing its international ideals. No one with whom I spoke could recall him; no one was even sure that he had actually been able to get out of Austria in time, although several told me generally of the P.E.N. attempts, under the presidency of Storm Jameson in the later thirties, to get as many writers out of central Europe as possible. Others told me that it was unfortunate I had not been able to talk with David Carver, the International Secretary of P.E.N. for many years who had died just a year or so before and would surely have known or known of Schalit. A novelist friend had suggested I look up

David Carver almost two years earlier, back when I was confining my inquiries to libraries and printed matter, and I realized one of the penalties of orderly research. I talked with a number of other writers: Gerda Charles, whose novels about Jews in England I had long admired; Catherine Dupré, who had nearly finished her biography of Galsworthy; a man whom I had met briefly some years earlier and who had a great deal to say about the Spanish Civil War. As most of the guests began to leave, Mrs. Watts came up to tell me how pleased she was that two people had agreed to read and comment on her book, her biography of her mother, the typescript of which was finished, before she submitted it for publication. She apologized for leaving, explaining that she had a dinner engagement. As I walked up the Kings Road, still in conversation about Galsworthy with Mrs. Dupré, we noticed a strong setting sun emerge from behind the grey clouds. "Isn't that lovely?," she said, "It looks as if our fabulous hot summer is coming back. Won't that be marvelous?"

In June, 1974, on our drive back from Bury to London, when Mr. Sauter had said that he and I might have been distorting Galsworthy by paying much more attention to the novels than we did to the plays, he had added: "You really ought to speak with someone in the theatre, someone who knew him well only as a dramatist or who acted in his plays. Perhaps you'll get another side of him." When I asked if he had anyone to suggest, he replied that the only one he could think of, still alive, was Dame Sybil Thorndike. "I saw her on television just a year or so ago. Over ninety but still articulate, to the point, with a good memory." On a very humid, sticky afternoon, three or four days after the P.E.N. reception, I walked, much more slowly, down the Kings Road, to the large block of flats in Chelsea Manor Street where Sybil Thorndike lived in her last years. As I went through the courtyard, a harassed looking, well-dressed man, jacket over his arm, tie loosened, car keys dangling in his hands, approached me and asked if I had seen the porter. When I said I hadn't, he muttered, "Damn. This place is supposed to have twenty-four-hour attendance. Just a line in the adverts to put more money in the pockets of property developers. Now the police will tow away my car if I can't find the attendant. I don't know what this country's coming to. One bloody swindle after another." As I got in the lift, I saw the porter politely approaching the man.

I was ushered into Dame Sybil's sitting room and saw her, seated upright in a small arm chair, tables on each side containing tissues, books, a telephone, an empty glass. She excused herself for not standing, mentioning her arthritis as if it were a troublesome mosquito, and shook hands firmly, as I noticed her still visible Viking-like beauty, her wide, warm smile and piercing bright blue eyes. When the woman who had shown me into the room asked what I would like to drink, Dame Sybil held up her glass and said, "I think I'll have just a bit more of mine to join him." I asked Dame Sybil about her first contact with Galsworthy, her playing the part of Mrs. Barthwick, the mother, in the Manchester production of *The Silver Box*, Galsworthy's first play. She smiled fondly, and said, "I loved that play—it was a great play. When Galsworthy first came to rehearsal, I went through it, thought I had Mrs. Barthwick right. I'd learned it, thought about it. Afterwards, Galsworthy called me over and said kindly and quietly, 'That was very nice, but now I'll show you what I want.' And he did. He was always clear, very certain what he was after. He came to rehearsals often because he always knew what he wanted. Perhaps a bit didactic, but I liked him so much and thought his work was so good. But he was remote, not what a lot of actors would call a 'good chap,'" and she laughed quietly as she said, "that means not the sort to join them in the pub after rehearsal. He was more an intellectual." As we talked further about her reactions to Galsworthy's plays and her sense of his uniqueness as a dramatist, she kept referring to her husband, Lewis Casson, to whom she was married for sixty-three years and who died at the age of ninety in 1969, in a tone that seemed to indicate that it was a great shame that I had just missed talking with him, as if he had stepped out only ten minutes before I arrived. When I asked her what she had liked about Galsworthy's plays, she sighed, and repeated, "Oh, I do wish you could talk to Lewis—he really understood Galsworthy, far better than I, and they so often talked about the theatre and ideas—often late into the night. We both loved Galsworthy's work, Lewis especially. It was new, a marvelous force then. Galsworthy was devoted to realism. All his work was so real, new in the theatre then, electric, wonderful. He wanted pure theatre without theatricality, and he was the first to do that. It was a genuine reform. Granville-Barker followed him. Granville-Barker was wonderful, just wonderful. Lewis and I both loved him, would have done anything for him, let him walk on our faces." When I told Dame Sybil that I sensed, in her remarks, an intense affection for Granville-Barker that rather exceeded the affection for Galsworthy, she paused a moment, and pondered, "Yes, I think that's true. Lewis really knew Galsworthy more deeply than I, was closer to him. Played the leader of the workers in *Strife*, something or other in *Justice*, other parts. I knew him more as a force in the theatre, a realist, a man of talent and intelligence who had a vision of truth that he stuck to. He always knew what he wanted, verbally and physically, too, and he got it. But I wasn't really close to him in the way Lewis was. I was just a bit afraid of him. He *hated* theatricality. Once, later, when Ann, my youngest child, was playing a child in *The Roof*, Galsworthy came up to me, when I was talking with Ann during a break in rehearsal, and said to me 'Don't teach her any of your theatrical tricks. She's fine.'" Dame Sybil laughed, and said, "That was the nearest thing to a joke I ever heard from him."

Dame Sybil continued to talk of Galsworthy's work: her great respect and admiration for the "realistic" plays, *The Silver Box*, *Strife*, *Justice*, *Loyalties*; her lack of interest in the fantasies like *Joy*, which she had always thought trivial. She was disappointed by *The Skin Game*, the first performance of which she hadn't liked (an opinion that differs from most others I have encountered, including Galsworthy's, which praised the "electric" performance of Meggie Albanesi) and which she hadn't seen or read since. She was fond of the film version of *Escape*, "the best film of his I can remember," which was done on location on Dartmoor and in which both her husband and her daughter Ann had played. Our conversation then shifted to Dame Sybil's reflections on both Galsworthy and Ada. She reported that Ada never came to rehearsals of his plays, that Galsworthy would not, she was quite certain, have wanted her to. "We really felt a *constraint* between the two of them. Ada wouldn't talk about herself; neither would Galsworthy. But there really was a constraint between them. Lewis noticed it, too. Sometimes, Ada would express a strong opinion, and Galsworthy would look as if he didn't quite agree, just make a hesitant, polite, 'not quite' sort of objection. So, of course, he wouldn't have wanted her at rehearsals. He knew what he wanted there exactly. Yes, we saw them socially. Went there to lunch a number of times. Ada was always charming, always very pleasant with me. I remember one lunch at their London place—was it Addison Road, then?—when I was pregnant for the first time, with my son John, that would be 1911. I talked about being pregnant at lunch, and Ada was fascinated, kept asking how I felt about temporarily giving up a career to have a child. Then, unexpectedly, she said, 'You must stay for tea,' and took me up to her bedroom after lunch and wanted to know all about it, all the intimate details about how I felt. Girl talk. I must say it surprised me at the time. I would never have expected her to talk that way, although I found it charming, delightful."

I suddenly realized that I had slightly exceeded the half hour I had been told, by her daughter-in-law, that I might stay, since Dame Sybil tired rapidly. [Dame Sybil Thorndike died, in her ninety-fourth year, in June, 1976.] As I stood up to go, Dame Sybil insisted on standing as well, holding her cane with her left hand as she shook hands again with her right, asking me to return again another time because she so enjoyed talking about Galsworthy, "Not that I don't like to talk about more recent people and plays as well. But I don't get as much chance as I'd like to talk about how we felt when the theatre seemed so new and suddenly changing." I walked quickly out into the baking street, then slowly up the Kings Road, looking at the people, dressed in open shirts or carrying heavy backpacks, who sauntered past the shops and wondering why I had been so pleased to find someone, who, quite unexpectedly, had seemed to have more emotional sympathy with Ada than with John.

As the weather continued hot, I worked mornings while the well of our flat was relatively cool and went on expeditions with my family most afternoons. We went to Hampton Court on a stifling day, lingering in the few cool rooms of the palace, waving away the thick midges circling about the topiary as we competed to see which one of us could first brush his way into the center of the maze in the Palace Garden. The next afternoon, I took my children out to Chessington, a few miles south and west of London, in Surrey, a park that combines a fairly large zoo with a miniature railway and other elements of an amusement park. The animals looked rather seedy and languid in the heat, and my children, perhaps because of a surfeit of the London Zoo in previous years, were more interested in the amusements. As they joined a queue to wait for an advertised half hour in a paddle boat on an artificial lake, I walked off by myself, passed up stopping at a refreshment stand that had run out of ice an hour or two earlier, followed a stream that led away from the artificial lake, sat down on the bank, rolled up my trousers, took off my shoes and socks, and put my feet in the water. I thought about Ada Galsworthy, and realized that my attitude toward her was beginning to assume something of the shape of a perspective. I pictured her as Ada Nemesis Cooper before her first marriage, a picture borrowed, for the most part, from Ralph Mottram's book. She was a talented, intelligent, high-strung girl; her father was a prominent Norwich gynecologist who had died by the time she was in her early twenties. She was shepherded about the Continent by her mother, most often described as silly and self-indulgent, looking for a wealthy and suitable husband for Ada. Catherine Dupré, in her biography of Galsworthy published in 1976, uses evidence from Norwich birth records, as well as the middle name of "Nemesis," to conclude that Ada was illegitimate. The gynecologist, Dr. Emanuel Cooper, was not her father and never legally married her mother, although he did bring up and provide for both Ada and her brother. This discovery, I thought, reinforced my interpretation of her character. I could imagine Ada's unease, her frustration, her need to develop the composure and the elegance that always characterized her. And, then, she had settled for Arthur Galsworthy, accepting his solid dependability while trying to ignore the facts that he was neither lively nor intelligent. Donald Wilson had understood all this well and sensitively in writing the first three episodes for the television series. Whatever had happened between Ada and Arthur in bed could probably never now be known, and that seemed to me to matter less than did the need in her to define her own kind of life, to use her hard won strength and her intelligence in some way that she could appreciate and respect. She was talented in music and literature, she was capable of intense application, and she needed to express these talents without violating the kind of security she recognized in all the Galsworthys, the vast clan of the prosperous middle class into which she had married. That the two most lively members of the clan, should become, first, her favorite cousins and then her best friends, was certainly predictable; that Ada's force should then center on their own favorite, their handsome and charming but still, at that time, rather indolent brother, Jack, was perhaps less predictable but clearly understandable.

I thought, too, of Galsworthy, in 1894, at twenty-seven, indulged, respected, and, in a sense, deferred to, as the oldest son of the oldest son, the potential patriarch of a large family, probably the kindest male in it, certainly the least competitive, still without any commitment to a career. He had never had to fight hard for anything, and, as with his lifelong mechanical ineptitude, he early learned to be charmingly self-deprecating about whatever he was not very good at. After Oxford, he had eaten his legal dinners and been "called to the bar" in 1890, but he had hardly ever practiced. He had, apparently, used his legal training principally when sent by his father to investigate a situation far away (in Vancouver, in St. Petersburg, in Australia). His letters back, which read like travel journals of an observant and thoughtful young man, rarely mention any legal issues or business, and no one, then or more recently, has made any attempt to conceal the fact that legal business was merely the pretense for his generally interesting and enlarging travels. Galsworthy had, as early as 1892, written the sister of a close friend that a writing career might be a "jolly good" thing, "the nicest way going" of earning a living, but there is no sign of serious application before 1894. In 1894, he fell in love with Ada, and it transformed his life. Her unhappy marriage with Arthur, her story, became the focus of a sympathetic susceptibility that had always been latent in him; her taut strength became the kind of center, the kind of force he needed for a career. At Easter-time in 1895, by her own account as recorded in Marrot's biography, Ada called to Galsworthy out of the window of a departing train in the Gare du Nord (she, with her mother, was to holiday further on the Continent, having seen something of him in Paris; he was about to return to London and was seeing her off at the railway station): "Why don't you write? You're the very person who ought to." And he began, seriously, working hours each day, studying and analyzing Maupassant and Turgenev to learn technique. Ada continued to be the center of his literary work, providing him with a sense of intellectual dedication he had not manifested on his own. Most people who knew him still did not know that he wrote seriously, and he published only under the pseudonym of John Sinjohn until *The Island Pharisees* in 1904. As late as 1898, he sent Conrad, by then a close friend with whom he spent frequent weekends, a copy of *Jocelyn*, his first published novel and his first attempt at dealing with the theme of adultery, although the adulterer, defended in the novel, is a man instead of a woman. Conrad wrote his own publisher that, although he knew Galsworthy well and thought him a generous and splendid man, "I had no idea the fellow wrote at all."

Ada had always remained an intimate part of Galsworthy's serious work. After their marriage, she became his only secretary, typing or writing out in longhand all his manuscripts, taking dictation (in longhand or on the typewriter) of well over half of his letters almost as rapidly as he could talk. I realized that my gratitude as a biographer, gratitude because her firm, straight handwriting is so much more legible than his, might play some part in my judgment, but I also knew, from conversations and from his diary, that she carefully edited and questioned almost everything he ever wrote. They had, as Rudolf Sauter had told me several times, long discussions about literature and other writers— the essays about Dickens and Tolstoy, as well as the formulations about puzzling new writers like D. H. Lawrence were, in a sense, theirs, the product of discussions in which two close reactions were sufficiently interfused as to be inseparable from the outside. He could like "bloods" and the comic dialogue in P. G. Wodehouse by himself, but attitudes toward serious literature were worked out together and held jointly. Throughout all I had read and heard, I felt that Ada was more committed to an idea of art, to a seriousness about literature, than Galsworthy ever was. The grace, the willingness to understand what he had not understood before, and the energy were his; the commitment, probably the firmness of the revolt against Victorian conventionality, and the sense of achievement were hers before he internalized them.

Attitudes toward Ada always differed widely, and some, particularly a number of theatre people, saw her as rigid and distant, keeping Galsworthy to his study and away from the conviviality he might enjoy. Most other writers, however, like Conrad and Ford, clearly respected her mind, her sensitivity, and her individuality. They found her sometimes less stuffy than he could be, less held in or impeded by a gentlemanly ideal or a sense of what should or should not be done. Conrad's letters to Galsworthy, for example (a correspondence carried on, almost without interruption, for almost thirty years), contain many fond references to Ada and frequent, rather coy, statements that, if JG cannot understand some abstruse or emotional point, Ada most surely can. In 1921, Arnold Bennett, writing to Galsworthy from his yacht, gloried in the pleasures of having been away from his wife for the past three and a half months. Bennett welcomed seeing little of his wife because "she hates yachting," began the letter with the statement that "I believe my wife still exists," and continued the tone of lamenting that wives so often were troublesome or dull. But Ada was apparently exempt from the general opprobrium, for Bennett concluded the letter with "My devoted homage to your wife to whom in my Midland way I am deeply attached, & I don't care who knows it." On the other hand, Compton Mackenzie, Rosamond Lehmann told me, talking with him often when she lived close to him in the country during the Second World War, found Ada "pretentious, boring, and remote," and thought that, although she always looked beautiful and dressed well, there was really nothing to her. Perhaps Edward Garnett's reaction was most typical of those from writers who did not know her intimately. Garnett was always closer to Galsworthy than he was to Ada. They had seen most of each other in Galsworthy's bachelor days when the two men took long walking tours together and discussed literature (although Garnett must have missed something in Galsworthy's fiction because he repeatedly argued that, in *The Man of Property*, Irene and Bosinney should run off together "joyfully" to Paris). When Galsworthy and Ada married, Garnett wrote, "Ada, you were made to be carried off in Chinese sieges by Mandarins" and added, to Galsworthy alone, that she "goes awfully well with a Byronic poem, 'Lara,' and with beauty and yellow silk trousers."

Like Garnett, Galsworthy was more comfortable in fiction symbolizing Ada, rather than characterizing her. He had once told Dorothy Ivens that he had never drawn a fictional portrait of her. For *The Forsyte Saga*, it is the story of Ada and what she represents, the symbol of beauty and art that cannot be owned or possessed by the acquisitive and ingesting Forsytes, which are important, not the complexities or possible ambivalences of her character. Just this fact—that Irene in the fiction is almost uncharacterized, is so patently a symbol with little relationship to the character of Ada—is, in the view of someone as perceptive as D. H. Lawrence, the fiction's fatal limitation. "Irene is a stick," Lawrence wrote, and "a parasite" and "a bitch," and, so, as *The Forsyte Saga* moves on, Galsworthy's "passion," initially genuine, becomes "faked." Galsworthy, I was convinced, never thought for a moment that he was characterizing Ada; he recognized, always, how entirely symbolic the character of Irene was. For him, the nature of Ada was too private, too much a part of their marriage, too much behind the barrier he drew between himself and the outside world, to be explored or dissected in something so public as fiction. The character of Irene, I realized, is useful to the biographer and the critic only in its significance for recognizing Galsworthy's particular kind of artistic displacement: she had made him an artist (such a carefully limited artist as he was, a water-colorist, not a painter, for he could never assign to the persona of himself the virtue of pure abstraction), and she could, therefore, be represented as beauty or art itself. Ada's story, too, the forcing, the raping, the violation of the self that, justifiably or not, she felt in her relationship to Arthur Galsworthy, was the central event of *The Forsyte Saga*. The implications of the event carried through generations, radiating into the themes of ownership and the sanctity of the private, as well as into all the complicated and troubled relations between generations. Melodramatic as Ada herself may have been about the event, particularly, as Rudolf Sauter had told me, in extreme old age when she repeatedly talked of the first husband she still could not forgive, and serious as Galsworthy's outrage must have been in his initial response to the story, I could not believe that the literal event itself had shaped the fiction as profoundly as did its symbolic ramifications. As Ada changed, Galsworthy changed his central focus from the symbol of Irene in *The Forsyte Saga*, the embodiment of beauty and of art, to the much more complex Fleur, the symbol of emotion and feeling in the second trilogy, *A Modern Comedy*. By her last appearance in the final trilogy, *End of the Chapter*, in which she is a minor character, Fleur has become a competent, stable, and understanding young matron. She is able to say, in reference to her father's raping of Irene, the seminal incident that led indirectly to Fleur's existence and influenced so much of her earlier life, that "the woman made a great fuss for nothing much." Galsworthy's edge of irony seems to be directed, in about equal proportions, against the remaining vestiges of Fleur's earlier rather flip and callow impercipience, against those who might think any issue, no matter how dramatic and significant, capable of remaining visible in the same terms through changes in time, and against any literal reading of his own intensity, against himself.

Some small element of the ironic thrust also seemed to be directed against Ada, for Galsworthy invariably could see all sides of any question, could dramatize, through his irony, his imagery, and all the many details of his world, a moderated version of all the possible reflective attitudes toward the experience he saw. I thought again that what he couldn't write was a convincing depiction of the singular intensity of strong rage or strong passion. I recalled having read, in the collection of his manuscripts at the University of Birmingham Library, a type-script of a story called "Heat" that he had written in the early twenties, at about the time of *To Let* and *Loyalties*, when he was writing at nearly his best. "Heat" begins with two maiden sisters, in their late forties, living economically in the south of France on a pittance their father, an English archdeacon, had left them. When their Italian maid becomes pregnant, the two sisters begin to argue, the older, the more earthy and masculine, amused by the situation and wanting the chance to bring up the baby, the younger, the more religious, appalled by the illegitimacy and wanting to badger the maid to tell who the father is. The maid won't tell and the baby is born, the two sisters resolving to take care of him. At first, the baby thrives, but then wilts in the sear-ing heat of the Mediterranean summer, as the two sisters, with increasing intensity, fight (at first, just verbally, finally physi-cally) over whether or not to have the baby baptised. This time, the religious sister wins, but, by the time of baptism, the baby is dead. The story begins plausibly and effectively. Yet, as it builds, as the sisters first argue, then scream, then tear each other's clothes in the intensity of their conflict, the story itself becomes as shrill as it is melodramatic. The prose is heavily wooden and elaborately rhetorical. Although Galsworthy emphasizes his point that addiction to orthodox religion is inhumane, his focus, his control, at the end of the story is badly blurred, as if the vio-lence and the passion he depicted had thrown off his usual sense of coherence and balance. On the top of the first page of the typescript, Ada had written in pencil, "not to be published by J.G.'s wish." His motive might have been a kind of reticence about exposing himself psychologically, since, in one possible reading, he seemed to be the baby destroyed by intensely com-peting dogmas. From the outside, I could respect his decision on the grounds of aesthetic judgment, could have no wish to see a story so shrill and melodramatic, material so ill-digested, pub-lished now. As I kicked my feet in the cool stream, I thought that Galsworthy was, in many ways, a writer very much like Anthony Trollope. Both could reach a wide audience, both in their own time and now, through their creation of a full social, political, and characterological world, the details all filled in.

Both displayed attitudes carefully moderated and balanced with an appreciation of different forms of human behavior and a wise skepticism that could puncture pretense, a perspective that could generate both fascination and comfort (the latter could be overemphasized when the novelist was read superficially) in an audience. Yet neither could depict searing passion or intensity; like Trollope, whose novel of the man of intensity, *He Knew He Was Right*, is one of the least psychologically convincing he published, Galsworthy, at his best in the long continuous series, could never adequately represent in fiction the extreme rage or violence he feared.

I thought, then, of the other side of rage or violence, the depiction of passion or sexuality, and realized that Galsworthy had never shown that directly either . . . partly the literary conventions of his time, but also a limitation within which he was generally comfortable. When he campaigned against censorship of the drama, he was campaigning for the freedom to discuss issues that were taboo, the freedom to allow the stage to become a forum that could generate wider rational argument and a wider range of sympathy, not necessarily the freedom to present sexuality more directly. In addition, Galsworthy was also, in part, carrying the campaign for his contemporaries writing the "new, realistic" drama at the Royal Court. It was some of the plays by Shaw, Garnett, and Granville-Barker that were refused licenses by the Lord Chamberlain, not those by Galsworthy. Although he certainly saw that the implications of censorship could easily extend to his own work, and that censorship is invariably arbitrary and accidental, he regarded himself as waging a campaign justifiable in general terms, as conveying a reforming or enlightened attitude rather than embracing a particular example of emotional necessity. As I looked up and saw a young couple strolling along the opposite bank of the stream, walking away from the Chessington crowds, I recalled that Galsworthy, although reticent about depicting sexuality directly or graphically, had never been Puritanical or particularly straitlaced about sex itself. I had seen ample evidence to assume that he had not been a virgin when his affair with Ada first began. Conrad's wife, Jessie, in her book of recollections, *Joseph Conrad and His Circle*, published in 1935, who had been very fond of Galsworthy and regarded him as their favorite and a "very easy" guest (her older son, Borys, echoing her fondness in a book published in 1970, recalled that "Mr. Jack" was his favorite among his father's friends and the first person to whom he wrote a letter), wrote of a weekend visit by Galsworthy to their cottage in Kent in the days before his affair with Ada. After lunch on Sunday, although he looked perfectly well to both Jessie Conrad and her husband, Galsworthy suddenly said he had a headache and retired to his room to rest for several hours before his train left. Later, Mrs. Conrad realized that a new housemaid, who she described as exceedingly pretty, was also missing most of the afternoon. When Mrs. Conrad later questioned the maid, the young girl hung her head and said, "Mr. Galsworthy asked me to stop and help him pack his bag." Mrs. Conrad used the story to illustrate Galsworthy's considerate sense of politeness and "inherent propriety."

It was not, I thought, that Ada rescued Galsworthy from a kind of incapacitating Puritanism or from an inability to feel. Rather, I suspected, that, in terms of the relationship, she legitimized some degree of intensity for him, became the person he could love. She had always been more intense than he, about time, about space (the various houses), about writing and art. I was, after some pondering, inclined to follow the relatives' judgment in not giving much credit to the charges of her hypochondria or her insistence on travel every winter when Galsworthy would have preferred staying in England, "writing alongside a fire of blazing apple logs, dogs at his feet," as Basil Dean had put it. In the first place, I had heard and read ample evidence that her illnesses were real, her asthma, her bronchitis, her need for warmth physiological as well as psychological. And I am always dubious about easy categories like "hypochondria," itself a Puritanical and self-righteous judgment that assumes one can separate the physiological from the psychological more certainly than any of us can. Ada's ailments may well have had a psychogenic or psychosomatic component, particularly in the light of the tensions and uncertainties of her early life, the consequent need for both distinction and stability. But few of those who labelled her "hypochondriac" made any distinction between imaginary or fabricated illness and real illness psychosomatic in origin. I wondered, too, about the physical nature of the imagination, all those people who have died of ailments their physicians could not find. I did not think that Ada's long life, in itself, refuted her own recognition of real debilities. In addition, from letters, diaries, and accounts of others, I was certain that Galsworthy welcomed the winter travels as much as Ada did. Typically, for example, when in the United States, they would spend a week in New York, about a fortnight on a lecture tour (Galsworthy did not, by all accounts, enjoy the lectures, although the fees helped make the trips possible), and then a solid six or eight weeks in Santa Barbara or Arizona where he could work without the interruptions of telephone or social engagements. Rather than these trips impeding Galsworthy's work (and he had also traveled at every opportunity before he knew Ada), they gave him a kind of energy, a breadth of understanding—he was, after all, far more a writer of exteriors than of interiors. He was also, and on this point numerous letters confirm the family's point of view, not above using, especially in his later years and with Ada's willing complicity, his "wife's indisposition" as a polite excuse for avoiding engagements he wanted to avoid. On the issues of both illness and travel, I saw a relationship unusually close, each invariably acting for and protecting the other, an intensely private relationship often impossible to penetrate from the outside. I thought of his brother Hubert's fury, as they modulated pronunciations of "charabanc" across the lunch table on his boat, at the private world in which they were capable of living together.

I realized, too, that the Galsworthys were not always so close, not always indistinguishable, particularly, as I had learned from both Rudolf Sauter and Dorothy Ivens, in the last years at Bury. Ada, kind as she was to the girls who worked for them whom she knew well and trusted, did not play the feudal lady to the generous feudal lord. She was not comfortable at charity bazaars or at the cricket suppers after the matches at the long tables set on the manor house lawn. She thought Galsworthy sometimes too generous, sometimes sentimental, supporting some people not worthy of support. As his letters show with a reasonable consistency throughout his life, he could, seen from the outside, seem too tolerant of both fools and spongers. There are letters exhorting old dishonest servants to hard work while providing them with another handout; there are letters explaining very carefully and politely to literal-minded clerics why he does not need their pity for the fact that he is not a Christian. In one correspondence from late 1914, when the Belgian painter deSmet and his family, refugeees from the German invasion, were staying with the Galsworthys at Wingstone, a Devon writer named Olive Katherine Parr kept writing importunate letters insisting that the deSmets be taken regularly to a Roman Catholic church that she thought suitable for them. Galsworthy began with two letters patiently explaining that he would be glad to take the deSmets to any church they wanted to go to, but they had no interest in going. After Miss Parr, in still another rather teasing and insinuating letter, continued to press that the deSmets attend her church, Ada took over the correspondence and told her to stop pushing them around and mind her own business. A lot of the Galsworthys' relationship could be seen in terms of protection, just as those ferocious dogs protected them both from the world. Within the relationship, Ada protected Galsworthy from himself, sometimes from a rather amorphous kindness and patience that could drift senselessly, just as he protected her from the ravages of climate he could so easily absorb. He was the one more in touch with others, with the outside world, more willing to defer to others or acknowledge their claims on him, more understanding and sympathetic; she was the one more in touch with herself, often both their selves, with the privacy of vision and dedication that helped transform the humane man into a writer.

I thought, too, of the fact that they had had no children, although all the novels attest to his constant interest in parents and children, in all the issues, emotions, and rebellions involved in transmitting attitudes and qualities from one generation to the next. Families were always a principal subject, their complexities, their tyrannies, their support, families as analogues for classes, then, in his later work, for nations. At first, I had tended to place, as some of the relatives and contemporaries had done, their not having had children on the consciousness of Ada's age when they married and his always demonstrable sense of consideration. But recent conversations with both Mrs. Ivens and Dame Sybil Thorndike had made me a bit skeptical. Perhaps Ada had wanted children and he, for some reason, had not, had preferred to work out what he knew were all the perplexing issues of parenthood in the safety of fiction; perhaps they had both wanted children at the time they married, and accident or some physical reason, either never known to them or never disclosed by them, had prevented conception. One could only speculate, realizing that, even if they knew all there was to be known then, the bedroom door was now just as firmly and permanently closed on this situation as it had been on whatever happened between Ada and Arthur back before 1894. The decorative *A*'s in Galsworthy's diary were a charming recognition of emotion and devotion, and did say something about the man, but they did not go very far in demonstrating the nature of what was clearly an extremely close, mutually necessary, and intensely private relationship for almost forty years.

As I realized that my children must have had more than their share of the paddle boats by this time, and collected my shoes and socks to go back to meet them, I thought that I had, almost unintentionally, become Ada's advocate—not as against Galsworthy, but rather as representing the best in him and providing the intensity that forced that into the best of his work. I imagined discussions between Galsworthy and his wife, discussions about writing and social engagements and sex, and, although I could construct a range of opinions, I could not always tell which argument came from which person. Having been married for twenty years, I knew how easily one switches sides in a marriage, how each assumes the position of the other until the two are indistinguishable on a particular question. Knowing again that I was projecting, I recognized how superficial and irrelevant are the forms of argument that maintain that one partner prevented the other from doing something or becoming something, that distinguish roles between the two. Galsworthy actually wrote all the work that carries his name, but the fiction, the myth in which they partially lived and by which he is memorable now, was, in large part, theirs together. As I met my children and we walked around to see the llamas and vicunas before trudging through the heat to the station for the train to London, I thought that there was still a question on which I needed to know more and think more about the relationship between Galsworthy and Ada, the question of politics, particularly the politics after the First World War. I was still uneasy about Orwell's charge and Priestley's fainter denigration. On political issues, I thought the relatives somewhat less helpful than on some of the other matters. The two most knowledgeable and sensitive of them, Rudolf Sauter and Dorothy Ivens, had been, particularly in the twenties, themselves apolitical, and neither found very much political implication in the work. Mr. Sauter saw the best work as impelled by the affair with Ada, by the compassion and the rebellion against Victorianism that the affair brought forth. Like Dwye Evans, he saw Galsworthy's work as basically about sex, although other questions about society, class, and justice radiated from this central concern. Mrs. Ivens sees the whole work as a vast "chronicle of feeling," done sometimes well, sometimes not so well, a record of "the days when feeling meant so much because so little could be said." Central as I knew these statements were, I thought something else still necessary, something more political, although not a matter of any faction or party, something perhaps more social, more particularly representative of England. And there, too, I thought, Ada was deeply involved.

Shortly after noon the next day, a blistering sun still making me feel that every movement must be compressed and conserved, I walked from the Knightsbridge flat toward Princes Gate, just off Kensington Gore, where Dame Rebecca West lives. I cut through the large yard of the small church just next to the Brompton Oratory, a yard I had often used as a shortcut to and from the Brompton Road when we had lived for a month or so in a mews flat next to the churchyard three summers before. I looked to see if the splendid cream 1931 Rolls Royce was still in the church car park as it had often been three years before. It was, in a line with black Austins from the fifties and varicolored cars of more recent vintage, still looking as if it was a condition to which all other cars aspired. I walked out of the churchyard through the back gate and, more slowly, up the slight rise of Ennismore Gardens, noticing that several pubs had put tables for lunchers and drinkers out on the sidewalk. This bit of Paris transported to London was even visible in front of a pub just off nearby Montpelier Square, where Galsworthy had installed Soames and Irene at the beginning of their marriage. Ennismore Gardens led to Princes Gate and the large, red brick house of elegant flats, facing Hyde Park. After I found the right court-yard, rode up the lift, and rang the bell, a maid led me into Dame Rebecca's sitting room, full of comfortable brocaded chairs, walnut tables, and antiques, with a bridge table, almost in the center of the room, on which glasses, bottles, and ice were set out for drinks. Almost before I had looked around the large and pleasantly crowded room, Dame Rebecca walked in quickly, carrying her cane as she strode over to me to shake hands. "What a miserable day," she said. "What a miserably hot summer." I agreed, welcoming the comments on the weather from one of the first of the English I had met who did not as-sume that Americans automatically welcomed hot, dry weather as a relief from the general English stereotype of cool rain. "Oh, yes," she continued, "all the Americans I'm fondest of come to London in the summer, if they can, to escape the heat. It's the wrong summer. Well, you'd better mix us drinks. I'm sorry I'm clumsy at it. I had an operation for cataracts this winter. The operation was a success, but what a nuisance. I couldn't work, couldn't read for five months. That was the worst of it, and I must make up for it now." As she talked, she kept switching from one pair of glasses to another, each held by a ribbon around her neck, impatiently trying to work out which was better so that she need not bother with them again.

After I mixed drinks, we sat down on two brocaded chairs in a corner of the room where a breeze was coming through the open window. I asked her immediately about the Orwell opinion that Galsworthy might have become some sort of "genteel Fascist" had he lived. "Rubbish," she replied. "Nothing to it at all. Just a lie. Ex-Communists always lie about politics. Once one has been too involved with the party, one way or another, even in rejection, truth disappears." We went on to talk more about Galsworthy himself. She hadn't, she said, known him before the First World War, and I suddenly and silently realized that in the years, between about 1912 and 1921, when she had been H. G. Well's mistress, Wells had generally brought his wife, Jane, of whom both Galsworthys were very fond, to visit at Wingstone. But Dame Rebecca had known Galsworthy well after 1921, worked with him on numerous P.E.N. committees. "Personally, he was fine. Almost as noble and generous as people said he was. Orwell couldn't have been more wrong. On politics, Galsworthy was utterly *sincere*, humane, genuinely left-wing. He was always both just and generous. Not just sentimental either. At one time, someone vaguely literary came to me with a sad story, wanting money. I was a bit suspicious, so I put him off for a week, knowing I was to see Galsworthy at a committee meeting that afternoon. When I told Galsworthy about it, he said, 'I think it sounds familiar, but I'll check and let you know.' A few days later, at the next committee meeting, he brought a cardfile of his charities, indexed, took me aside and said, 'Now, what was the fellow's name again?' We looked him up, and there was the same sad story, briefly summarized on a card, dated several years earlier. 'Yes,' he said, tapping the card, 'that's a bad one. You'd best stay away from it.'"

We began to talk more about P.E.N. in the late twenties and thirties. I had known of Galsworthy's efforts, in the growing political conflicts after 1921, to keep the organization antiideological, like his rather tepid letter to Admiral Horthy interceding against the persecution of two Hungarian writers (some had wanted him to write a more militant ideological protest and circulate a petition worldwide). I had also known that H. G. Wells, who became the president of P.E.N. after Galsworthy died, had issued a number of more militant statements, from 1934 on, asserting the principles of freedom of expression and of making no judgments on the basis of a person's origin or creed. I asked

Dame Rebecca if she had thought Galsworthy as profoundly committed to an anti-Fascist point of view, as deeply antiethnic, as Wells was. "Oh, yes," she replied rapidly, signalling me to mix myself another drink in which she would not join. "Galsworthy was just as deeply antiethnic, as you put it, as Wells was. He would never make a judgment on race or creed or class. Their styles were just different. Each did whatever he could for writers, for all refugees. In a way, it was easier for Wells, easier after 1934, when we all knew certainly what the Nazis were. Galsworthy handled P.E.N. well, very well given the times. He was democratic, listened to others, relied on experts when that was appropriate, yet he kept a firm hand on the organization's direction, and did whatever he could for all writers trapped by governments and ideologies." I asked Dame Rebecca if she had known Ada Galsworthy or had any sense of her role, in the late thirties, in helping refugees. "Oh, yes," she replied. "Ada Galsworthy did a great deal. She helped, and I heard that often. I didn't know her well personally. She wasn't, I gathered, an easy person to know. But when, in the late thirties, my husband and I were trying to help as many people as possible get away from the Nazis, putting up some, being willing to underwrite them with the Home Office, writing letters, giving money, we knew of Ada Galsworthy as someone one could count on, absolutely."

The maid knocked timidly and entered to tell us that lunch was ready. As we walked slowly out into the hall, Dame Rebecca told me more of the efforts she and her husband (to whom she had been married for almost forty years and who had died five or six years before) made to help refugees from the Nazis, both during the middle and late thirties and after the fall of France in 1940. She spoke bluntly of writers who had been grateful and of some who had not, who seemed to resent the dependency they required. In the hall, she broke off and excused herself, saying that she had to go into her bedroom to get some pills. "I take fourteen of them a day now. Various pills for the various ailments of age. Infuriating, isn't it?" I walked into the large dining room, thin curtains billowing in a breeze from the open bay window, the large oval table rather formally set with three places. As the maid gathered the third setting to put it away, she asked me to choose what wine I would like, adding that Dame Rebecca would not drink any. Dame Rebecca soon entered, saying, "I expected you would bring your wife." I could recall having told her, when I introduced myself, that I was in London with my wife and children, but I could not remember, either in that conversation or in the subsequent phone call, any invitation to bring my wife. I lapsed into momentary silence, annoyed at myself for having missed a possible implication of an invitation, or, rather, half annoyed and half guilty, knowing that, when I returned to the flat to tell her, my wife would wish I had gathered a clearer indication of whether or not she was to be included. And, then, quickly burying my own compound of occasional lack of directness and fear of imposing on people for the boring self-consciousness it doubtless was in a muttered apology, I turned the conversation back to Galsworthy.

As we ate our soup and, then, a delicious and heavy ragout, which my wife would not have enjoyed so early on a hot afternoon, we talked more of Galsworthy's work. As I had rather anticipated, she had liked Galsworthy personally better than she had liked his work. "I was never moved by *The Forsyte Saga*. I always found the characters stock. The work is well plotted, and he had a good sense of structure. What one could learn by labor, he did. The television version was really, I think, better, more imaginative, than the novels. My husband always said that Galsworthy read better in German, and I think that's probably true, something about his kind of imagination linked to the structure of a language. My husband was bilingual. Others who are have said the same. I don't really know for myself, since my German is not that good and I've no ear at all for French." She stopped and laughed at herself, "I probably should not have been literary at all had I not happened to be born English." We talked further about Galsworthy's prose, agreeing that it had a rather heavy quality, a lack of deftness, a lack of pungent conviction, that made it seem more English from nonEnglish perspectives. As we went on, Dame Rebecca said, "You know, perhaps his real limitation was in the fact that, both in fiction and in life, he had no sense of humor. He couldn't see an absurd situation as simply absurd and reduce it accordingly in his prose.

In a way, he was profound, always thinking around things, seeing all the implications of an issue or a point of view, judiciously examining the whole question. But some issues don't deserve that profundity, and he didn't see the humor of that. In life, it was the same. One day, going to a P.E.N. meeting, I was in the lift with Galsworthy, Radclyffe Hall—you know, the author of *The Well of Loneliness?*—and her companion, Lady Una Troubridge, and the lift stuck for about ten minutes between floors. Galsworthy pressed the emergency button. He did the right thing. I suppose I was a bit nervous and looking for something to say, so I cracked, 'What a great loss to English literature if we don't get out!' Galsworthy stiffened. He didn't think it was funny. I suppose any such statement would require far too many qualifications and comparisons before it could be accepted or rejected." I realized, as we were talking, that, in one sense, Dame Rebecca was certainly right, that Galsworthy had not been capable of capsulizing a situation in the kind of striking reduction that indicates a sense of humor, or, when he occasionally did so, sounded rather flat and banal. What he called jokes were never funny, a quality I find sometimes in other good fiction, Doris Lessing's for example. Sometimes, when he tried to write satire, as in *The Burning Spear*, his 1919 novel which lampooned a super-patriot who dashed about England whipping up enthusiasm for the War, the target seemed rather trite and obvious. The character in *The Burning Spear*, rather like Voltaire's Dr. Pangloss, suffers many misfortunes, confuses identities, gives long illogical speeches about his patriotic obsession, and never, in this rather repetitious roustabout absurdity, loses his enthusiasm for the War. That Galsworthy published the novel under a pseudonym (A.R. P-M.) and did not publicly acknowledge it as his own until the Manaton edition of his works in 1923 seems to have been less a matter of hesitancy on any literary standard (as, perhaps, it should have been) than apprehension about the novel's unconventionality in 1919. Yet, still thinking and talking of Galsworthy's lack of a sense of humor, I recognized another side, the refusal to reduce anything, the curiosity about everything human that insisted on examining all implications, even those, perhaps, not worth examining, the constant insistence on his own vulnerability. He would not (perhaps could not) let himself repose in the safety of a humorous reduction. It was as if, I thought, Galsworthy was the alter ego for Evelyn Waugh in some kind of mythically universal English literary mind.

Over fruit and coffee our discussion continued to jump from Galsworthy to comparisons with other novelists and, then, to talk of the other novelists themselves. Dame Rebecca's opinions were direct and forceful: "Tolstoy's the most overrated one of all. I find Anna, for example, completely unmotivated. What supposedly sane person would throw herself under a train because her lover had jilted her? I certainly wouldn't. Would you?" She agreed with me that Rosamond Lehmann's novels were fine and generally undervalued, but said she could not understand the vogue for praising Elizabeth Bowen's work. She welcomed argument, and we found ourselves delivering crisp judgments back and forth. She thought, as I do, that the "influence of Bloomsbury," particularly as represented in its manifesto, "Mr. Bennett and Mrs. Brown," had not been healthy generally for the reading public, that it had, particularly in the academies and in America, led to an easy and uninformed dismissal of Bennett and Wells as well as of Galsworthy. "But, you know, Bennett was, in a way, just the opposite of Galsworthy. An awful man, but he could be absolutely brilliant, both as a novelist and as a reviewer. As a man, he was entirely *mercenary*, really cared about his yacht and talked about it just as men at a golf club would. Galsworthy couldn't talk that way. Bennett's work was uneven, never labored like Galsworthy's, but it could be marvelous, moving." Dame Rebecca was also interested in whom else I had seen and talked to, wondering if I had ever met Bennett's second wife who was then still alive, adding that it doubtless would not serve my purposes very well. When she heard that I had spoken a good deal with Galsworthy's surviving relatives, she seemed surprised and asked me, "But weren't they awful, dreadful people?" When I asked what she had in mind, she brushed the question aside quickly, "No, no. I'm sorry. I don't know the ones alive now, the ones in the next generation. I was thinking of his parents, vague memories of stories about them, Forsytes and all of that. Perhaps, he never fully recovered from that. They seemed to have such a hold on him. The way he, even as a man of talent and presence, when he was over sixty, still talked about his parents."

We walked slowly back to the large sitting room. Dame Rebecca took me out onto a balcony where she was growing some ferns and flowers, "nothing much this year. I do most of my gardening at Eynsford, in the country." The balcony overlooked Hyde Park where we could see masses of delphinium, gladiola, and dahlia resplendent in the sun coming from over the building behind us. We then moved back into the sitting room and out another balcony facing east rather than north. This overlooked a courtyard, surrounded by other wings of the apartment house. "You know," she said, "the wing straight across. That was the American Ambassador's residence between the wars. There, that stone wall. You know the famous picture. All the Kennedy children seated in a line along the wall. I have a copy of it somewhere. Such a shame. And, there, the wing in back is almost all Arab now. They've bought it out, just recently. The ones I've talked with are fine people. Intelligent and gracious. They're a bit nervous in London. Understandably so. After someone broke into one of the flats in that wing, they installed a full security system, searchlights on the roof as well. Makes it more difficult to sleep sometimes, particularly on these hot nights, but I suppose it benefits us all." We returned to the sitting room, to the chairs in the breezy corner, and Dame Rebecca repeated her respect for Ada Galsworthy. "Yes, I'm sure he was lucky to have married her. Quite different, I should think, from the Forsytes. Much stronger, more humorous, less insulated from the world." We talked, in a more rambling desultory manner than we had been talking, of families, the war, children, and universities, Dame Rebecca wanting to know if I, as an American professor who had lived for some time in England, would like to see my children go to Oxford or Cambridge. When I said that I would, if they wanted to, she replied, "Yes. That's still good. Still the best possible thing, although it didn't work very well for my granddaughter. Maybe she just isn't the right type for it. But it gets so complicated. So many different ways in which children have to revolt from their parents. More and more all the time. Harder for them, too." Soon afterwards, I rose to go, but Dame Rebecca signalled me to remain. "No, no. I never work until late in the day, at least after tea. I like to sleep late, then be social, talk to people over lunch and afterwards. I can work better after I've been engaged in conversation." She asked me what I had thought of any plays I had recently seen, regretting that her eye operation had caused her to miss almost all of the past theatre season. I asked her how she had reacted to the original productions of the Galsworthy plays she had seen. She laughed, and said, "I've been waiting for you to ask me that. Of course, they had a sense of theatre, of plot, an excitement. But they weren't even as good as the novels, unfortunately. Too melodramatic, unrealistic, even at the beginning. Have you talked to others about their first response to the early plays?" When I mentioned Dame Sybil Thorndike's feeling that the plays were new and exciting because they were "realistic," she replied, puffing out her lips, "Oh, Sybil's a goose. A dear, of course, lovely and sweet and genuinely talented, but a goose as well. Galsworthy's plays were never realistic. The excitement was all theatrical, melodramatic, and, unlike the novels, handling the issues melodramatically as well. Even *Loyalties*, which I suppose is his best. What is the date again? 1922? Well, you see, on the right side in noticing and opposing English anti-Semitism, especially that early in the twenties. But it blurs the issue. A prejudiced Englishman of the middle classes wouldn't have assumed that Jews steal, just that they talked too much." I wondered then, as I wonder now, if Galsworthy's use of stealing, a metaphor for usurpation, for the alien impinging on the native land, wasn't a closer representation of a kind of truth. "But," said Dame Rebecca, "you're relying on metaphor again. And, then, he had to turn it on crime. Make the prejudice into a criminal act rather than just wrong and inhumane feeling. Melodrama." We agreed to disagree.

We talked further of plays, Galsworthy's and others', and then I realized that it really was time to go. Dame Rebecca walked me to the front door, then out to the lift, shaking my hand repeating that, next time, I must be sure to bring my wife to lunch. As the lift door closed, I could just see her turn, placing her cane imperiously before her, going back inside her apartment to work. I walked quickly down Ennismore Gardens, oblivious to the heat this time, eager to return to the flat and, before speaking or taking off my jacket, write down every word I could remember. Only about two hours later did I loosen my tie, unbutton my collar, and apologize to my wife for the mix-up that had caused her to miss the lunch. She laughed at my too scrupulous concern and suggested that we go out to dinner at a nearby, cool Alsatian restaurant, with tile floors and ceiling fans, without the children.

The next afternoon, as I was walking along Walton Street toward the Knightsbridge station of the Underground on my to tea with Mrs. Watts in her Hampstead house, I passed a wine shop. The year before, when we had lived only a street away, the shop had been called "Separate Tables" and had displayed many varieties of elegant glass and chrome coffee, end, and dining tables. My daughter, Kate, then seven, finding few children her age in the vicinity and always able to accommodate to any social world around her, had stopped at "Separate Tables" almost daily on her way home from the school bus stop on Brompton Road. She would enjoy an extended tea and long talk with Sarah, the attractive and fashionable young woman who ran the shop, which had never seemed busy. Kate had also, through the year, received postcards from Sarah written from country-house weekends about the animals she had seen or from a pre-Easter skiing holiday in Zermatt. Now, as I walked in the shop, I saw gaily decorated bins full of cheaper French wines along one side wall, the more expensive still wines lined on full shelves along the other, and the champagnes racked carefully behind the counter. The young man standing by, who told me he was Sarah's brother-in-law, explained: "The tables didn't do very well. We were a bit late. They were trendy in the late sixties. Bit late with the wine, too. The time for that was when we first entered the Common Market, '72 or '73. We'll have to spot things better. Any ideas? Sarah, you know, is married now. Living pastorally in Gloucestershire, idyllically happy. She only comes up to town about once every two months. She still talks occasionally about her young American partner in Mad Hatter teas. She'll be pleased to know you've asked." I bought a bottle of wine to bring to Mrs. Watts.

Mrs. Watts, smiling, led me up her narrow stairs, deposited the wine in her kitchen, and briskly brought me out to the large dining table, set in the bay window, on which she had placed the typescript of her book about her mother in carefully organized piles of pages. "I've put some bits out that you might want to read before we go out in the garden for tea." I read a statement that Galsworthy had carefully written for delivery at his last P.E.N. Congress, the 1932 meeting in Budapest, in which he articulated the ideals on which P.E.N. was founded and to which it "must remain faithful." The ideals included "Literature in the sense of Art (not of journalism, not of propaganda)," humane conduct, friendship with writers of all other countries, and doing nothing that might promote war, concluding that P.E.N. had "nothing whatever to do with State or Party politics." A letter to Mrs. Watts's mother, Mrs. Dawson Scott, in 1926, objected to the attempt, by some members of the P.E.N. to find a permanent house or club for meetings, Galsworthy writing that he would quit the presidency if they insisted on a home, for "P.E.N. is an idea or it's nothing." When I said to Mrs. Watts that the chastity of this idea did not seem to have survived among the P.E.N. members, she laughed and replied, "Well, I suppose he was a bit too stiff about some things." Still another letter began with a detailed plan for seating arrangements for an international dinner, cautiously trying to avoid offense and complaining that the Russians, in particular, were more interested in politics than in literature. The letter goes on to object strongly to all discrimination, all ideological persecution, stating that no one, no matter what he believes "*deserves* to be exterminated." I asked Mrs. Watts if she thought that Galsworthy's strong aversion to totalitarianism applied equally to the Soviets and the Nazis, granting the fact that during his lifetime so much less was known and discussed about the Nazis. She lifted her head to the side for a moment and looked up. "Oh, yes," she said, "certainly he hated any totalitarianism. One could always see him wince at any statement that defended a government's discrimination. But, of course, since I saw so much less of him after 1926, I remember mostly the statements about how difficult the Russians were. But also Admiral Horthy, who was anti-Semitic. I think the 1932 statement is against his ideas, too. In the twenties, you must remember, the Bolsheviks seemed the greater danger. Galsworthy, like us, like my mother and me and many writers, leaned toward the left automatically, and so the Soviet ideology was the greater danger. Galsworthy never went for the Bolsheviks at all. Early in the thirties, my husband and I, like so many young people in those days, leaned quite far left, *not* all the way. But, after my husband died, I didn't pay much attention to politics for a long time. I had too much else to do with three young children. I had little interest until after the war and the nonideological things like the National Health. I'd be certain, though, that Galsworthy would never have given even tacit support to any governmental ideology."

As we gathered the brewing teapot, the hot water, the cakes and sandwiches and plates, loading them onto the large silver tray to carry them out to the garden, I mentioned that I had also noticed the difference in tone between two letters, one written by Galsworthy and one by Ada, congratulating her on her engagement in December, 1924. Galsworthy's was more formal and distant, Ada's warmer, fuller, more graceful. "Yes," she laughed. "That surprised me, too, as I was sorting things out to see what I wanted to include in the book. I always saw her as so elegant and distant. I must have been rather frightened of her." I asked Mrs. Watts if she remembered Ada talking politically, displaying any aversion to totalitarianism on her own or any dissent from Galsworthy's opinions. "No," she replied laughing, pointing out the hazards in the stone steps as she led me, carrying the tray, into the more level back portion of the garden. "I can barely remember anything she *said* at all. Yet, now that I think of it, one would simply have assumed that she would have no patience with any kind of political discrimination or ideology. She just wouldn't tolerate it, *at all*." Mrs. Watts pursed her face severely and arranged a small table and chairs, in the shade backing against large bushes of rich hydrangea, completely without the litmus paper look their color so often has in the northern United States, while I held the tray until the space was ready.

Still talking about politics, as we ate and drank our tea, our conversation hopped among other writers, both in and out of P.E.N., and what their political attitudes in the thirties were. I brought up Henry Williamson and his support of Oswald Mosley. Like Rudolf Sauter, Mrs. Watts thinks of Williamson's work as his early nature writing, *Tarka the Otter* and *Salar the Salmon*, not in terms of any political point of view, not his *A Chronicle of Ancient Sunlight*, the series of fifteen novels, written in the fifties and sixties, that trace the growth of a character through England of the last eight decades and is now beginning to interest a number of readers and critics. "Of course, the Mosley period, 1935, '36, '37, was just when I was most out of touch. But I've known Henry Williamson for many years. He used to come to the Tomorrow Club my mother organized in the First War; I probably knew him as early as 1917. He was a difficult man, awkward, now that he's eighty he's quite a curmudgeon. My mother was always kind to him, probably because he was so awkward. At one time he signed his letters with a drawing of an owl. There've been a number of marriages and children. He lives, all higgledy-piggledy, in a cottage in Devon. His daughter won't go there. I think he's managed to quarrel with all his children. He and I are now friends. We haven't always been. He was very helpful about my book, and he can be flattered. But, you know, I just never have thought of him as having any kind of politics." Our talk returned to Galsworthy and politics, Mrs. Watts saying that she had not, in the twenties, read *A Modern Comedy* with any political implications. "I may have missed something. Perhaps I should reread it now. But I didn't really enjoy it then. Not like the wonderful old Forsytes. Fleur and Michael never came alive. I *do* agree with you about *Flowering Wilderness*. Yes, I thought that very good. It came out after I was married and had children." Mrs. Watts associates politics far more readily with Galsworthy's plays than with the novels. "Yes, I went to the first nights in the early twenties. One of my boyfriends was a drama critic. The Galsworthy I remember best, and liked best, was *Loyalties*. And it was political. Quite a controversy about it at the time. You know, of course, that I'm not a critic. But I did love *Loyalties*. I identified with the Jewish man, the victim of prejudice. And I thought that Galsworthy did, too." We talked further about the controversy, people of his own class, station, background, who might have thought that, in 1922, he was making a rather melodramatic fuss over nothing, might have accused him of writing propaganda. None of the plays he wrote that were performed later in his life engendered any social or political controversy—none seemed at the time to generate much response at all. I said that I thought that, particularly after 1922, Galsworthy had perhaps come to see his social and political feelings as sufficiently complicated to belong only in novels. He had always felt that the drama was the more obvious and immediate form, the one closer to propaganda, and this left him often without a new or challenging subject for the stage. Mrs. Watts looked puzzled at my distinction between fiction and drama, and said, "But you see, he didn't *entirely* react against his background, at least in the days I knew him. He wasn't bitter or a rebel. He was just a humane man who tried to deal with the evils he saw. He tried," and then she paused, groping, holding her hands in front of her and then drawing them in toward her thin cotton dress, "to bring everything in, to hold everything, all sides, into himself." We talked for a while about this absorptive quality of Galsworthy's, as if he had somehow the responsibility for everything, had to contain everything, and we wondered if this, along with the growing discomfort of undiagnosed illness, had led to his increasing personal silence of his last years. "Yes, yes," said Mrs. Watts. "Increasingly withdrawn. There is a letter I found from my mother to Hermon Ould, the permanent secretary of the P.E.N. then, written, oh, about 1930 or '31, in which she says, 'You must realize that Galsworthy is shrinking away from us.' My mother, as I've told you, was much more vital than Galsworthy, much more active. Always moved and spoke quickly, was so enthusiastic. They complemented each other so well. Still, she only outlived him by a little more than a year."

Mrs. Watts went back to the kitchen to heat more water to replenish our tea while I moved the chairs and table out of the sun's slanting rays that had encroached on us, back toward the corner of the garden, near the high brick wall against which dark red climbing roses had bloomed earlier in the summer. Mrs. Watts came back bearing the pitcher of hot water, smiling, saying "You know I was just thinking about a question you once asked me concerning Galsworthy's use of French. I don't think I ever finished answering. He didn't do much of the French correspondence at the P.E.N. Sometimes Ada did. He felt he was lost in languages with international committees. But he did speak French a bit. He could get along. He rather liked to make speeches in French, though he wasn't adequate at real conversation. What I was remembering was how much he enjoyed speaking at the 1924,—no, that was in the U.S.A.—at the 1925 P.E.N. Congress in Paris, in French, on the charms of the French language. Ford Madox Ford was so funny—it's in 'The Apotheosis of John Galsworthy'—do you know that piece?—Ford was so funny about Galsworthy's gaffes. The French were delighted, charmed. Galsworthy was completely unaware, an innocent about all his unintentional double meanings. Only he could have carried it off." We talked further in the hot waning sunlight, passing from French to other languages to Galsworthy's "innocence" to the question of his lack of a sense of humor. "Oh, but he did have a sense of humor," Mrs. Watts insisted. "When we were planning to get married and furnish a flat, I liked modern furniture and my husband didn't. Finally, my husband said one day that, all right, we could go to Heal's to look about. Heal's was one of the largest showrooms of modern furniture at the time. The next day, Galsworthy happened to ask me how the argument over furniture was resolving itself and I told him that my husband was conceding at least a visit to Heal's. 'I see,' he replied, 'you're bringing him to heel.'" She laughed. When even an attempt at politeness could not fully cover my stony-faced response, Mrs. Watts looked at me quickly and said, "Yes, I suppose it's not really very funny. Just that, from Galsworthy, such a remark was so unexpected, so out of keeping with the rest."

Back in the sitting room, Mrs. Watts let me borrow some letters and an article on Galsworthy that her mother had written, material I promised to return before leaving England. I recalled our leave-taking the summer before, after her dinner party, and

said that I was pleased that she had finished her book long before
I had finished mine. "Yes," she said, clasping my hand "I'd
wanted to finish it quickly. I worked hard on it both here and in
Cornwall. But now that I have I'm not sure it was wise. I shall
miss it. I shall have to think of something else to do." And she
lifted her head, smiling brightly and briskly, as she walked me
to the door. As I rode back on the Underground, I thought far
more of her unconscious gesture in bringing the space around
her into herself to demonstrate Galsworthy's absorptive quality
than I did about Galsworthy's "jokes." When the train approached the station at St. John's Wood, I recalled my earlier
vague intention to stop, perhaps, and watch the last few overs
of a cricket match at Lord's. But, looking at my watch, I realized
that it was late and that a cold shower would be more welcome
than twenty minutes of sitting in the sticky sunlight.

Later that night, sorting notes in the kitchen of our flat, I
tried to think of Galsworthy's political and social attitudes in a
consistent framework that relied on something other than the
word "humane." I pictured him, between 1908 and 1914, having earned his place as a member of a literary and political establishment with a novel like *The Man of Property* and plays like
The Silver Box and *Strife*, having lunches with ministers, taking
a part in writing reform bills, and expressing reasoned opinions
on questions of the day in frequent letters to the *Times*. Simultaneously, he organized himself with sufficient consciousness
and care to convey his strong sense of immediate social concerns
in plays like *Justice* and his more thoughtful, less dramatic analyses of society and its direction in novels like *Fraternity*, *The
Patrician*, and *The Freelands*, the last a particularly searching
novel about what had happened to farming communities and
what might, in socialistic terms, be done about it. With the
shock of the First World War, however, its family internments,
its skepticism, its cruelties, he knew that the days of an enlightened Liberal establishment were over, and he became very much
more private. Whereas, during the war, H. G. Wells wrote a great
deal of propaganda for the English government and Arnold
Bennett became, in 1918, the Minister for Propaganda under
Lloyd George, Galsworthy wrote almost none—just an article or

two analyzing and working out the details of plans for Englishmen growing their own food. He was, as always, generously charitable and concerned. He contributed all his American earnings, which, at the time, were larger than his British earnings, to causes like servicemen's rehabilitation or relief for those widowed by the war; he edited the journal, *Reveille*, under the Ministry of Pensions, that combined short literary works with articles on prosthetics, education, job-training, and other information useful to wounded and other veterans; he turned over one of the houses his father had left him, in Cambridge Gate, bordering Regents Park, for use as a servicemen's club. He also spent five months in France in the winter of 1916-17, working as a masseur and a counselor in a small hospital for the shell-shocked near Grenoble. Ada went along as housekeeper and seamstress. But, in spite of all these generous contributions of time and money, he held the major share of his writing to himself, focused on private themes and, near the end of the war, wrote the satire of patriotism, *The Burning Spear*, and began to resume his chronicle of the Forsytes. I had thought of *The Burning Spear* as a rather watery *Candide*, until I noticed in Dorothy Ivens' typescript, *A Sketch of a Relationship*, that she said the novel "has a flavour of Galsworthy and Bertie Wooster." She and I agreed that the "book lacks force and is often factitious," but, I thought, her comparison with Bertie Wooster was unquestionably more apposite than mine.

The comparison also seemed to describe an element in Galsworthy's thinking after the war, a quirky quality, unusual and perhaps even eccentric causes that he would argue for logically without taking entirely seriously. He wrote of a number of these individualized issues that had no connection with any political party or public program, like the half-serious endorsement of the scheme to ameliorate unemployment or overpopulation by encouraging emigration to the Commonwealth (dramatized as "Foggartism" and treated with the gentle, charitable satire of the resigned in *A Modern Comedy*), or several carefully worked out agricultural plans for England to grow more of its own food and become less dependent on commerce and trade. In a way, his life at Bury, his position as the benevolent feudal lord over a

small area, satisfied both his sense of agrarian socialistic experiment and a desire to manage or control apart from the governments and cartels of the modern world. He wanted a kind of
omnipotence, his own charitable version of his father's role as
the Victorian patriarch. His measurement of the heads of visitors
to gauge cranial capacity, on the other hand, was quirky individualism on a more obviously Bertie Wooster level. Galsworthy
also subscribed to a number of personal rituals; the Muller exercises he performed daily; the riding jackets, dark green or maroon, color-coded to match the horse he rode that day; dinner
clothes selected as appropriate for the different houses. I
thought I saw something of that same kind of gentle quirkiness,
the eccentricity without the desire to impose on others, the
logic applied to an independent issue in full knowledge of the
fact that most of the world will ignore one's position, in some of
the current members of the family. There were the Ivens on their
boat in Scotland and his nephew Hubert on his boat talking of
arguments with Sir Gerald Nabarro or the Russians planting acres
of dandelions. Important or trivial, never argued for or presented
with intensity, all the public issues Galsworthy brought up after
the war (with the exception of the international issues, the
League of Nations, the P.E.N., all of which he always held with
the restrained fervor he had applied to so many issues about
England and Art before the war) were far from the center of
general English political consciousness. And he was skeptical
about the intensity applied to issues that were, the strikes in
which he thought both sides were wrong, the party strategies
and squabbles that didn't matter. All Galsworthy's causes were
so individualized, so far from an establishment or public consensus, because he thought that government in England had
become, since the war, increasingly removed from people and
problems, assuming and propagandizing stances in the intensities
of its own concerns, becoming abstract and aggressive in its certainty. He saw the English government, the establishment the
legal system, as forms of more or less benign tyranny, and he
revolted in the only way an aging, still unresigned, and socialistic gentleman could, by becoming more and more private, living
more in his myths both fictional and real. In fiction, he showed

this in *A Modern Comedy*, the trilogy of the mid-twenties. Although occasionally tendentious and even more occasionally
boring, *A Modern Comedy* is structurally and often dramatically
thorough and profound, on many simultaneous levels, about the
government and management of the self, of marriages, of classes,
of societies, of the country. Galsworthy is constantly concerned
with management, with the dilemmas produced by the attempts
to control experience, dramatized in those brilliant trials in
which the legal truth, the social truth, and the individual truth
are never identical, examined in all those events and relationships
in which motive and consequence have little connection amidst
all the perplexities of the "modern comedy." His range extended,
he wrote trilogies, he brought in businessmen, social workers,
schemes to eradicate the slums. More and more, Galsworthy's
impulse to manage, to be omnipotent, like Trollope's in his
multiple series of novels, created a vast simulacrum of England
in which he, the author, could live and reign benevolently. He
was "wider" than his father, patriarch only for a large family,
and a capitalist as well. It was all a "comedy," he knew it could
never be real, yet the "comedy" was seldom funny. Dame
Rebecca West was right in stressing his lack of humor as a central limitation. His incapacity to reduce anything to absurdity,
his incessant seriousness and vulnerability, his attempt to see all
sides of almost any question, was a failure of one dimension of
intelligence, as if one of the four corners of the literary mind,
the quickest one, was simply absent, requiring an ever more
careful cultivation of the other three. The lopsided square held
more than he needed of sympathy for others, of guilt, of a refusal to impose himself, but rather less than he, as a writer,
needed of the confidence of genius. His only humor was dependent on class or on obvious topicality, the humor of the golf
club or the genteel smoking room, the rather patronizing sense
of what Dorothy Ivens had referred to as his very occasional
"vulgarity." Most of the time, he chose to abandon that form of
social isolation and protection, but he never saw that humor can
also protect and reveal a more unique and complicated self.

One of the difficulties with trying to define Galsworthy's
political and social positions of the twenties, the difficulty in

trying to describe his kind of skeptical middle-class socialism or in authenticating his early anti-Nazism, was, I knew, the increasing silence of the last few years, a silence pervasive enough to make the fiction a principal source for biography. All his relatives report an increasing withdrawal, a look almost of desolation, few words, particularly in his last year and a half. The brain tumor of which he died was not diagnosed until his last weeks, and even then not very clearly, while, in the meantime, doctors had ordered painful treatments like having all his teeth pulled. No one now can really tell when the brain tumor began to affect him. A number of people noticed an increasing slowness, a diminution of energy, and silence even in the mid-twenties. In October 1926, Arnold Bennett, writing in his *Journal*, commented, after a dinner at the Galsworthys, that he "was very quiet. He talks, but talks more quietly than ever." This seemed to Bennett, who was fond of Galsworthy personally although not often of his work, quite a different man from the one who, a guest at a dinner at Bennett's in 1918, interrupted by an air-raid, had hastily gathered all the fruits and chocolates from the table before going down to the basement to pass them around to the cooks and other servants. The increasing silence led Ada to take over more and more of his correspondence. From 1929 or 1930, as the letters in the Scribner Archives demonstrate, she had written most of the letters to old friends like Charles and Arthur Scribner and Maxwell Perkins, and her letters were far more expansive than his had been for many years. I thought of Ada's later work helping to vouch for Jewish refugees from Germany and Austria. I also recalled some of her letters written to Scribner's even before Galsworthy died—her assertion, as early as 1930, that it didn't matter if the trains ran on time, her report of the changed atmosphere on the Continent, the intensities and hatreds that depressed her both in themselves and because they indicated that all the privations and disasters of war might well have to be endured again. From these letters, from some suggestions in numerous stories the relatives had told me, and from the final trilogy, I began to think more certainly that Galsworthy, in his last years, in spite of the silence and the illness, perhaps combined with them in increasing depression, was, like Ada, sharply

sensitive and unequivocally opposed to the implications of
Nazism and Fascism spreading over Europe. Orwell, in truth,
could not have been more wrong.

Galsworthy had always deplored chauvinism. From the time
of the Boer War, all his statements on public issues and all his
campaigns strive against any easy or comfortable satisfaction
with one's role or class or country. Looking over my notes, I
came across a typical example of his kind of reaction to public
events in a letter he had written to Dorothy Ivens in August,
1917:

> A revolution is no picnic. Revolution in a vast country
> like Russia is taking the lid off a cauldron with a ven-
> geance. Russia is in for years, perhaps a generation of
> dishevelment and chaos. All the same I say Heaven be
> praised. Very likely there will be dictatorships, fur-
> ther revolutions, something very like disruption; pos-
> sibly a splitting up into several countries. All this was
> inevitable when and wherever the old bad order went
> by the board. And only those who know something
> of the utter cynical dejection of spirit in which Russia
> lived under the old regime will see that all that may
> be coming was better than that. I have little patience
> with those who can only look at the case and future
> of another country through the lens of how it suits
> their own. This is the reason of all the heart burning
> of the British—nothing impersonal or cosmic whatever
> in their attitude. Even if Russia is beaten out of the
> war the thing was a blessing.

Although later events and further revolutions caused Galsworthy
to qualify some of the attitudes he expressed in that letter, he
remained insistent, throughout all his work in the P.E.N., that
political issues and changes in other countries should not be seen
through the perspective of England. The central objections to
various forms of chauvinism are even more visible throughout
Galsworthy's work. *The Forsyte Saga* is, in a way, a representation of the evils of male chauvinism extended to a class, the

Forsytes, whose sense of themselves is entirely involved in manifest forms of self-justification. A good early play, *The Fugitive*, excoriates male chauvinism in English society even more simply and directly. In *A Modern Comedy*, the objection to chauvinism is expressed in the focus on the need for civilization and tolerance, for the willingness to abrogate the insistence on self, both personally and socially, that is characterized in the central figure of Michael Mont. At the end of the trilogy, when he guesses that Fleur has been unfaithful to him and has been rejected by Jon, Michael articulates his response, his knowledge that he will absorb and accept the situation, in terms that are both personal and historical:

> All his life he had detested the ebullient egoism of the *crime passionnel*, the wronged spouse, honour, vengeance, 'all that tommy-rot and naked savagery.' To be excused from being a decent man! One was never excused from that. Otherwise life was just where it was in the reindeer age, and pure tragedy of the primeval hunters, before civilization and comedy began.
>
> Whatever had been between those two—and he felt it had been all—it was over, and she 'down and out.' He must stand by her and keep his mouth shut.*

Michael, as persona, has been elevated to the son of a baronet. All the more reason, in Galsworthy's terms, for him to need to absorb, both personally and socially, everything that life throws at him.

For me, I realized, the implications of the kinds of anti-chauvinism and anti-Nazism that Galsworthy finally came to represent radiate most fully and impressively from his final trilogy, *End of the Chapter*. Establishing the central perspective of an initially naive young English girl, Dinny Charwell, the cousin of Michael Mont, a member of the country aristocracy and

---

*John Galsworthy, *A Modern Comedy* (London: Heinemann, 1962), p. 735.

rather on the fringe of contemporary English life, Galsworthy chronicles all the influences, moral and material, of English civilization on other civilizations. His sense of management extends to other societies, other races. In the first novel, *Maid in Waiting*, Dinny's brother, Hubert, a military man, has killed a native in self-defense while on a South American expedition; in the second, *Flowering Wilderness*, Wilfrid Desert, the poet who was in love with Fleur in *A Modern Comedy* and is now engaged to Dinny, himself privately agnostic, has been forced at knife point, while in the Middle East, to become a Muslim convert; in the third, *Over the River*, Dinny's younger sister, separated from a brutal husband, spends a night in a car with another man. In all three, the central issue can be seen, from certain obvious points of view, as trivial. But Galsworthy is less interested in the issues themselves, in fact doubtless chose their triviality deliberately, than he is in the fact that, in civilized society, individual political, religious, and sexual issues ramify, must be judged and acted upon in terms of the wide social or political contexts implicit when other nations or societies are involved. None of the characters is able to act solely in terms of intensely individual integrity, although all are capable of following strong feelings. At the same time, respectability, convention, acting out a consensus of opinions so freely discussed in London clubs and drawing rooms is even more clearly not the solution. Galsworthy has little patience with the "establishment" answers, colonial or otherwise. Rather, as Dinny finally sees in each separate novel, the adjustment between society's claims and individual integrity is complicated and difficult, requires working through separately in terms of each individual issue. For example, although the ethos of colonialism is given some defense in the second novel, because the religious fanaticism confronting Wilfrid Desert is seen (by Galsworthy, not by Wilfrid) as the greater danger, colonialism is only a rigid imposition in the first novel, no matter how honest and committed its practitioners may be. In all three novels, whether the assault on what Galsworthy regards as "civilization" is violent or verbal, whether the specific issue is political, religious, or sexual, he deals centrally with the theme of imposition. His contrasts explore all the complications and varieties of one

social code impinging on another; his attitude maintains a sometimes fine distinction between inevitable impingement and imposition—in the latter bullying is implicit. The kind of social
control Galsworthy advocated and imagined invariably avoided
bullying, became a form of utopian socialism that never involved
constraint.

In his treatment of all the dense questions concerning varieties of uncivilized imposition and possibilities for opposing
them or mitigating their effects in contemporary life, Galsworthy
had found, I thought, his fullest and deepest theme, conveying
it most crisply and cogently in *Flowering Wilderness*. Only the
final novel, *Over the River*, in which, as Dorothy Ivens has written, "there is a shadow, a sense of philosophy instead of life,"
shows any sign of the physical deceleration and lack of precision that marked Galsworthy's last year or two. I thought of the
confusion of titles I had once or twice seen in bookshops, people
assuming that *Over the River* and *One More River* were two
separate novels. After Galsworthy's death, I had discovered in
the Scribner Archives, Ada had published the novel as *Over the
River* in England, and the plates, following the customary practice, had been sent to Scribner's in New York. Just as the novel
was going to press, Ada cabled Scribner's to change the title to
One More River. Scribner's complied. Afterwards, when it was
too late to change the title back again, Ada explained that
Marrot had confused "over the river" with "up the river" and
convinced her that, in America, the original title would mean
going to Sing-Sing—clearly, a sensitivity to phrases gone slightly
awry. The three novels of *End of the Chapter*, despite the defi-
ciencies of the last, need to be read together. In one way, taken
together, they are Galsworthy's final answer to Kipling, his intellectual antagonist ever since the days of the Boer War, a statement that a "civilized" society can transcend both chauvinism
and a capitalistic sense of purpose. In another way, they are also
a dense yet cogently shaped description of the individuality and
sometimes quirky particularity of England, of the undemonstrative and unaggressive insistence on the privacy of self that, with
an added dimension of luck, held out against intensity, dogma,
and bombs in 1940. It seems, in terms of my own myths of

1940, all the more English in its deliberate rejection of chauvinism and imposition, an instance of a nation (again, partly attributable to simple good fortune) momentarily transcending itself. That the principal characters are aristocrats is, perhaps, the trilogy's least convincing element, for the characters share Galsworthy's essentially middle-class concerns with behavior, ethics, and control. As Garnett said back in 1909, he may never really have known the aristocracy. Yet, for Galsworthy, the Charwell family is a symbol, a family unlike the Forsytes (or the Galsworthys) that could absorb so much, learn so much of other people and races, care so much, and still survive. In his final trilogy, Galsworthy wrote the family he wished he had had, one of gentle anthropologists and radical clergymen who could change and care, one in which aristocracy was not a matter of striving or class superiority, but one of calm responsibility and socialistic concern. The early novels diagnosed the ailments in English society: Forsytism, Pendycitis (defined by Galsworthy in his 1907 novel, *The Country House*, as the Old Tory landed gentry's "bull-dog tenacity to have one's own way"). The final trilogy proposes the antidote, the undemonstrative, private, never bullying Englishness that can occasionally transcend itself. This kind of Englishness is not official or realizable in political terms, although, as Galsworthy knew and we have seen frequently since, political parties have tried to coopt it often enough.

As I gathered the sprawled papers together, I suddenly realized that *End of the Chapter* was not Galsworthy's last work. He had, in the autumn of 1932, before his illness stopped all writing, been working on a play he called *Similes*, the unfinished half or two-thirds of which Ada had published in 1935. The play begins with a wealthy lady realizing that she had negligently left her pearls at the hairdresser's; in the next scene, the manicurist, having borrowed the pearls for a dance and lost them, is too frightened to confess. But, as the issues develop, the pearls may have been paste and metaphors for the false jewel of the wealthy lady's marriage and the false gift of her husband's business success. In addition, as the manicurist begins to confess, Galsworthy encourages speculation about which relationships are false, which genuine, what the similes simulate in both economic and sexual terms. One cannot tell, from the fragment, how he would have worked out either the plot or the imagery of the play. Was he, I wondered, reaching for a concept of economic justice in 1932? Was he moving toward a dramatic indictment of a society that insisted on the visible manifestations of class distinctions throughout the terrifying slump, Baldwin's immobility, Macdonald's overwhelming pleasure in his own advancement? No. I stopped myself. The play gave no clear indications, and, thinking about it again, I realized that it was closer to Maupassant's strikingly ironic similitudes than to any representation of British social and economic life in 1932. I was in some danger, especially at this hour of the early morning, of forcing Galsworthy into what I wanted him to be. I went to bed.

When I awakened late the next morning, a Wednesday, I was acutely conscious that we had only forty-eight hours left in England that summer. I had already known that we hadn't time to meet with Hubert Galsworthy again and cruise down the Thames in his boat, and I had had to phone Mr. Sauter, who had been dispossessed from his house for a week or so by the woodworm exterminators, breaking my promise to bring my wife and children to Stroud again for the day. Since, in the shade of our well-like garden, it seemed a degree or two cooler than it had been the day before, I decided to take my son to a cricket match at the Oval. We were disappointed that we were not to stay in London long enough to see the Australians against England in the final test at the Oval, although we had seen one day of the earlier test at Lord's, a day on which England had batted rather better and more tenaciously than expected on the kind of dry wicket that favored the Australians, England looking composed and dignified, coming close in a cause they could not win. Galsworthy had watched his cricket at Lord's, had never, so far as I could discover, been to a match at the Oval. I preferred the Oval, the stumpy wooden stands and the small, decaying, ornate Victorian pavilion on the grounds surrounded by gas works, a small electrical supply factory, and council houses in South London, in Kennington just on the edge of Brixton. I had first come to enjoy cricket and learn about it there, early in the summer of 1952, staying, after my year in Glasgow, with Miss Quartz in Brixton, often stopping at the Oval in the late afternoons, let in free, to watch the last dozen overs or so before I walked to Miss Quartz's for something to eat. I once persuaded Clifford, Miss Quartz's actor son, to join me in watching the end of a match. He watched an over or two, eyes glazing over, and then fell asleep sitting in the warm sun. When sporadic applause awakened him, he laughed and said, "That's just what I always did when we played cricket at school. But, then, I was supposed to be fielding." My son, too, had watched his first cricket match at the Oval, three summers before, fascinated by every movement of the game, allowed, in that more casual ground, as all children were, to sit on the field just behind the white-washed boundary circle, backing up a fielder when the ball occasionally came toward that spot on the circular boundary. My wife's introduction to cricket at Fenner's in Cambridge during the first year of our marriage, a greener and more sedate ground, had been quite different. Primed by my explanations with match sticks on the kitchen table and immediately catching my interest in the statistics, she had applauded enthusiastically and cheered, jumping up, when a young Cambridge player reached a century. The frozen stares of the other spectators near us had dampened her enthusiasm considerably. She decided to spend a final afternoon with Kate at the exhibition of prints, wallpapers, and furnishings held for Liberty's centenary celebration. James and I took the Underground to the Oval.

The match was Surrey vs. Yorkshire, neither side having been particularly impressive that year, quite unlike the fifties and early sixties when those two sides had almost dominated county cricket. We arrived after lunch, my Yorkshire-born son sprinting down to sit in a vacant spot just behind the boundary, turning and pointing to the scoreboard to show me that Yorkshire had been batting very well, that, even nearing the end of its innings now, it had piled up an impressive score. I sat back and watched the mechanical Surrey bowling and rather lazy fielding allow Yorkshire to finish adding even more runs than it should have done, my son applauding each Yorkshire four lined through the fielders. When the inning ended and the sides took a short break before Surrey batted, James came up to me to say that he far preferred the Oval to Lord's. "Lord's is too formal and far away. They won't let you sit on the ground and it's hard to see the scoreboard because of the posts. I feel as if I'm not supposed to be there." He ran back to the field as Surrey came in to bat. In spite of the dry wicket, Surrey's batting was lunging and erratic, desperate to make quick runs to catch up and trying wild strokes that missed entirely or popped the ball straight up in the air for an easy catch. At the tea interval, they had already lost four or five wickets for only forty runs or so, had virtually no chance to catch Yorkshire. When my son joined me, looking for something cold to drink, he said, "Why do you vote for Surrey? They're terrible." When I explained, as I had before, my sentimental allegiance to the side I had first watched and learned the game from watching, a side of crisp, sure bowlers of various paces and a carefully strategic and intricate defense, the side that had won the County Championship in every year from 1952 through 1958, James looked at me sharply, and said, "But that's no reason. Just because they won in the fifties. It's exactly like the New York Yankees, and you never vote for them. You're certainly not consistent." I opened my mouth to reply, and then decided to accept the charge because, trivial as it was, I knew it was true. Emotionally, I was the iconoclast I pretended to be only on my own turf; on alien ground, no matter how often I might revisit it or how carefully I might once have tried to deny it, I've always seen in myself some tendency to fall gently toward the establishment. I wondered, suddenly, if that might distort my view of Galsworthy.

That evening, my wife and I went to a play with Simon and his wife, then afterwards to a new restaurant on Walton Street, one that we had discovered, with full mirrors and deep armchairs, cool and muted, where one could get an excellent late supper. We enjoyed finding new restaurants for Simon and his wife, since he had, when we first married, astounded us by discovering every good new French restaurant that opened in London after all the years of rationing and older restaurants serving, at best, overdone and dried out slabs of flannel-tasting lamb with two veg and two different kinds of potato. The Walton Street restaurant was even better than it had been on the night we had tested it, and we lingered long over coffee. He kept asking questions about my interviews, and, when I responded, he said, "Last year seemed to be your year of southern England, and this was a Scottish year, almost like when we first became friends and you would come down from Glasgow and tell me about Scots Nationalism and slumps in the shipbuilding industry." I said that I thought Galsworthy combined both the southern English and other perspectives, might stand for something or incorporate something British in spite of the specifically southern English locales of his origin and his settings. Simon asked me how I saw Galsworthy's point of view socially and politically. I started to develop my answer slowly, aware, even after almost twenty-five years of friendship, that I was on foreign ground. I was suddenly conscious of the fact that it was Simon, who for Christmas in 1955, had given us a copy of Graham Greene's *The Quiet American* and, convinced us later that, caricature though the portrait of the American, Pyle, might be, it still represented a valid English way of looking at American innocence, a point of view that seemed more and more accurate over the years. As I warmed to my own words, I stopped needing to guard against my own possible innocence and completed my picture of Galsworthy as representing the private anti-totalitarianism so firm and yet so absorptive in 1940, so anti-ideological and yet so curiously unbudgeable. Simon replied slowly, "Yes. I think, without ever saying it or defining it, I've always seen Galsworthy in a way something like that. Curious country, old England. It would be very hard for it to produce a Hitler or a Stalin who gained any large number of followers. Or even a General Amin or an Ian Smith who stayed." He stopped and laughed, then continued, "Of course, ten or fifteen years ago, I'd have laughed, we'd both have laughed, about what you've been saying. We'd have made jokes about the 'spirit of Dunkerque' or 'we happy few,' jokes with a bitter edge at the time of Suez. But I saw something of the opposite in myself the last few years, especially when I was just back from Persia and could be swayed by newspapers and politicians about Communists in the unions and slogans like that. The Galsworthy point of view came back by itself." He turned his chair to include our wives in the conversation, laughing and reminding Joan that he was hopelessly addicted to trains running on time. He looked back smiling at me: "Oh, I still get furious at times, at all the waste, the inefficiency, the kindly, sweet old men who just won't move. I'm sure I'm much more impatient than you are. I get so angry at 'muddle' and the people who'll use it as an excuse for anything. But I suppose I'd rather miss it if it weren't here. And, besides, the more intense places, the ones that believe their ideologies or are totalitarian, have just as much 'muddle,' if not more. They just don't admit it. I know—I've lived in and been fascinated by those places long enough." He and his wife went on to tell us of some of the magnificent scenery and canyons in Iran until we became conscious that we were the last people still sitting in the restaurant.

The next day, I was busy finishing my reading of the typescripts and books I had borrowed, writing long letters about them, and mailing them back. I was particularly interested in Dorothy Ivens' *Tantalus*, the 1923 novel about a middle-aged clergyman during the war, surrounded by a devoted and conventional wife and daughters, who falls in love, in defiance of his own scruples, with a French governess hired to take care of his sister-in-law's children on a long visit to his home. The "affair" between the clergyman and the governess is manifest only in a few passionate kisses by the sea, in anguished romantic discussion about a relationship impossible before it has begun, and in long passages of tormented self-castigation in the clergyman's mind. The family forces the clergyman to give up the girl, and the novel ends with him preaching a sermon on the theme that no one in his family or his flock understands. In spite of the abrupt quality and rather flat message of the end (the implications of the clergyman's renunciation are never really worked out), I found the novel full of fine, crisp writing, tersely handled similes that suggested far more than they said, and many perceptive moments, particularly those concerning the elaborate defenses characters establish to conceal from themselves what they feel. I thought about whether or not the characterization of the clergyman might have been modelled on Galsworthy.

Although I noticed a few similarities, the reticence, the tendency to think of others and to punish himself, I realized that the characterization really contained very little of Mrs. Ivens' view of her "uncle," almost nothing of the charm, the talent, the breadth of interest, and the careful dedication to his work that she so clearly saw. And Ada had certainly no connection with the clergyman's dull, placid, conventional wife. Fiction, I knew, and I knew that Mrs. Ivens knew, was a great deal more complicated than any one-to-one correlation between character and person would allow.

As I was writing to Mrs. Ivens, the second post arrived with a thick letter from Mr. Sauter. Between a long paragraph describing the pressure pumps and the smelly foam used to exterminate woodworm and another long paragraph politely recording his disappointment that we would not be able to visit Stroud again and his warm good wishes for us, he inserted the single sentence, "I came across these poems of Vincent Marrot's which I think answer the question you asked as to why he was chosen to do the Biography." Mr. Sauter had included a photocopy of six short poems, two of them sonnets, that Marrot had written in February, 1933. Although doubtless expressing genuine grief at Galsworthy's death, the verses managed to combine many of the stock phrases of soulful "poetic" expression, self-pity, a sycophantic reverence for the three survivors, and fulsome assurances that because Galsworthy had such a truly great mind and a truly great heart "his glory will live on." Later that day, after I had carted my letters and packages to the post office, and just as we were ready to go out for our final London dinner, Mr. Sauter and Mrs. Scrivens phoned. He first wanted to know if the Marrot poems had arrived, and what I thought of them. As I began trying to express my criticisms of the poems gently, he interrupted, saying, "Yes, yes. They are terrible. I'd forgotten how bad until I saw them again. Now, that's what I mean by 'sentimental.' Death masks are much less so, much harder, mean much more." He also wanted to say goodbye, both he and Mrs. Scrivens talking to both my wife and me. He asked all about the details of the flight, the times and the size of the plane. At one point, as he was talking to Joan, I was reminded of one of

Galsworthy's last letters to Dorothy Ivens, which I had read earlier that day, written on shipboard on his way to America in 1931. The short letter was dry and withdrawn, citing only the tonnage of the ship, the date of arrival, and a list of the eight lectures he was to give after his rest in Arizona, the letter of a man retreating more and more into himself. But, as soon as I was on the phone again, I realized that the nephew, though fifteen years older than Galsworthy had been when he died, was not at all like that side of his uncle. Mr. Sauter's interest in all the detail was warm and humorous, interspersed with comments about art exhibitions and plays, and a reaching out, not a withdrawal, a gesture to confirm the fact that we were friends apart from anything of his uncle that I had come to learn or he had wanted to perpetuate. I very much hoped that I would be able to visit him soon again. [Rudolf Sauter died suddenly of a coronary in June, 1977. His last Christmas card had a drawing he had done of a golden bird in flight on the cover, a drawing of himself, firm lines holding the chin downward, and one of his new poems inside. An accompanying letter expressed concern for us because he had just heard of the PBB contamination in Michigan. He also wrote of various ailments among his friends, adding "I seem to be the only lucky one."]

The next morning I felt the intense heat very early as I loaded our luggage into the taxi and fended off the driver's importunate arguments that it would be easier for all concerned if he drove us all the way to Heathrow. We were relieved to get rid of our luggage and be assured of the airplane seats we wanted at Victoria Air Terminal. As we sat on the top level of the double-decker airport bus, winding through Pimlico and Chelsea to the river before it cut north and west again, I noticed that Joan was dry-eyed, moving her face to try to catch any possible faint breezes, for once not quietly crying because we were leaving England, unlike our other departures on cool and rainy days. I spent the plane journey, leaning back, determined not to smoke, withdrawn in the 747's insulation out of time and temperature, hoping that the weather in England would break soon.

Not until several weeks after we had returned to America did I learn that the cool westerlies had reasserted themselves and broken the hot spell. A letter from Dame Rebecca West, adding a few details to something she had told me about Galsworthy, details she said she remembered waking up suddenly in the middle of the night, concluded by saying "You did well to get out on Friday. Friday and Saturday were the worst days." I learned that, before the heat had broken, vandals had spilled oil all over the pitch at Headingley in Leeds, forcing cancellation of the Test Match before the final one at the Oval. A long letter from Dorothy Ivens had told me about the mixture of models for the clergyman in *Tantalus*, particularly about a clergyman in Kent who was silently and conspirartorily delighted to have recognized himself. She also, in response to a question that James had put at the bottom of my letter, "Is there really a Loch Ness monster?," had replied, cryptically, "Please tell James there is nothing doing with his 'Monster' just now." Shortly after I read that the final Test Match had been played on schedule at the Oval, both newspapers and letters from friends reported that the cooling rains of autumn had begun. I realized that, before I had begun to work on Galsworthy, I never paid much attention to the weather, had to make a deliberate effort to recall whether the day on which an event took place was hot or cold, wet or dry. Although I had been in England often before, almost the first day with which I could associate heat was a blistering and still day in September, 1973, shortly after we had come to London for the year, when a London taxi-driver had told me that this was the hottest September since 1940, a fact the newspapers verified statistically, and then rapped his "wooden" head to ward off the omen. Perhaps that was when I had begun to associate the weather and Galsworthy, to think of the static continental masses of heat as connected with dogma and intensity, the shifting, prevailing westerlies, alternating sun and shadow and rain, as connected with resilience and absorption. Standing up to a heat wave or against a dogma reminded me of the pictures Dwye Evans had shown me more than a year before, Galsworthy, bat in hand, standing grim and composed against the bowling, determined not to flinch, knowing that he might well lose his wicket, that life is loss, but that at least he could do so without sentimentality.

I recalled, too, the year before when I had been living in England, all the competing theories, the escalated intolerance, the feeling in all the journals and newspapers that a government or society needed to be decisive, to pin everything on a rate of economic growth or an energy policy. And I saw many parallels with life and discussions in the thirties, parallels on economic issues, parallels in intensity. Yet, over the past two years, I had seen, more and more, that static, assertive, and consistent theory, what most people seem to mean by decisive government, might only impose on people, eliminate what is left of villages like Bury or some of those in Devon or the fishing villages that nestle against the hills along the Scottish lochs. Galsworthy had clearly seen the perils of imposition, of artificial or bullying certainty, just as each of the older people I had talked with had seen them in his or her own, very different, terms. Not one of them had much faith in a calculus that could engineer human beings, Galsworthy, perhaps, least of all. I thought of him always baffled by machinery, in fact and in metaphor. I pictured him at Bury, building houses for others and helping them, in part because of his own guilts and inadequacies and poses and wish-fulfillment, holding firm his little piece of earth. Yet the kindnesses themselves were real, and he always knew that he was doing at least as much for himself as he was for others. Resilience and a capacity to live with contradiction were the other side of his acute sensitivity. What he represents might, I thought, possibly still survive, something of the English climate and light and landscape in all its moderated movement, its inconsistency, its minute daily changes.

The next winter left me less time than I had anticipated for thinking or writing about Galsworthy. I did do some library work, and was able, by serendipity, to settle a question that had nagged in some recess of my mind since the P.E.N. reception several months earlier. While checking a list of periodical articles on Galsworthy that someone else had compiled, just to make sure I was missing as little as possible and not expecting very much, I came across a short article by Leon Schalit in the *Contemporary Review* of February, 1943. The article was fond, soft, and unexceptionable, containing nothing one had not thought of often before, but its first paragraph did demonstrate that Schalit was living in the sanctuary of London in 1942. Contemporary news from England seemed less than heartening. Inveraray Castle burned. The pound kept falling on the international exchange. The restaurant in Walton Street, where we had enjoyed our long supper with Simon and his wife, exploded with a bomb planted by the I.R.A., numerous people badly injured by slivers of flying glass. And, as I finally had the time to work myself entirely into Galsworthy again, I heard the news of the extensive mass of very hot, dry air suspended over all of Western Europe, another parched Wimbledon (without even the partially redeeming presence of Arthur Ashe in the finals), months of blazing sun, browned pastures, sere hedgerows, even, this time, a shortage of potatoes. I wondered about my confidence at the end of the summer before, my feeling that the westerlies and moderation were likely to return again and again. I wasn't altogether sure they would, now. I had no great retrospective fondness for the moments of confidence in my own past. I could still recall, with a lingering bite of shame, the bright morning in May, 1940, when my friend from next door stopped in our kitchen to walk with me to high school and gloomily pointed to the *New York Times* and its headline about the advance of the Nazi Blitzkrieg. I had pompously opened the newspaper to an inner page, pointing to a map that showed the advance of the day before superimposed upon a line showing the furthest advance of the German Army in 1914, the 1940 line not yet having quite reached that point. I said, with an arrogant and callow assurance that I hope I would not have been capable of much past my fourteenth birthday, "Nonsense. When the Nazis reach the 1914 line, which they won't, I'll begin to worry. Not before then."

I also wondered, as I reread and thought about all my notes, if I should really be as confident as I sometimes was that I could tell when to identify closely with Galsworthy and when to pull away, when I could trust my reaction to parallel his and when I could not. From my reading and my conversations and my imagination, I had constructed a picture of Galsworthy, the favored son, never having had to work, yet of whom much was expected, on whom the middle-class family line was thought to depend. Little wonder, I thought, given his background that he should, after a long period of charming aimlessness, fully indulged by his family because of their view of his promise for the future, turn toward "Art," toward just what it would be most difficult for his parents to understand; little wonder too, that he should later emulate his father's patriarchal role in very different ways. Yet, he would always feel, in some way, inadequate, feel that he had received more than he deserved, economically (he always knew that he was writing both of and for "that tenth or so of the population whose eyes are above the property line," as he said in the preface to *A Modern Comedy*), emotionally, and in terms of his artistic reputation. I thought, at times, that I could understand this, feel this, because of some similarities in my own background, high expectations and gentle treatment, the moral strictures and the distant indulgence. Although I had not been the charming aimless man-about-town, I had not had to be driving or assiduous either. I could not afford not to work for a living, and the difference in time and class between me and Galsworthy was considerable. But I could sketch a shaky parallel between his well-nourished early days about London and my own wanderings about England and Western Europe in the first six or eight years after the Second World War, my position as an American not connected with a commercial or military enterprise, just looking around, bought drinks and offered beds and engaged in long drifting conversations just because I was there, a postwar comaraderie I loved and had not earned. Like Galsworthy, I felt that, both economically and emotionally, I received more than I deserved, more than I could give. And, at other moments, I felt guilty.

Suddenly, in the midst of those speculations, I stopped, sounding ludicrous to myself. I was, I thought, simply being presumptuous, imposing myself on a man I had known only through his writing and through others. I was also riding the dragging coattails of the famous. I needed to repeat: John Galsworthy,

Englishman, 1867-1933, novelist and dramatist. Nothing fit me except the initials, the most common and superficial resemblance of all. I felt again, as I had felt on a number of occasions during the last several years, once in particular standing with Mr. Sauter, taking pictures, on the hill above Bury, that I was intruding myself where I should not, publicly invading the privacy of a man whose writing combined expression and concealment.

I deliberately buried the self-consciousness, knowing that following it would the sure way to do nothing. My thoughts returned to Galsworthy as a young man, looking around him, observing, reacting, understanding, but not wanting to give out, to be, until he was sure he had it right. Then, he fell in love, and Ada told him that he ought to write. He had absorbed and absorbed, and she recognized that he needed to express, needed the control and the definition that writing might provide. He worked at it carefully, laboriously, scrupulously, writing, as he did everything else, like the conscientious gentleman who would offend neither others nor himself, who would faithfully represent all he had seen and understood. For a time, the understanding and the expression, the taking in and the giving out, were balanced, and he was able, simultaneously, to travel, to be kind, to write novels and plays, and to champion causes. Then, beginning with the First World War, the world threw more and more at him that required understanding: the war itself, family internments, knowledge of new customs and new cruelties, conscious assaults on civilization, aging, and, finally, debilitating illness. He took it all, absorbed it all. He even shaped a form, the vast trilogy which he connected to other trilogies, in an attempt to control, express, and surmount all of it, all he had taken in. The tension between absorption and expression still, in parts of *A Modern Comedy* and in the whole of *Flowering Wilderness*, created some of his finest work, work that was "profound" (in Dame Rebecca West's sense of the term, as seeing and representing, in conceivable and coherent shapes, all possible sides of the issues he treated). Yet, as I suspect he had always known, he lacked the quick touch of genius, the immediate sense of crystallized apprehension that is entirely new and that no amount of conscientious labor can create. He never really transcended the middle-class worrying of ethical debate or the desire to fence off and thereby control every acre of his vision. When he tried directly for the stroke of genius, the apotheosis, as in *The Dark Flower* or *Beyond*, he seemed at his least convincing, to wallow heavily in the merely soulful or trite. He could not impose on the world by insisting on himself and, thus, perhaps transcending himself, could only represent, judiciously, sometimes self-effacingly, sometimes brilliantly, what his world was. When, in the last few months of his life, he learned that he had been awarded the Nobel Prize and began to write his acceptance speech, a curiously humble and flaccid talk that he was not well enough to travel to Stockholm and deliver, he seemed overwhelmed by depression. He had taken in and taken in, understood, but then, at the end, seeing that the conscious sanity of internationalism was failing, ill and slow in mind and body, knowing surely that he had missed genius, he, in a sense, did not want the Nobel Prize he would never have been truculent or ungenerous enough to refuse. In his own terms, he did not deserve it.

As I developed this construction of Galsworthy's life, I recalled, again, Rudolf Sauter's statement back during our second conversation, that he often thought that Galsworthy would have been "shattered" by the events after his death, by the concentration camps and the war, because he was so sensitive to suffering. When I first heard the speculation, I was inclined to be skeptical, for I had emphasized Galsworthy's "balance" simply as his scrupulous understanding and his capacity to absorb and had assumed that he, as long as he lived, could have continued to take it, could have managed the distance necessary for survival. Later, understanding more, through Mr. Sauter and others, reading more carefully, I came to accept Mr. Sauter's statement, to appreciate the fact that Galsworthy's "balance" required a visceral sensitivity to suffering that could "shatter" a man, that his understanding could have dislodged him, that a man can be more fragile than he looks, his interior not represented by composed photographs. Now, speculating further, I was still inclined to accept Mr. Sauter's basic statement, but I wanted to qualify by changing the metaphor suggested by "shattered." Galsworthy had taken in and taken in, but, toward the end, with incapacity compounded by illness, he could seldom any longer find a way to express or control all that he understood, the balance leaned more heavily toward absorption as his limited and conscious, always too conscious, strength to express could not continue to grow. He cultivated Bury and he wrote the final trilogy, he lived as much as he could in terms of his myths, and he knew he was not the great artist that he wanted to be. And still the world kept flooding in: more cruelties, more assaults on "civilization." Saturation, I thought, more than shattering, a surfeit that choked him into silence. The incapacity to break out, the prisoner to his mold, seemed, finally, to me, a better metaphor than fragmentation. I thought of his sympathy for prisoners in solitary confinement, the "cause" that, before the First War, he had worked on most tirelessly and the one that had yielded the most tangible result.

I pulled my typewriter out from the corner of the room, opened it, and placed it on my desk, pile of fresh paper (ripped from the empty backs of student blue-books unreclaimed) on one side, sheafs of sorted notes on the other. I did not know if I was vicariously close enough to Galsworthy, or ever would be, to take a very minor version of what lesson I could from his career, just as I did not know when England's anticyclonic air mass might shift, or what next year's weather or the next decade's climate would be. I might well be projecting and imposing myself on him, in spite of all my conscious worrying about closeness and distance and in spite of all the help I had had from those filters and catalysts closer to him than I. But, momentarily at any rate, I had absorbed as much as I could sustain. As Joan had told me often enough, I had to begin to write.

Index